Praise for *In Search of Monsters to Destroy*:

"With *In Search of Monsters to Destroy*, Christopher Coyne offers readers a crisp, concise, and devastating indictment of American imperialism. His provocative proposal for a nonviolent 'polycentric' approach to national security comes as a welcome bonus."

—**Andrew J. Bacevich**, President and Chairman of the Board, Quincy Institute for Responsible Statecraft; Professor Emeritus of International Relations and History, Boston University

"Why go overseas to slay monsters? Whether it's corruption and cronyism, bureaucratic pathologies and perverse policies, mechanized terror and murderous militarism, the monsters are right here, America. Luckily for us, in *In Search of Monsters to Destroy*, Coyne faces them down with courage and clarity. So should we."

—**William J. Astore**, Lt. Col., USAF (Ret.), author, *Hindenburg: Icon of German Militarism*

"Christopher Coyne has long been the leading voice in economics on the folly of American military interventions overseas. In his remarkable new book, *In Search of Monsters to Destroy*, he gives unpopular but deeply compelling arguments why such interventions are a threat to liberal values both at home and abroad."

—**William R. Easterly**, Co-Director, Development Research Institute, New York University

"Coyne argues in his tightly written examination of America's global meddling, *In Search of Monsters to Destroy*, that these interventions almost inevitably cause more harm than good because America lacks both the interest and knowledge to do otherwise. It is not 'Mission Accomplished' but 'Mission Impossible'."

—**Harvey M. Sapolsky**, Professor Emeritus of Public Policy and Organization and former Director of the MIT Security Studies Program, Massachusetts Institute of Technology

"Christopher Coyne's *In Search of Monsters to Destroy* is a timely book. Completed on the heels of the undeniable failure of America's longest war in Afghanistan, it comes out in the midst of the United States' and NATO's dangerous effort to destroy yet another monster, this time the Russian bear in Ukraine. Sadly, we continue to need Coyne's reminder of the folly of even well-intentioned empire and the urgency for a new, non-imperial approach to national and international security."

—**Michael C. Desch**, Packey J. Dee Professor of International Relations and Brian and Jeannelle Brady Family Director, Notre Dame International Security Center, University of Notre Dame

"*In Search of Monsters to Destroy* is a bold necessary book that examines the costs and failures of U.S. military interventions in Afghanistan, Iraq, Libya, and beyond. Coyne reveals the false assumptions and political and economic cronyism that for decades have sustained what he calls the 'imperial national security state.' The book also offers solutions, outlining alternative, polycentric defense strategies, including civil resistance, that promise greater security at less risk of war. A well-written compact volume that makes a valuable contribution to the debate on national-security strategy and the need for military restraint."

> —**David Cortright**, Director of Policy Studies, Kroc Institute for International Peace Studies, Keough School of Global Affairs, University of Notre Dame

"Christopher Coyne's very important and timely book, *In Search of Monsters to Destroy*, reminds us once again that *all* wars bring taxes and the expansion of the power and scope of government. When the wars end, the taxes remain. The new powers remain. The new additional government functionaries remain. State power ratchets upwards and rarely back down. War is truly the health of the state."

> —**Grover G. Norquist**, Founder and President, Americans for Tax Reform

"With his book *In Search of Monsters to Destroy*, Coyne uses key insights from political economy to deliver a major broadside against interventionist American foreign policies. He argues that we have unproductively adopted an imperial approach that undermines both liberal ends and our security needs. Agree or disagree with his analysis or recommendations, readers will find Coyne's challenges to traditional approaches well worth pondering."

> —**William P. Ruger**, President, American Institute for Economic Research

"*In Search of Monsters to Destroy* presents a detailed and tellingly accurate anatomy of the American warfare state and its consequences for both the United States and other nations before laying out a thought-provoking case for an alternative to Washington's current, counterproductive militarism."

> —**Charles W. Freeman, Jr.**, President Emeritus, Middle East Policy Council; former U.S. Ambassador to Saudi Arabia; former Assistant U.S. Secretary of Defense for International Security Affairs

"*In Search of Monsters to Destroy* is a spirited, and often passionate, analysis and assault on American interventionism, nation-building abroad, and militarism at home and abroad, which are collectively conceptualized as much of the substance of the American empire. The book challenges much in orthodox studies and owes a debt to important dissident writers Coyne obviously respects: especially Friedrich A. Hayek, Charles A. Beard, William Appleman Williams, C. Wright Mills, Arthur A. Ekirch, Jr., and Robert Higgs. Even readers often preferring interpretive orthodoxy will find

Coyne's chapters on the failed drug war in Afghanistan and on the menacing use of drone warfare both compelling and unsettling."

"Christopher Coyne's book *In Search of Monsters to Destroy: The Folly of American Empire and the Paths to Peace* offers a clear and comprehensive analysis of the concept of 'liberal imperialism.' Coyne's compelling elucidation of what is essentially a contradiction in terms, completely at odds with the contours of reality, is then illustrated through a detailed consideration of two cases of major foreign policy failures in the twenty-first century: the efforts by U.S. occupiers to stanch opium production in Afghanistan, and the use of lethal drones to kill people throughout the Middle East. These examples show how military intervention in the name of liberal values has sown misery and exacerbated many of the problems which it was supposed to solve. Yet foreign policy elites, undeterred by their long string of orchestrated disasters, persist in insisting that the United States is the 'indispensable' nation. Under this assumption of 'American exceptionalism,' all of the attendant hypocrisies inherent to liberal imperialism continue to be condoned, even as 'public bads' multiply. There is, however, an alternative to the dominant, state-centered security approach: polycentric systems of security grounded in individual and community action, which, being intrinsically coherent, are far more likely to succeed than the reflexive use of state military force. The challenge remains to spread the word, and Coyne's timely book greatly contributes to that worthy cause."

"In this groundbreaking new book, *In Search of Monsters to Destroy*, Christopher Coyne presents us with both a crystal-clear history of the modern American Empire and a brilliant, innovative policy manual. Interweaving his deep expertise as an economist with theoretical and policy insights drawn from international relations, classical-liberal thought, business theory, psychology, and many other fields, Coyne [He] has written a scholarly masterpiece which stands much of contemporary American international relations theory and practice on its head—most particularly where he suggests fundamental changes in the way conflict and violence can be managed and lessened, both at home and abroad. This superb and beautifully written book should be read and re-read by anyone concerned with the dangerous world which the American Empire has made more dangerous and anyone interested in fresh policy prescriptions offering workable and peace-generating 'alternatives to empire'."

—T. Hunt Tooley, A.M. Pate, Jr., Professor of History, Austin College; author, *The Great War: Western Front and Home Front*

"The U.S. government spent almost $9 Billion over 20 years in Afghanistan to eliminate the poppy crop used to produce opium and heroin. The result? Opium poppy production quadrupled. This failed war on drugs is just one subset of the failed war on terror that Christopher Coyne documents in his book, *In Search of Monsters to Destroy*, his masterful analysis of the follies of the American Empire. What we imagine to be a necessary, efficient mechanism for protecting American freedoms and spreading liberty is, as Coyne artfully details, a massive, corrupt enterprise that suctions money from American taxpayers into the accounts of a few monopolistic corporations and, in the process, extinguishes the liberties and, too often, the lives of millions beyond our borders. It is essential reading for all who hope to be informed Americans—a vital roadmap for charting a more effective, more just foreign policy."

—Joseph Cirincione, Distinguished Non-Resident Fellow, Quincy Institute for Responsible Statecraft; former President, Ploughshares Fund; former Director for Non-Proliferation, Carnegie Endowment for International Peace

"Christopher Coyne's *In Search of Monsters to Destroy* calls to us to imagine alternatives to empire. It is timely, sobering, and provocative. A century and more ago, anti-imperialists warned our republic against the corruption, militarism, jobbery, and vanity of a misconstrued national greatness premised on imperial expansion. Coyne challenges all skeptics of empire and lovers of liberty to reassess where we are, how we got here, and where we go next. Ideological interventionists, nation-builders, and regime changers have to be held accountable for the word they promised and the world they made."

—Richard M. Gamble, Professor of History and Anna Margaret Ross Alexander Chair in History and Politics, Hillsdale College

"Christopher Coyne's *In Search of Monsters to Destroy* is a devastating critique of Washington's arrogant and blundering foreign policy. Too often, U.S. policymakers succumb to the temptation to launch military crusades for regime-change or supposedly humanitarian goals. The debacle in Afghanistan is the most recent example of how populations in targeted countries pay a very high price in blood and treasure for the hubris of America's policy elites."

—Ted Galen Carpenter, Senior Fellow, Defense and Foreign Policy Studies, Cato Institute

"Step by careful step in his book *In Search of Monsters to Destroy*, Christopher Coyne makes a powerful humanitarian and economic case against U.S. empire. He shows that it has caused huge destruction of life, liberty, and property abroad and substantial destruction of life, liberty, and wealth at home. Coyne applies Friedrich Hayek's analysis of the problems with centralized information to foreign policy, showing that, whatever the U.S. government's intent, government officials cannot know enough to intervene productively in other countries' affairs. Moreover, government officials usually have perverse incentives that cause them to act badly. Is there hope? Read his last chapter."

> —**David R. Henderson**, Emeritus Professor of Economics, Graduate School of Business and Public Policy, Naval Postgraduate School; Research Fellow, Hoover Institution

"As Christopher Coyne convincingly demonstrates, militarism and imperialism impose harsh costs on human populations, including those in the imperial heartland as well as the direct victims of intervention. At a time when the United States and its rivals are gearing up for a new era of military competition and conflict, Coyne's superb *In Search of Monsters to Destroy* provides a powerful antidote to our culture of endless-war preparation."

> —**Michael T. Klare**, Professor Emeritus of Peace and World Security Studies, Hampshire College

"'Imperialism' is an ugly word to most Americans, connoting the malevolent practices of European powers. Alas, as *In Search of Monsters to Destroy* tells us, the practice is very close to home. In a revealing and easy-to-read style, author Christopher Coyne describes the dark side of U.S. foreign policy, particularly since the 9/11 attacks. His discussions on Afghanistan and Iraq are extremely well done. For anyone with an interest in U.S. foreign policy, its implementation, and the near mind-boggling results, this book is a must-read."

> —**Donald L. Losman**, Professorial Lecturer (Ret.), Elliott School of International Affairs, George Washington University; former Professor of Economics, The Eisenhower School, National Defense University

"Using telling examples such as the 'mechanized terror' of drone warfare and with hard-hitting prose, Christopher Coyne's book, *In Search of Monsters to Destroy*, offers a scathing critique of the way that America's efforts to spread liberalism and democracy undermine the values it claims to promote."

> —**George C. Herring**, Professor Emeritus of History, University of Kentucky; author, *From Colony to Superpower: U.S. Foreign Relations since 1776*

"In Search of Monsters to Destroy is an apt and engaging dissection of the follies and of the often decidedly illiberal consequences of American military interventions abroad. It concludes with a provocative assessment of the potential value of other approaches to the provision of defense and security including non-violent ones."
    —**John E. Mueller**, Woody Hayes Senior Research Scientist, Mershon Center for International Security Studies, Ohio State University; author, *The Stupidity of War: American Foreign Policy and the Case for Complacency*

"In the aftermath America's failed and costly effort to pursue 'regime change' and 'nation building' in Iraq, Afghanistan and the rest of the Greater Middle East by employing U.S. military power, we are now facing growing pressure in Washington to launch new Cold Wars against Russia and China as a way of continuing to maintain U.S. global hegemonic power. To apply what Talleyrand was supposed to have said of the Bourbons, it seems that the members of the U.S. foreign policy establishment 'have learned nothing, and they have forgotten nothing.' Against this backdrop, Christopher Coyne provides us in *In Search of Monsters to Destroy: The Folly of American Empire and the Paths for Peace*, with a wide-ranging critique of U.S. military interventions in the Middle East and elsewhere, a historical tour d'horizon and an intellectual exercise that reflects the author's classical-liberal worldview. Not only does Coyne explain how we got here, how contrary to the aspirations of the Founding Fathers, the U.S. has become a military empire and the devastating effects this has had on our political economy and civil liberties. He also offers us a path forward, proposing a set of alternative policies that would allow America to affect the world along the lines of its liberal values, so it could become the shining city on the hill instead of ending up in the graveyard of empires."
    —**Leon T. Hadar**, Washington Bureau Chief, *Singapore Business Times*; author, *Quagmire: America in the Middle East* and *Sandstorm: Policy Failure in the Middle East*

"Christopher Coyne has provided us with a timely – indeed urgent – examination of why America failed in Afghanistan. But more even than that, he has given us a historical perspective on how the American empire developed after two world wars. I was stunned by the chapters on the drug war in Afghanistan, and the ultimate horror of drone warfare as the final expression of technological efforts to make the world safe for democracy."
    —**Lloyd C. Gardner**, Charles and Mary Beard Professor Emeritus of History, Rutgers University

"In Search of Monsters to Destroy provides an incisive and timely critique of U.S. imperial practice abroad, encompassing America's frequent foreign interventions as well as the nation's permanent global military network. Author Christopher Coyne finds the roots of imperialism in the expansive nature of America's 'protective state.'

And he carefully traces its growth from the early spurts of western expansion, to the initial claims of extra-territorial authority during the 19th and early 20th centuries, to the ongoing bid for global hegemony following the Second World War.

Coyne employs a libertarian analytic while also drawing deeply on a range of other critical approaches in international relations, security studies, and peace research. He argues convincingly that a consistent libertarian viewpoint must necessarily be anti-imperialist. *In Search of Monsters to Destroy* also serves more broadly to illuminate pivotal recent instances of US foreign policy malpractice.

Especially worthy are Coyne's incisive critiques of US efforts at 'nation building' in Afghanistan and the broader practice of drone warfare. Clear, rigorous, and comprehensive - I have read none better. More than reviewing a litany of missteps and deadly mistakes, Coyne astutely clarifies the dynamics of recurring disaster. In so doing, he explains why these practices are irredeemable. Equally worthwhile is his examination of the US military-industrial complex as epitomizing crony capitalism. He elucidates why the constituent industries routinely deliver less capability than promised at greater cost—often much great cost—than initially estimated.

Coyne ends with a provocative introduction to various options for 'polycentric defense' which stand as alternatives to centralized statist efforts at securing Americans against threats, both domestic and foreign. 'Polycentric defense' involves individuals and non-state associations operating freely at various levels to provide different types of security—active and passive, physical and electronic, armed and non-violent forms. For examples of the latter, Coyne draws on the influential work of political scientist and strategist Gene Sharp. While readers will find the proposals for 'polycentric defense' both innovative and challenging, Coyne excels at showing the varied ways this approach is already operating effectively at levels ranging from neighborhoods to the global commons."

—**Carl Conetta**, Co-Director, Project on Defense Alternatives, Commonwealth Institute

IN SEARCH OF
MONSTERS
TO DESTROY

INDEPENDENT
I N S T I T U T E

INDEPENDENT INSTITUTE is a non-profit, non-partisan, public-policy research and educational organization that shapes ideas into profound and lasting impact. The mission of Independent is to boldly advance peaceful, prosperous, and free societies grounded in a commitment to human worth and dignity. Applying independent thinking to issues that matter, we create transformational ideas for today's most pressing social and economic challenges. The results of this work are published as books, our quarterly journal, *The Independent Review*, and other publications and form the basis for numerous conference and media programs. By connecting these ideas with organizations and networks, we seek to inspire action that can unleash an era of unparalleled human flourishing at home and around the globe.

100 Swan Way, Oakland, California 94621-1428, U.S.A.
Telephone: 510-632-1366 • Facsimile: 510-568-6040 • Email: info@independent.org • www.independent.org

IN SEARCH OF
MONSTERS
TO DESTROY

The Folly of American Empire
and the Paths to Peace

CHRISTOPHER J. COYNE

INDEPENDENT
I N S T I T U T E

OAKLAND, CALIFORNIA

"America, with the same voice which spoke herself into existence as a nation, proclaimed to mankind the inextinguishable rights of human nature, and the only lawful foundations of government. . . . Wherever the standard of freedom and Independence has been or shall be unfurled, there will her heart, her benedictions and her prayers be. But she goes not abroad, in search of monsters to destroy. She is the well-wisher to the freedom and independence of all. She is the champion and vindicator only of her own. She will commend the general cause by the countenance of her voice, and the benignant sympathy of her example. She well knows that by once enlisting under other banners than her own, were they even the banners of foreign independence, she would involve herself beyond the power of extrication, in all the wars of interest and intrigue, of individual avarice, envy, and ambition, which assume the colors and usurp the standard of freedom. The fundamental maxims of her policy would insensibly change from liberty to force. The frontlet upon her brows would no longer beam with the ineffable splendor of freedom and independence; but in its stead would soon be substituted an imperial diadem, flashing in false and tarnished lustre the murky radiance of dominion and power. She might become the dictatress of the world: she would be no longer the ruler of her own spirit. . . . Her glory is not dominion, but liberty."

—**John Quincy Adams**, Address to Congress on U.S. Foreign Policy, July 4, 1821; 8th U.S. Secretary of State (1817–1825), 6th President of the United States (1825–1829)

Independent Institute
100 Swan Way, Oakland, CA 94621–1428
Telephone: 510–632–1366
Fax: 510–568–6040
Email: info@independent.org
Website: www.independent.org

Cover Image: John Parrot/Stocktrek Images
Cover Design: Denise Tsui

Library of Congress Cataloging-in-Publication Data

Names: Coyne, Christopher J., author.
Title: In search of monsters to destroy : the folly of American empire and the
   paths to peace / Christopher J. Coyne.
Other titles: Folly of American empire and the paths to peace
Description: 1st Edition. | Oakland, California : Independent Institute, [2022] |
   Includes bibliographical references and index.
Identifiers: LCCN 2022016451 (print) | LCCN 2022016452 (ebook) | ISBN
   9781598133479 (Cloth) | ISBN 9781598133493 (epub) | ISBN 9781598133493
   (mobi) | ISBN 9781598133493 (pdf)
Subjects: LCSH: United States--Foreign relations--Philosophy. | Intervention
   (International law) | Militarism--United States. | Imperialism--United States. |
   Liberalism--United States. | United States--Politics and government--1989-
Classification: LCC E183.7 .C675 2022 (print) | LCC E183.7 (ebook) | DDC
   327.73--dc23/eng/20220525
LC record available at https://lccn.loc.gov/2022016451
LC ebook record available at https://lccn.loc.gov/2022016452

Contents

Dedication

Acknowledgments

THIS BOOK BUILDS, integrates, and updates over a decade's worth of independent and coauthored scholarship. The following list of articles serve as the background and foundation for the chapters that follow:

Ammons, Joshua D., and Christopher J. Coyne. 2018. "Gene Sharp: The 'Clausewitz of Nonviolent Warfare,'" *The Independent Review: A Journal of Political Economy* 23(1): 149–156.

Coyne, Christopher J. 2018. "The Protective State." In, Peter J. Boettke and Solomon Stein (eds.), *Buchanan's Tensions: Reexamining the Political Economy and Philosophy of James M. Buchanan*. Arlington, VA: Mercatus Center at George Mason University, pp. 149–169.

————. 2020. "Introduction: Symposium on Polycentric Systems in a Free Society, *The Independent Review: A Journal of Political Economy* 25(2): 229–234.

Coyne, Christopher J., Abigail R. Hall, and Scott Burns. 2016. "The War on Drugs in Afghanistan: Another Failed Experiment with Interdiction," *The Independent Review: A Journal of Political Economy* 21(1): 95–119.

Coyne, Christopher J., and Steve Davies. 2007. "Empire: Public Goods and Bads," *Econ Journal Watch* 4(1): 3–45.

Coyne, Christopher J., and Nathan Goodman. 2020. "Polycentric Defense," *The Independent Review: A Journal of Political Economy* 25(2): 279–292.

Coyne, Christopher J., and Abigail Hall. 2016. "Empire State of Mind: The Illiberal Foundations of Liberal Hegemony," *The Independent Review: A Journal of Political Economy* 21(2): 237–250.

————. 2018. "The Drone Paradox: Fighting Terrorism with Mechanized Terror," *The Independent Review: A Journal of Political Economy* 23(1): 51–67.

————. 2019. "Cronyism: Necessary for the Minimal, Protective State," *The Independent Review: A Journal of Political Economy* 23(3): 399–410.

Coyne, Christopher J., and Garrett Wood. 2020. "The Political Economy of Foreign Intervention." In, Stefanie Haeffele and Virgil Storr (eds.), *Government Responses to Crisis*. Cham, Switzerland: Palgrave Macmillan, pp. 89–109.

I would like to thank my coauthors (in alphabetical order)—Joshua Ammons, Scott Burns, Steve Davies, Nathan Goodman, Abigail Hall, and Garrett Wood—for their collaboration on these previous projects.

I am grateful to the Independent Institute, and especially David J. Theroux, Christopher B. Briggs, and George L. Tibbitts, for their support of this project. I thank Barton Bernstein, Laurie L. Calhoun, and Ivan Eland for providing detailed comments to improve the text. Stephen Thompson deserves special mention for his extensive editorial work and, more importantly, for his encouragement and guidance throughout this project. The final book is vastly improved due to his efforts.

Portions of this book were presented at the Institute for Humane Studies at George Mason University in early March 2020. I would like to thank Joshua Ammons for inviting me, the Institute for hosting my talk, and the participants for their feedback. I would also like to thank Yahya Alshamy, Amy Crockett, Nicole Melnyk, Matthew Owens, and Kathryn Waldron for their suggestions and assistance in completing this project.

I would also like to extend my gratitude to my colleagues in the F. A. Hayek Program for Advanced Study in Philosophy, Politics, and Economics at the Mercatus Center at George Mason University. I am fortunate to work in an intellectually exciting environment where I am free to pursue my research interests with constant support and encouragement.

Finally, I am grateful for the constant love and support of my family— Rachel, Charlotte, and Cordelia.

Preface

THIS BOOK PROVIDES a critical analysis of American empire, which I have been studying for two decades. The attacks of September 11, 2001, occurred during the first semester of my PhD studies at George Mason University. The subsequent response by the US government—the expansive, transnational "war on terror"—served as my entry point to study the ability, and limitations, of the US government to militarily intervene in other societies to "export" liberal values and institutions abroad (the topic of my dissertation and first book). From there, I turned my scholarly focus from the effects of a proactive, militaristic foreign policy abroad to the, often pernicious, impact on domestic life. This book incorporates and extends that research into a cohesive exploration of American empire.

The scholarly analysis of American empire has a long and rich history. I approach the study of empire through the lens of the economic way of thinking. This approach holds that people act purposefully in pursuit of their goals, that they face constraints—i.e., limitations on what they can achieve—that they respond to incentives—i.e., changes in perceived costs and benefits—and that different contexts shape constraints and incentives in different ways. The conclusions I draw stem not from first principles—preexisting foundational assumptions about empire—but rather from applying the economic approach to the various aspects of empire and my interpretation of the results of that exercise.

Some of my main personal intellectual influences in the study of this topic include (in alphabetical order): Charles A. Beard, Elise Boulding, Kenneth Boulding, James Buchanan, Arthur Ekirch, F. A. Hayek, Robert Higgs, Gabriel Kolko, Walter LaFeber, C. Wright Mills, Ludwig von Mises, Franz Oppenheimer, Elinor Ostrom, Vincent Ostrom, Murray Rothbard, and William Appleman Williams. These interdisciplinary scholars are diverse in their scholarly approaches and ideologies. While I have my areas of disagreement with each (some more than others), I have benefited from their work in my own study of American empire.

The diversity of these thinkers highlights that there is much common ground to be found—both across scholarly disciplines and across the ideological spectrum—in the study of American empire; that is what makes it such a fascinating topic of study. Despite their differences, one of the unifying characteristics of these scholars is that they questioned, to varying degrees, the orthodox understanding of their respective fields and disciplines. I take this as a source of inspiration in my own work.

The study of American empire has broad "real-world" implications. In American politics, there tends to be a strong consensus among the political elite in their support for and propagation of American empire. At least since World War II, with some exceptions along the way (e.g., Barbara Lee's single vote against the Authorization for Use of Military Force of 2001), there has been unity and support among the two main political parties regarding the necessity of American empire. There are certainly differences of opinion on certain topics and issues—e.g., how military-related funds should be allocated, how and where military force should be deployed—but the necessity of American empire and US military primacy is taken as a given and unassailable. Simply put, when it comes to matters of American empire, Republicans and Democrats look alike, and there is bipartisan continuity in their shared commitment to American empire. Given this overwhelmingly strong support, it is imperative to study, understand, and appreciate the realities of American empire, given the enormous reach and welfare consequences at home and abroad.

In the chapters that follow, I do not cover all aspects and nuances of American empire, foreign policy, and international affairs. For instance, the historical discussion in Chapter 1 is intended to provide an overview, in contrast to a detailed historical treatment, of the evolution of American empire. Further, I do not go into great detail about the various nuances of nuclear weapons—their development and actual use in 1945, the size of nuclear arsenals, and the various types of weapons—pertaining to American empire and foreign policy. I should also note that my discussion of constitutional matters in Chapter 2 offers one interpretation of these issues, which may differ from others regarding the military and security activities of the state.

That all said, I do offer a cohesive treatment of what I believe are key themes and topics related to American empire. I also discuss possible paths to peace that I believe are neglected in both scholarly literature and policy discussions. In doing so, I hope to provide an entry point for a constructive interdisciplinary and cross-ideological conversation about the realities, costs, and consequences of American empire for achieving a stable peace.

Prologue: American Global Interventionism Buried in the Graveyard of Empires

ON AUGUST 31, 2021, the last US soldier left Afghanistan, officially ending the two-decade American occupation. The occupation ended as it began, with the Taliban in control. Like much of the occupation, the days leading up to the withdrawal were chaotic and fraught with ineptness. The US government overestimated the strength of the Afghan government and military while underestimating the Taliban. The Taliban, which had been consolidating its control of territories throughout the country for years prior to the US withdrawal, quickly recaptured the capital city of Kabul in mid-August. Afghan President Ashraf Ghani chose to flee the country as his government disintegrated. The Afghan National Army, which was trained by the US government at the cost of over \$80 billion,[1] collapsed with little resistance. US troops rushed to evacuate embassy staff who were frantically attempting to destroy sensitive materials to avoid them falling into the hands of the Taliban. Despite efforts by US political leaders to save face, the reality is that the US government and its foreign policy of military imperialism are the latest victims of the "graveyard of empires"—a label given to Afghanistan following the defeat of superpowers Britain (1839–42, 1919) and the Soviet Union (1979–89).[2]

The costs of the US government's occupation of Afghanistan are substantial. The Costs of War project at Brown University estimates that 176,000 people were killed in the Afghanistan war between 2001 and 2021. That figure includes 4,155 US military personnel and contractors, 46,319 civilians, 69,095 Afghan military and police personnel, 1,144 allied troops, 52,893 opposition fighters, 74 journalists and media personnel, and 446 humanitarian workers.[3]

Although perhaps counterintuitive, it is important to include opposition fighters because, "[a] lot of times," says Stephanie Savell, codirector of the Costs of War project, "there are political incentives for governments to undercount civilians and put people in the category of 'opposition fighters' or 'militants' because politically that looks a lot less bad."[4] And, frankly, we will never get a clear count of the civilian dead.

Why? One reason is the expansive use of drones. A key component of the US government's "war on terror," which included the US occupation of Afghanistan, was the widespread use of drones to carry out offensive strikes. But the US government's drone program is mired in secrecy, making it difficult to access accurately the number of civilians harmed. Despite this purposeful obfuscation by the government, however, we know that innocent civilians were harmed by US drone attacks, as evidenced during the withdrawal from Afghanistan.

On August 29, 2021, two days before the final exit, a US-government drone blew up a car carrying a suspected terrorist in Kabul. US intelligence indicated that the target vehicle contained an ISIS bomb, which posed a threat to Americans at the Kabul airport. The intelligence was terribly wrong. It was later discovered that the car contained Zemari Ahmadi, an aid worker who was delivering water to those in need. In addition to killing Ahmadi, the drone strike murdered nine others, including seven children.[5] In the immediate wake of the strike, General Mark Milley, the chairman of the Joint Chiefs of Staff, called it a "righteous strike." Two weeks later, when the full details were made public, he referred to the strike as "a horrible tragedy of war."[6] Throughout the twenty-year occupation, some innocent civilians throughout Afghanistan suffered a similar fate with little recognition from the US government and media.[7] Beyond Afghanistan, and across all post-9/11 wars, total deaths, many of them civilian, are estimated to be in the 897,000–929,000 range.[8]

Another human cost of the war is displacement, which refers to people forced to leave their permanent residence to seek safety either in another domestic area or abroad. The Costs of War Project estimates that the war in Afghanistan produced 5.9 million displaced persons.[9] Further, it is estimated that all post-9/11 wars resulted in at least 38 million displaced persons.

Regarding the financial costs, the Costs of War Project estimates that the post-9/11 US wars in Afghanistan and Pakistan cost $2.3 trillion for the

FY2001–FY2022 period. This number includes war budgets (Department of Defense and State Department), care for veterans of the Afghan War, and interest on war-related borrowing.[10] The cost of all post-9/11 wars is estimated to be $8 trillion.[11]

What about the benefits of the US occupation? The US military reduced the capability of al-Qaeda in Afghanistan, which was an initial motivation behind the invasion. However, that didn't stop al-Qaeda from carrying out terrorist attacks. As Dylan Matthews, a journalist, noted in 2021, "[E]ven with that degraded capability, global deaths from al-Qaeda, ISIS, and Taliban attacks have not fallen since 9/11."[12] Granted, these attacks have not struck the American homeland, but the goal of the war on terror was more grandiose. In a speech to Congress on September 20, 2001, President George W. Bush emphasized that "[o]ur war on terror begins with al Qaeda, but it does not end there. It will not end until every terrorist group of global reach has been found, stopped and defeated."[13] With these comments, not only did Bush formally begin the war on terror, but he also set the ambitious benchmark for success—the complete eradication of terrorism. From this standpoint, the war on terror has failed.

Also relevant is the important distinction between correlation and causation. It is true that there has not been another major terrorist attack in America since the start of the war on terror. But that does not mean, however, that the war on terror caused that outcome. There are other factors that might also explain this result, such as the difficulty of planning, coordinating, and executing a large-scale attack or the heightened alertness by ordinary citizens, which serves as an effective deterrent. The 9/11 attacks were a rare occurrence, an outlier, as far as domestic terrorism within American borders is concerned.[14] The likelihood of domestic terrorism by extremists was minuscule before September 11 and remains so today. It is unclear that the war on terror has had a major and significant causal effect on this post-9/11 reality.[15]

Another frequently cited benefit of the Afghanistan occupation was gains to certain groups of Afghan citizens, especially women. Education and literacy rates for women increased in certain parts of the country—but the preoccupation baseline was extremely low under the repressive Taliban regime.[16] In addition, many of the gains to women were concentrated in the capital and other major cities in Afghanistan. With over 70 percent of Afghans residing outside of cities, the benefits did not extend to many women throughout the country.[17] Instead, the presence of US occupiers in rural areas often led to violent conflict that made the lives of many women worse through instability, perpetual fear of harm, and the death of innocent family and community members.[18] The gains experienced by women living in the major cities were fleeting as the US-established Afghan government quickly collapsed following the advance of the Taliban into Kabul. This highlights the inability of foreign occupiers to consistently nation build, to construct the complex array of institutional arrangements necessary for the maintenance of a free society.

In total, we can conclude that the US government has certainly failed in achieving the goal of eradicating terrorist groups around the world. There have certainly been instances of individual success in certain cases. But even here, the magnitude, extent, and sustainability of these benefits are dubious. At the same time, many of the costs—human and monetary—of the occupation are real, observable, and significant.

The failures in Afghanistan present a unique opportunity. The curtain has been pulled back on the American empire once again, offering us yet another chance to critically assess the features and realities of empire—and to chart a new course. This book does just that. I explore the various aspects of the American empire, including the nature and limits of military imperialism abroad, and the harmful effects of militarism at home.

I also offer a potential path forward, an alternative way of thinking about security in a free society. For many, my proposal may appear radical, but it is far less radical than the erroneous, yet pervasive, belief that the world can be shaped and controlled at gunpoint: the belief that liberal values can flourish where illiberal methods are adopted as the means to promote those principles. As a result of the Afghanistan debacle, Americans have caught a glimpse of the graveyard of empires. The question now is whether we will allow those who wield control over the levers of political power to repeat these mistakes. The risk is that one day we may not be able to extract ourselves from the graveyard; our most cherished freedoms and institutions may be lost due to atrophy and overreach.

The American empire will not change on its own; militarism and imperialism are the raison d'être of the expansive US national security state. Yet, we are not helpless; the source of change is us. The citizenry can avoid the traps of empire by throwing off the shackles of militarism and exploring alternative means, not reliant on state military imperialism, for resolving conflict and providing security. The first step in this journey is recognizing the realities of empire.

I

The American Empire

AFGHANISTAN IS ONLY the most recent example of failed US military imperialism. In March 2011, a NATO-led coalition, which included the United States, began a military intervention in Libya. The intervention involved the naval and air forces of participants enforcing a no-fly zone to protect rebels, attacking Libyan military targets, and establishing a naval blockade. The operation lasted about seven months and ended in October after the brutal death of Mu'ammar al-Gadhafi, then the prime minister of Libya. Initially hailed as a success by Western politicians and pundits, Libya quickly fell into chaos. Consider, for example, two headlines from the *New York Times* four years apart, which capture the highs and lows of the Libya invasion.

In 2011, the *Times* ran an article entitled "U.S. Tactics in Libya May Be a Model for Other Efforts," suggesting that the success in Libya would serve as a template for future military interventions. Four years later, the newspaper published a story with the headline "ISIS' Grip on Libyan City Gives It a Fallback Option." The initial intervention led not only to civil unrest in Libya, but also to growing violence in the region, affecting countries as far away as Mali to the southwest. One unintended beneficiary was the Islamic State of Iraq and Syria (ISIS), which US foreign policy elites claimed was an existential threat to America and liberal values around the world.

Reflecting on the Libyan intervention in 2016, President Barack Obama said, "So we actually executed this plan as well as I could have expected: We got a UN mandate, we built a coalition, it cost us $1 billion—which, when it comes to military operations, is very cheap. We averted large-scale civilian casualties, we prevented what almost surely would have been a prolonged and bloody civil conflict. And despite all that, Libya is a mess."[1]

As an isolated case, Libya serves as an illustration of how well-designed and well-executed military interventions can cause severe negative consequences. More broadly, Libya reflects the foreign policy mentality of US government elites, which holds that liberty, freedom, and peaceful order (on a domestic, regional, and global scale) require a proactive, omnipresent US military presence.

Historically, American government officials have provided numerous justifications for proactive foreign military interventions, including concern for suffering, spreading freedom and democracy, fixing broken societies and nation building, and retaliating against perceived threats and enemies. President Woodrow Wilson's phrase—"The world must be made safe for democracy," justifying American entry into World War I—is perhaps the most famous. Intervention in Libya was no exception to this overarching tradition, specifically with regards to the removal and death of a former ally turned enemy, Gadhafi. Certain interventions have succeeded in achieving some of their goals; however, many others (like Libya) have tragically failed.

Nonetheless, at their core, American global military interventions require a mentality that is inherently at odds with traditional liberal values. Liberalism, from the Latin word "liber" or "free," is the philosophy of individual freedom.[2] It is the "theory of a society consisting *entirely*, if ideally, of free people."[3] Liberal values emphasize the primacy of individual freedom, deep respect for human dignity and intellectual humility, an appreciation for voluntary choice and association, freedom of expression, economic freedom, toleration, pluralism, cosmopolitanism, spontaneous orders, and a commitment to peaceful solutions to interpersonal conflict. As the US government's shocking actions showed at the Guantánamo Bay detention camp and Abu Ghraib prison, the interventionist mindset can lead to the adoption of extremely vicious and repugnant illiberal tactics of coercion and brutality, masked by the rhetoric of noble liberal intentions.

Liberal Hegemony

The United States has been described as a "liberal empire"[4] with the US government's imperial strategy described as "liberal hegemony."[5] From this perspective, the US government uses its global power to exert influence over others while promoting Western liberal values.[6] The centerpiece of liberal hegemony has been the US military, which requires "a sustained investment in military power whose aim is to so overwhelm potential challengers that they will not even try to compete, much less fight."[7]

At the heart of any empire is imperialism, an ideology and related set of policies focused on one nation's government projecting its economic, political, and social power over other societies. Imperialism entails a commitment to hard (military) power, with soft (diplomatic) power playing a complementary role.[8] The argument for an imperial, interventionist America is usually grounded in a Hobbesian view of the natural aggression between nations (according to Thomas Hobbes, life was "solitary, poor, nasty, brutish, and short"[9]), an aggression which needs restraining. The underlying assumption is that a liberal international order cannot emerge spontaneously but requires imperial design and, when necessary, the use of force.[10]

Proponents of empire contend that the liberal hegemon provides collective goods—that is, goods where many people share in the benefits on a global scale. Standard examples of such goods include a stable world monetary order; protections against pirates, organized crime, "rogue states," and other predators; and a stable set of rules for transnational trade and finance, diplomacy, and conflicts.[11] In the Western Hemisphere, the United States had been the regional hegemon since the late nineteenth century. Since the 1940s, the United States has been the global hegemon.

Liberal hegemon supporters say that there is also a need for "nation building" to counter the Hobbesian world. This becomes necessary when an officially recognized state is too weak or corrupt to provide collective public goods.[12] Such "failed states" are a problem not only for those forced to live under them, but also for the world, because they undermine a stable international order. The list of "failed states" typically includes Haiti, Somalia, Afghanistan, and Yemen, but is often broadened to include almost all of Africa and much of Latin America, the Middle East, and Central Asia. Proponents of liberal empire thus argue that failed states necessitate intervention by outside powers in order to bolster global and local stability and provide a value-added service by supplying liberal public goods. This is well documented in a growing body of studies by social scientists exploring the benefits of foreign interventions.[13] However, their work is often one-sided, focusing on the public goods but not the public bads or substantial costs of empires.[14] This book contributes to correcting this imbalance.

The Origins of American Liberal Empire

The evolution of the American empire can be understood in three phases.[15] The first involved continental expansion in the early to mid-nineteenth century. This westward expansion included the Louisiana Purchase, the Florida Purchase, the annexation of Texas, the Oregon Treaty, and the Mexican Cession in 1848. "Manifest destiny"—the belief that American settlers were meant to expand west, based on a unique set of virtues and a duty to spread them—was one animating principle during this phase, and it set the stage for the more expansive ambitions that would follow.[16]

The second phase began with the Spanish-American War in 1898, and was marked by overseas imperialism focused on the Western Hemisphere.[17] The American government intervened in Cuba, Puerto Rico, and the Philippine Islands due to internal instability associated with the Cuban War of Independence against Spanish colonizers. The American intervention was a resounding success and set the stage for a pivotal moment in this phase of American empire.[18] In December 1904, when President Theodore Roosevelt outlined the main tenets of what would become known as the Roosevelt Corollary to the Monroe Doctrine:[19]

> Chronic wrongdoing, or an impotence which results in a general loosening of the ties of civilized society, may in America, as elsewhere, ultimately require intervention by some civilized nation, and in the Western Hemisphere the adherence of the United States to the Monroe Doctrine may force the United States, however reluctantly, in flagrant cases of such wrongdoing or impotence, to the exercise of an international police power.[20]

In addition to specifying his famous "big stick" foreign policy, Roosevelt indicated that the US government would serve as the Western Hemisphere's protectorate, using military force when necessary. The official announcement of the Roosevelt Corollary can be understood as a foreign policy declaration based on military primacy, which had already begun.[21]

There were two key events that provoked Roosevelt's Corollary to the Monroe Doctrine. One was the German involvement in a blockade of Venezuela, after the Venezuelan government threatened to default on outstanding debts in 1902.[22] The Venezuelan crisis raised the prospect of continued European interventions in Latin America in response to future debt defaults. The other was the prospect of an isthmian canal, creating the need to protect the "Canal Zone," allowing American investors to reap vast benefits and excluding other rival projects.[23]

As Serge Ricard, a professor of American civilization, notes, "[U]ntil the 1890s, Americans generally considered a coastal defense of US shores sufficient protection from foreign attack."[24] Roosevelt's "big stick" approach to foreign policy resulted in a tectonic shift—not only in the political and economic relations between the United States and Latin America, but also in the relationship between the United States and Europe. The United States government would no longer focus simply on defending its national borders, but also the broader Western Hemisphere.[25] The wider ramifications of this policy shift are still evident today.

The Roosevelt Corollary would be used by Roosevelt, as well as subsequent US presidents, to justify numerous interventions in Latin America.[26] What were the results of the military interventions in Latin America that occurred after the official announcement of the Roosevelt Corollary? Some scholars conclude that the results were positive because these interventions brought financial and governmental stability to the Caribbean (if not in Latin America more generally), as demonstrated through higher average sovereign debt prices.[27] However, given the overlapping complex systems that constitute the world, foreign interventions never do just one thing. They set off a chain of consequences—domestically and internationally—the effects of which are long and variable. Indeed, a closer examination of the Roosevelt Corollary reveals a different, murkier outcome of repeated US government interventions in Latin America.

In most cases, the pattern was for US government intervention to lead to short-term improvements in the financial stability of governments, followed by a "relapse" into bad ways and the necessity of further intervention. Moreover, as time passed, it became clear that active intervention by the United States government as a hegemonic power had produced several severe and adverse long-term consequences, seen (for example) in the Dominican Republic,[28] Cuba,[29] Nicaragua,[30] Venezuela,[31] and Colombia.[32]

In the context of mid- and late twentieth-century geopolitics, this led to further direct US government interventions, making the situation even worse and more intractable. The underlying principle was that existing states had to be sustained and major unrest to the existing political order averted—major unrest always being a challenge to the American political elite's vanity of control and pretense of knowledge, and never being good for the prices of financial assets in the short term. This underlying presupposition was widely accepted, with the result that any unrest was especially likely to be hostile, thereby strengthening the original rationale for imperialism. In that case, the principle of preserving the established "order" through American imperialism becomes self-rationalizing.[33]

The pattern of intervention and its consequences is clear when one takes a longer historical perspective. It then becomes apparent that US government interventions have not been one-offs, but have led to further intervention. Moreover, the results have not been widespread political liberty, social and economic development, or the spread of liberal ideas and institutions promised by the proponents of liberal empire—in fact, just the very opposite.

The cumulative effect of a century of direct and indirect US interventions in Latin America is a continuing series of "inevitable revolutions."[34] Given the repressive nature of the political and social systems—the result of prior interventions—the only mechanism of political and social change is through political or violent uprisings. This, in turn, leads to a situation where political or military threats to US-friendly (although typically illiberal) regimes are met with subsequent direct or indirect US government interventions. The vicious circle of initial US interventions, the resulting negative consequences, and subsequent repeat US interventions becomes a self-perpetuating trap of empire.[35]

Yet another negative consequence of continued US government intervention in Latin America is the ideological backlash against liberal democratic political, economic, and social systems. Not only do many indigenous people view revolution as the only means of change, but they also despise the idea of liberal capitalism because, in their view, it is associated with ". . . a brutal oligarchy-military complex that has been supported by US policies—and armies."[36] This ideological backlash against US-style economic and political institutions make any movement toward sustainable liberal institutions that much more difficult and unlikely, which is fundamentally at odds with the liberal outcomes promised by proponents of American empire.[37]

The creation and support of repression-perpetuating arrangements is a hallmark of US government interventions. Consider the Dominican Republic during the US government occupation from 1916–1924. As historian Frank Moya Pons notes, "[T]he [US] military government had been a government of occupation and, as such, had taught the advantages of repressive methods, especially to the members of the police who were now in charge of maintaining order in the country."[38] These lessons were institutionalized in the thirty-year rule of Rafael Leónidas Trujillo, who came to power via a military coup in 1930. Trujillo trained with US occupiers before climbing through the ranks to general and commander in chief of the US-created Dominican Army. This positioned Trujillo to orchestrate a coup and take control of the country.

Similar illiberal consequences can be found in other US government interventions in Latin America. For instance, during the 1927 occupation of Nicaragua, the United States created the "Guardia Nacional de Nicaragua."[39] The creation of this National Guard was intended to provide stability, suppress civil war, and support political institutions. However, three years after the exit of US occupiers, Anastasio Somoza García—whom the United States government had placed in charge of the Guardia—used the military apparatus to seize control of the country's political institutions. Somoza García established a repressive regime and remained in power until he was assassinated in 1956, when his son, Luis Somoza Debayle, succeeded him and continued his father's illiberal rule.

Despite the repressive and illiberal nature of their rule, the United States government was supportive throughout the Somoza family reign because they typically acquiesced to US demands. US policymakers were fully aware of the family's repressive methods. When asked in 1939 "how he could support that son of a bitch [referring to Anastasio Somoza García]," President Franklin Roosevelt reportedly responded, "Somoza may be a son of a bitch, but he's our son of a bitch."[40] The United States government may have benefited from this stability in Nicaragua's political ruling class, but many ordinary people certainly did not. Similar stories can be told for much of the rest of Latin America.

As the Latin American experience indicates, US interventions beget subsequent US interventions, generating a continued pattern of short-term stability and long-term instability. This pattern creates short-term benefits for some, but significant long-term costs for others. The promise of American empire is that its actions will produce widespread liberal outcomes. However, the historical record of American imperialism in Latin America invalidates this idea of liberal outcomes and demonstrates that imperialism is often the *cause* of illiberalism abroad.

The Rise of a Global Liberal Empire

The third phase of the American empire can be traced to World War II, and marks the beginning of a global hegemon defined by military primacy and the US government's self-identification as the world's policeman. Historian Stephen Wertheim documents how, in the early years of World War II, prior to the Pearl Harbor attack, some US policymakers and intellectuals crafted a blueprint of global "armed primacy" based on the idea that "the superior coercive power of the United States is required to underwrite a decent world order."[41] The belief in the necessity of US military supremacy continued after World War II, when the US government's focus shifted to the supposed global threat from its former wartime ally, the Soviet Union. As historian Michael Hogan notes, "[I]n the national security ideology, then, the nature of the Soviet regime put a premium on military preparedness, the immediacy of the Soviet threat made preparedness a matter of urgency, the long-term nature of that threat required a permanent program of preparedness, and the danger of total war dictated a comprehensive program that integrated civilian and military resources and obliterated the line between citizen and soldier, peace and war."[42]

Through the enactment of the National Security Act of 1947 and amendments added in 1949, the US government reorganized to counter the Soviet threat. These reforms had long-term effects, both internationally and on the relationship between US citizens and their government. The National Security Act of 1947 and later amendments created such household names as the Department of Defense (DOD), unified the military under a new position called the secretary of defense, and established the Central Intelligence Agency, the Joint Chiefs of Staff, the National Security Council, and the Armed Forces Security Agency, which was the forerunner of the National Security Agency (established in 1952).[43] The goal was to centralize the state's defense and security operations in order to reduce waste and duplication, and to improve capacity and efficiency to wage a total global war.[44] In this regard, the National Security Act of 1947 and amendments did what its designers had planned, creating "all of the leading institutions of the US national security bureaucracy, except for the Department of State."[45] The imperial national security state and associated "deep state"—the labyrinth of government agencies, private contractors, and industries associated with the security state—were born.[46]

Although the liberal American empire has matured, the original animating spirit remains. The Roosevelt Corollary also had a lasting influence on US foreign policy in general, serving as a precedent for subsequent US government interventions around the world.[47] Serge Ricard contends that the corollary influenced and guided "diplomacy throughout World War II and during the Cold War."[48] One can also see a lineage between Roosevelt's 1904 rhetoric of using the US military to establish a "civilized society" in Latin America and Woodrow Wilson's 1917 call to use the military to "make the world safe for democracy."[49] The spirit of the Roosevelt Corollary can also be seen one hundred years later in the "Bush Doctrine" after September 11, 2001, in which US foreign policy aimed to "seek and support the growth of democratic movements and institutions in every nation and culture, with the ultimate goal of ending tyranny in our world."[50] Today the spirit of global empire continues to flourish, with open-ended conflicts spanning the globe.

Imperial National Security State

The imperial national security state, the backbone of the American empire, is a political apparatus with centralized war-making powers and a significant scope to act outside of the constitutional rules intended to limit abuses of power.[51] Numerous historians have highlighted the "imperial presidency" by analyzing expansions of power in the executive branch associated with war making.[52] Following the 9/11 attacks and the US government's transnational "war on terror," Schlesinger noted that "[t]he American presidency has come to see itself in messianic terms as the appointed savior of the world whose unpredictable dangers call for rapid and incessant deployment of men, arms, and decisions behind a wall of secrecy. . . . The impact of 9/11 and the overhanging terrorist threat gives more power than ever to the Imperial Presidency and places the separation of powers ordained by the Constitution under unprecedented, and at times unbearable, strain."[53]

The Executive, however, is just one piece of the broader imperial national security state. There is also a vast network of government agencies and departments, as well as private firms, contractors, and consultants, that constitute the national security state. A detailed study by journalists Dana Priest and William Arkin found that the post-9/11 security state was so vast and secretive that no one was sure of its exact magnitude, how much it cost, or what actions the different actors, many of whom have security clearances, were performing.[54] This poses obvious issues with countering abuses of power by bureaucrats, contractors, consultants, and the like, who possess both access to sensitive information and the ability to influence foreign policy, including those related to war making. Taken all together, this deep state acts outside of electoral politics, spanning administrations and government agencies.[55]

The presidency itself has become reliant on the deep state to provide crucial information on foreign affairs—namely threats, challenges, and intelligence. This gives the deep state an asymmetrical advantage in presenting certain information while withholding other information.[56] This information asymmetry further limits the effectiveness of Congress to check abuses of power (if a majority in Congress wants to fulfill that role). Members of Congress are often reliant on members of the deep state for the very information they use to oversee their activities, which leads to obvious conflicts of interest.

Another difficulty for the President and members of Congress with regard to monitoring the deep state is its sheer size and scope. It is nearly impossible to stop abuses of power when you don't understand the vast, secret complexities of an organization. Similarly, voters with even less information are unlikely to pressure their representatives to increase or improve oversight over the national security state. Consequently, the operations of the security state are too often at odds with the rule of law. The rule of law requires governance by jurisprudence, not arbitrary power. It also requires that no person be above the law, including those in power. Instead, the deep state requires that officials not be constrained by laws because they must be free to respond to unexpected events. This gives rise to rogue actions, rampant illegality, and political opportunism under the guise of advancing the "national interest."

Historically, the courts, protectors of constitutional rights, have been a weak check on both the Executive and deep state in wartime. Louis Fisher, a political scientist, argues that "federal courts have consistently refused to reach the merits in war power cases," holding that these were political matters to be resolved by the other branches of government.[57] The result is that the judiciary is often a passive onlooker of imperial national security state activities in times of war and peace.

A Domestic Culture of Militarism

Passage of the National Security Act of 1947 and its amendments forced "a growing militarization of the American government and an increase of presidential and Executive Branch power normally associated with wartime."[58] As new national security agencies rapidly took over foreign policy, it bled into other areas of government and America's identity, which are now synonymous with militarism and empire.[59] As historian Andrew Bacevich notes, today the "American public's ready acceptance of the prospect of war without foreseeable end and of a policy that abandons even the pretense of the United States fighting defensively or viewing war as a last resort show clearly how far the process of militarization has advanced."[60]

This reflects a broader culture of domestic militarism, defined as an ethos in which people "rank military institutions and ways above the ways of civilian life, carrying military mentality and modes of acting and decision into the civilian sphere."[61] There has always been a tension between militaristic and antimilitaristic sentiments in America; for much of US history, antimilitarism was a vital force.[62] This changed with the two world wars, when militarism became a leading part of American life.

As General David M. Shoup, who was awarded the Medal of Honor in World War II, noted in the wake of the world wars, "[T]he American people have become more and more accustomed to militarism, to uniforms, to the cult of the gun, and to the violence of combat."[63] Similarly, Colonel James Donovan noted that, following the world wars, "America has become a militaristic and aggressive nation embodied in a vast, expensive, and burgeoning military-industrial-scientific-political combine which dominates the country and affects much of our daily life, our economy, our international status, and our foreign policies."[64] This militarism was further entrenched with the onset of the Cold War. According to Bacevich, the result is that "[t]oday as never before in their history, Americans are enthralled with military power. The global military supremacy that the United States presently enjoys—and is bent on perpetuating—has become central to our national identity."[65]

Militarism enables the operation of the imperial national security and deep state and is actively reinforced by their operations. Militarism grants those in the state a privileged position in society, providing significant freedom to act with weak or nonexistent constraints. At the same time, militarism is directly reinforced by the activities of the deep state, promoting actions at home and abroad in the name of protecting the American populace from alleged threats to liberty and safety.[66] As the activities of the security state become normalized, they change what Americans will either tolerate or support in empire-related activities, both domestically and internationally.[67]

A Permanent War Complex

Another domestic component of the American empire is a massive, permanent war complex involving an array of entanglements between public and private actors. At the core of this arrangement is the perpetual war economy that emerged in the wake of two world wars.[68] In the face of total global war, US government leaders determined that continual preparations for wars, threats, and future conflicts were necessary. This, in turn, required a permanent war economy involving conflict-related research and development, defense production, and the honing of expertise and administration in military matters. The US government spends a significant number of resources on military-related activities. Proponents of maintaining the status quo, or even increasing military spending, like to point out that as a percentage of gross domestic product (GDP), military spending is in the 4 to 5 percent range. This makes it seem as if military spending is relatively small compared to overall economic activity.

However, consider an alternative perspective. Fiscal year 2019 expenditures on defense-related activities by the US government were $1.25 trillion.[69] Some argue that the US government needs to maintain or increase military spending due to looming threats from China and Russia. Yet, this is far from clear when one considers that the US government's 2019 military expenditures accounted for 38 percent of the total world military expenditures. To provide context, consider that the government of China, which is second to the US government in military spending, accounted for 14 percent of the world's military expenditures. The world share of military spending by other governments—India (3.7 percent), Russia (3.4 percent), Saudi Arabia (3.2 percent), France (2.6 percent), Germany (2.6 percent), and the UK (2.5 percent)—is minimal compared to the spending of the US government.[70] Indeed, if the US government cut military spending in *half,* it would still be greater ($366bn) than that spent by the governments of China and Russia combined ($326.1bn). For 2019, the US government spent approximately $2.80 for every dollar of military expenditures made by the Chinese government and about $11.24 for every dollar spent by the Russian government on military expenditures.

The permanent war economy has real effects on the dynamism of the market economy. Like all other government services, military production requires the transfer of resources—money, capital, labor—from the private market to the military sector. Private citizens and producers cannot simultaneously use military-industrial base resources for private production. This is not simply a matter of one-to-one crowding out. Private markets are dynamic because participants can rely on competitive market prices and profit and loss to gauge the opportunity costs of alternative courses of action. There is no analogous set of mechanisms under government-directed economic planning, which is a defining feature of the military sector.[71]

The funding of military activities does more than simply transfer resources from the private to the military sector. Government expenditures create new, and often undesirable, profit opportunities. Like any other government program, military expenditures create vested interests who not only benefit from immediate government expenditures, but who also seek to influence and manipulate future political decisions for their own narrow benefit. The existence of what President Eisenhower termed the "military-industrial complex" (more accurately described as the military-industrial-congressional complex) is well known, but the implications are often neglected: much of the government spending on what is categorized as "defense" is more often related to political privilege and corporate welfare.

An entire industry of defense-related companies has emerged and grown due to military expenditures by the security state over the preceding decades.[72] Many of these companies are dependent on government-provided defense contracts for their survival. There is a massive network of dedicated companies and subcontractors that have emerged to participate in and perpetuate the permanent war economy. The resources employed in this flourishing war economy are not only monetary, but also human, in the form of ingenuity and effort. Indeed, one of the main overlooked costs of the war economy is the redirection of entrepreneurial alertness from satisfying private consumers to satisfying government officials who award lucrative military contracts.[73]

Waste, fraud, and cronyism are defining features of the military sector. Decades ago, A. Ernest Fitzgerald, a management engineer for the US Air Force, heroically exposed this massive waste and fraud despite efforts by the Nixon administration to silence him and ruin his career.[74] More recently, the efforts in both Afghanistan and Iraq have been plagued by significant waste, fraud, and corruption.[75] The magnitude of these systematic tendencies was evident when the Pentagon finally met the requirements of a federal law to submit its financial documents for an audit (two decades after the law went into effect!) in 2017. When the results of the audit were released in 2018, former Deputy Secretary of Defense Patrick Shanahan told reporters, "We failed the audit, but we never expected to pass it."[76] He went on to suggest that the Pentagon's compliance with federal law was, in itself, cause for celebration— "It was an audit on a $2.7 trillion organization, so the fact that we did the audit is substantial."[77] A lawless environment where even the most basic accounting practices are ignored is ripe for extensive, narrow opportunism undertaken in the name of protecting "the nation."

An imperialistic foreign policy requires a large military, necessitating military spending and contributing to increases in the scale (size) and scope (reach) of government. Many proponents of "small government" are comfortable critiquing government expenditures, programs, and interventions in domestic areas of life—e.g., healthcare, education, and finance. Yet many of these same critics are also proponents of an active, militaristic foreign policy that consumes significantly more resources and contributes to the growth of government on a variety of margins that they purport to find undesirable.

Global Military Sites, Status of Forces Agreements, and Special Ops

The US government maintains a global network of military sites that allows it to project its military power around the world. According to the Department of Defense's (DOD) annual *Base Structure Report*, for FY 2018, the DOD possessed over 500 sites in foreign countries and an additional 4,200 sites in the United States and its territories.[78] Anthropologist David Vine calculates a much higher total number of US bases on foreign soil: "Today there are around eight hundred U.S. bases in foreign countries, occupied by hundreds of thousands of U.S. troops."[79]

The DOD's total real estate portfolio is enormous, with the agency being "one of the Federal government's larger holders of real estate managing a global real property portfolio that consists of over 585,000 facilities (buildings, structures, and linear structures), located on 4,775 sites worldwide and covering approximately 26.9 million acres."[80] These foreign sites enable a forward-deployed military that is used by the US government to project power by enabling rapid deployment of military force. This arrangement is justified on the grounds that it serves as a deterrent against threats while enabling efficient responses to threats with military force as required.[81]

Complementing the government's vast real estate portfolio are status of forces agreements (SOFAs), which refer to arrangements between a host nation and a foreign nation to station the latter's troops there. These agreements formalize the rights and privileges of foreign troops and cover such things as "criminal and civil jurisdiction, the wearing of uniforms, taxes and fees, carrying of weapons, use of radio frequencies, license requirements, and customs regulations."[82] The US government is currently a party to one hundred status of forces agreements with countries around the world.

While formal agreements create a contractual military relationship, allowing the US government to project influence over foreign societies, the involvement of the US military in foreign countries is not limited by these arrangements. Consider, for instance, the case of the United States Central Command (CENTCOM), which has twenty countries in the Middle East and Central Asia under its area of responsibility. Status of forces agreements exist with eleven of these countries. However, "[t]here are no such agreements with several nations in the region with which the United States has significant military relationships."[83]

The United States government has increasingly deployed special operations forces around the globe as an influence-projecting tool. The United States Special Operations Command (SOCOM) oversees the special operations aspects of each branch of the US military, with a total command of about 70,000 personnel. This means the size of American special ops forces is, by itself, the same size or larger than many countries' entire armed forces. US special ops are active around the world. One review of the global use of special ops forces concludes that, during the year 2020, US special operations forces were deployed to 154 countries, which constitutes about 80 percent of the world's nations.[84] These deployments are largely undertaken in secret, meaning little is known about the magnitude, specific activities, or goals of the interventions. The nature of these forces and the way they are utilized allows the US national security state to quickly and covertly project influence around the globe.

None of these instruments—real estate, status of forces agreements, and special ops—are utilized to engage in territorial acquisition, as in the case of past empires. Instead, they are methods by which the American government projects influence and control around the globe through military means. These forms of power projection vary greatly and include anything from small-scale special operations missions to the permanent presence of troops stationed for nation building, assistance, or regional influence.

Arms Sales, Aid, and Geoeconomic Policies

The US government is the world's largest arms dealer. Consider international arms transfer agreements that represent orders for the future delivery of weapons. According to the Stockholm International Peace Research Institute, "[B] etween 2010–14 and 2015–19, exports of major arms from the USA grew by 23 per cent, raising its share of total global arms exports to 36 per cent. For the 2015–2019 period, total US arms exports were 76 per cent higher than those of the second-largest arms exporter in the world, Russia. Major arms transferred from the USA went to a total of 96 countries."[85] This included the transfer of weapons to authoritarian countries like Saudi Arabia, who received 73 percent of their weapons imports from the US government. In terms of regional effects, half of the US government's arms sales during the 2015–2019 period were to governments in the Middle East.[86] Such arms sales are a means for the US government to project imperial power abroad in the name of "balancing power" and creating "global order" and "stability."

Arms sales are complemented by US government foreign aid, which is "the largest component of the international affairs budget and is viewed by many Members of Congress as an essential instrument of U.S. foreign policy."[87] In absolute terms, the United States government provides the most foreign aid of all the world's governments. For FY 2018, the US government accounted for $33.8 billion of official development assistance (ODA). This accounts for 20 percent of total ODA from major donor countries. To put this in perspective, the German government ranked second, providing $25.7 billion in ODA while the United Kingdom ranked third, providing $19.5 billion.[88]

Historically, the US government has justified foreign aid in terms of advancing national security, promoting the commercial interests of Americans, and addressing humanitarian concerns. The overall flow and allocation of each type of aid is driven by the political considerations of gatekeepers in the US government, who determine how aid will be distributed to achieve their goals.[89] From this perspective, aid is viewed as a tool for shaping and influencing people in other societies, as one part of a master blueprint to design the world according to the visions of interveners.

Beyond aid, the US government employs a variety of other geoeconomic policies to project power.[90] This includes policies associated with trade, investment, the monetary system, energy, and commodities, as well as the use of sanctions. As with arms sales and foreign aid, the purpose of geoeconomic policies is for members of the US government to use their economic power to influence political, economic, and social outcomes around the world in order to advance liberal values (at least in rhetoric).

A Road Map for Understanding Empire

The subsequent analysis of empire proceeds as follows: The next chapter, Chapter 2, explores the interventionist mindset associated with the American empire. This approach to foreign policy contains an inherent tension. Its adherents claim a commitment to liberal values, but successfully implementing the strategy requires, attracts, and reinforces an illiberal mentality and the adoption of illiberal methods in fundamental opposition to those values. Even if deemed liberal in its intentions, empire is an inherently illiberal enterprise. In discussing the illiberal foundations of liberal empire, I explore five ways through which the activities of empire, justified in terms of protecting the liberty and rights of citizens, can generate antiliberal results at home.

Chapter 3 explores the extensive cronyism inherent in American empire. Cronyism, which refers to favor-generating entanglements between private and political actors, would be prevalent even if government were solely limited to providing minimal protective functions. American empire goes beyond providing basic protection, so cronyism should be expected to be ubiquitous and especially rampant. With its rent seeking, rent extraction, and revolving door, the US military sector at the foundation of American empire is the poster child for state capitalism writ large.

The subsequent chapter, Chapter 4, analyzes the limitations of imperialism. I consider two broad categories of constraints—knowledge and incentive. Knowledge constraints, which refer to limits on the use of human reason to design the world, matter because interveners cannot fully grasp the complexities of the world in our own society, let alone in other societies. Even *if* we assume the best of intentions on the part of interveners, they do not know how to go about designing liberal institutions and a global "liberal order." Furthermore, foreign interventions suffer from significant incentive problems. The industrial organization of an empire, which is Big Government writ large, often produces perverse outcomes that prevent imperialists from achieving their goals. These include the various frictions and pathologies in democratic politics resulting in waste, persistent resource misallocation, and inertia in policies and daily operations.

The following two chapters illustrate the limits of foreign intervention and the realities of empire. In Chapter 5, I analyze the US government's effort to combat opium production in Afghanistan. Despite spending billions on drug interdiction efforts in Afghanistan since the 2001 invasion, opium production grew substantially. The US government's policies of drug eradication not only failed to end the opium trade, but they also undermined the goals of the war on terror. By creating numerous perverse consequences, the US interdiction efforts strengthened the Taliban insurgency and undercut the stated goals of the occupation. This is a powerful case study because it illustrates the dramatic failure of a well-financed, well-staffed government initiative with a clear, straightforward overarching goal. If the American empire fails so dismally in this case, what should be expected of more complex and grandiose instances of imperialism?

In Chapter 6, I turn to the US government's drone program, a defining feature of America's global military strategy as part of the broad and open-ended "war on terror." I discuss the harm caused to innocent civilians, contrary to the claims made by many US policymakers. I then consider a tension: the US government justifies drones as an efficient method for weakening, and ultimately ending, the threat of global terrorism. However, drones create and spread terror among foreign populations. Drone strikes may annihilate specific targets, but they do not eliminate terror, which is propagated by the US government's drone program. This case study illustrates how military imperialism frequently contributes to unseen costs and negative consequences that foster illiberalism and make Americans less safe.

Each of the first six chapters concludes with a list of points summarizing the realities of empire. The purpose is to reiterate key themes, both within each chapter and across the broader analysis of the American empire.

The final chapter asks you to rethink empire. I discuss the importance of shifting focus from a culture of militarism to cultures of peace (the plural is used to emphasize the many possible paths to peace). Central to this shift is the consideration of alternatives to empire through alternative means of security provision. As a first step, I consider one possible alternative—polycentric defense—in both conceptual and practical terms. Finally, the epilogue discusses renewed calls for a reinvigorated American empire in light of perceived challenges posed by China and Russia, and offers reasons to resist the siren song of empire.

The Realities of Empire

- It is simplistic and utopian to imagine that an interventionist apparatus and polity will act only in the good cases and avoid the associated bads. A complete analysis of empire must go beyond a focus on the narrow signs of potential goods.
- The analysis of empire must recognize the limitations of knowledge regarding institutional and social change, the pathologies of democratic politics in the intervening countries, and the deleterious consequences, or "public bads," of imperialism.
- Foreign interventions promote a way of thinking among the elite and others that leads them to see the world as a competitive zero-sum game.
- Imperialism and interventionism deemphasize the role of spontaneous forces, while elevating the importance of centralized control for order and coercive force as the basic means of social relations and dispute resolution.
- Failed states often arise because of earlier imperialism.
- Imperialism has long been associated with bellicose masculinity, xenophobia, and racism, and liberal imperialism has been no exception.

2

Illiberal Foundations of a Liberal Empire

LIBERAL EMPIRE IS not only illiberal in practice, but it also threatens the very foundation of liberalism *everywhere*, both abroad and at home. Military imperialism in particular harms humans, badly and often forever.[1] Although US foreign military interventions are usually justified by proclaiming liberal ideals, the truth is that such interventions are inherently illiberal. The very idea of an international liberal order—created and maintained by the American military since 1945—is a misnomer. To the extent that an American-created international order exists, it is a result of illiberal activities, including systematic violence, the threat of force, violations of international law, and partnerships with brutal, authoritarian regimes.[2]

Moreover, the job of running the liberal empire falls on a largely lawless, illiberal group of American government officials and political elites, who are given wide, discretionary power (largely outside of the US Constitution) over the lives of peoples and nations, including their fellow citizens. Many excel at their jobs and rise naturally through the government ranks. In fact, it is a necessary leadership skill for any aspiring imperialist that he or she has the capacity to downplay or ignore other people as human beings deserving of individual sovereignty and dignity. Instead, "the government" and "the nation-state" are elevated above the individual, both at home and abroad. The very idea of emergent orders, free of government control and violence, is alien to them. Should asymmetries exist between the goals of the intervener and the will of the targeted populations, mechanisms of social control are prescribed to raise the cost of resistance and noncompliance. Examples of social control by the US government in foreign interventions are many, and include massive use of military force, troop presence ("boots on the ground"), surveillance, curfews, segregation, bribery, censorship, suppression, imprisonment, and torture of local populations.

To pull it all off, interventionists must believe their vision is superior to any alternatives, including the status quo; otherwise, the intervention would not be undertaken in the first place.[3] This outlook of superiority is multifaceted, predicated on the belief that the interventionist possesses (1) better technological knowledge compared to foreigners, (2) better preferences to those held by foreigners, and (3) better moral insight than foreigners in general. Taken together, this overarching sense of superiority doesn't further liberal values, but promotes illiberal disorder instead. Political scientists Simon Reich and Richard Ned Lebow analyze the US government's reliance on its military in international affairs and conclude that "we . . . characterize the United States as constituting as much a threat to global order and stability as it is a possible pillar of its preservation."[4]

The overly confident interventionist is comfortable using an array of means to get his or her way. Typically, this includes some combination of soft power—the ability to attract and persuade—and hard power—force and coercion. In certain cases, hard power can be brutal; tools of the trade include torture, long-term incarceration without due process, and the killing of innocent civilians categorized as "collateral damage."[5] Where such extreme tactics are employed, proponents of liberal intervention fail to understand or acknowledge that these vicious illiberal methods destroy liberalism itself.

Interventions are typically complex, broad, and oversold as humanitarian. Yet even where humanitarian motives do exist, interventionists too often lack compassion and empathy toward the targeted populace and will injure and kill them—whether intentionally or unintentionally—to get their way. As prime examples, consider the US government's military interventions in Afghanistan and Iraq. Part of the justification for these interventions included improving the well-being of citizens and promoting democracy. These interventions had indeed generated certain, if limited, improvements in certain areas—unsurprising given the significant sums of money spent by the US government on the occupations, which included an array of humanitarian programs.

Despite these improvements, concern for the safety of Afghan and Iraqi citizens never appeared to be the highest priority. As US General Tommy Franks once remarked when discussing the number of people killed by US forces in Afghanistan, "[W]e [the US government] don't do body counts."[6] Discussing the injury and death of innocent Afghan civilians at checkpoints at the hands of American and NATO occupiers, General Stanley McChrystal, then senior American and NATO commander in Afghanistan, noted that "[w]e have shot an amazing number of people, but to my knowledge, none has ever proven to be a threat."[7]

In addition to combatant and inevitable civilian fatalities, foreign interventions bring other, nonlethal costs on local populations: family displacements, the onset and spread of disease, malnutrition, communal violence, and a variety of short- and long-term psychological problems. These costs may outpace any potential humanitarian benefits generated by interveners. There is a tendency to focus too narrowly on the lives lost and monetary costs incurred by the intervening nation, while excluding the larger costs that fall on the targeted surrounding populations.[8] This approach severely underestimates the costs of intervention while encouraging moral apathy on the part of the intervener.

Finally, in addition to directly adopting harsh techniques of social control at home and abroad as a means of spreading liberal empire, the US government has historically partnered with brutal authoritarian regimes to achieve short-term imperial goals, thus violating and undermining the liberal values it claims to uphold.[9] In short, the interventionist must be willing to consider employing all illiberal means available in order to succeed, under the age-old canard that "the [liberal] ends justify the [illiberal] means."

Why Illiberals Get on Top of a Liberal Empire

Liberal imperialism requires that a small group of government elites hold fast to the belief in their ability to redesign other societies according to a grand "global order" blueprint. Moreover, a certain hubris is needed to believe that this blueprint can be implemented like any other engineering plan. For example, the very idea of externally imposed "nation building" exemplifies hubris. Despite its noble stated aims, a liberal empire needs the same type of people to run it as any other empire. Given imperialism's authoritarianism, militarism, and the overall illiberalism required for an empire's growth, a certain type of individual rises to top leadership positions.[10]

In his discussion of economic planning in the 1930s, economist Frank Knight noted that economic planning authorities would have to "exercise their power ruthlessly to keep the machinery of organized production and distribution running" and that "[t]hey would have to enforce orders ruthlessly and suppress all disputation and argument against policies."[11] He went on to argue that "the probability of the people in power being individuals who would dislike the possession and exercise of power is on a level with the probability that an extremely tender-hearted person would get the job of whipping-master on a slave plantation."[12]

Economist F. A. Hayek, a future Nobel laureate, made a similar argument, emphasizing that under a regime of government economic planning, the worst people in society were the most likely to rise to positions of power. Planning grants significant discretionary power to those tasked with making decisions about the allocation of resources. Who, Hayek asked, is most likely to flourish in a system characterized by wielding such power over others? Like Knight, his answer was that "the unscrupulous and uninhibited are likely to be more successful" in such a system.[13] That is, those who feel comfortable exercising power and control over other human beings are most likely to advance in a system of unconstrained, discretionary decision-making.

Knight and Hayek also pointed out that, irrespective of the type of person who entered the system, success ultimately required that they behave in a defined way. The incentives created by central planning would either initially attract the type of people who already behaved as Knight and Hayek described, or would require otherwise "good" people to act in an unscrupulous manner to flourish. People who were uncomfortable being paternalistic and authoritarian were unlikely to desire leadership positions in the first place, or they would soon be replaced by more ambitious candidates.

A similar type of government official is found in empire building and military interventions. People in key imperial positions will either possess the interventionist mindset or have the incentive to acquire it quickly in order to fulfill bureaucratic mandates and objectives, achieve promotion, or simply keep their jobs. The required mentality is further dependent on the bureaucratic pecking order because "[f]unctions within the bureaucracy arrange hierarchically, so that higher authorities always control those with less power at lower levels, and decisions and policies always sift from the top down."[14]

In the context of foreign policy, those further up the hierarchy of empire are those who decide where and when to intervene and determine the specific techniques and strategies for carrying out those interventions. Those further down the hierarchy, cogs in the imperial machine, will tend to possess fewer of these characteristics but must have some to execute the intervention.

There are four related factors that promote widespread adoption of the interventionist mindset. First, people are attracted to work for an organization where they fit in with its culture, and government and bureaucracy are no exceptions to this rule. Government employment is a way of life, attracting thousands of willing applicants every year.

Second, those in government bureaus are actively indoctrinated to follow orders. The military is the model. Colonel James Donovan notes that US military training "stresses the fundamental obligation to serve the nation loyally and without question to carry out the policies and orders of the President, who is Commander in Chief, and the orders of his appointed officers."[15] Philosopher Jack Conrad Willers emphasizes that those entering bureaus soon realize "[s]uccess within bureaucracy requires not only skill and expertise and knowledge but also above all, an apparent devotion to the bureaucracy and unquestioning loyalty to its goals."[16] Former National Security Advisor and Secretary of State Henry Kissinger noted that, once embedded in the foreign policy bureaucracy, "[s]erving the machine becomes a more absorbing occupation than defining its purpose."[17]

A third factor encouraging adoption of the interventionist mindset is the desire for personal advancement within government bureaucracy.[18] As in any organization, those employed in government agencies advance their careers by developing the appropriate skills and reputation, while signaling these abilities to key decision-makers. Again, the military is the ideal. General David M. Shoup noted that in the US military "[p]romotions and the choice job opportunities are attained by constantly performing well, conforming to the expected patterns, and pleasing the senior officers."[19] Similarly, Colonel James Donovan emphasized that to advance, the bureaucrat "must become known as a faithful disciple of his service. To promote the organization and its success, he has to compete for goals other than dollar profits, within the fields of operational doctrines, service doctrines, roles and missions, defense appropriations, new weapons programs, and service prestige."[20] This incentive generates peculiar, and often undesirable, imperial outcomes.

In the context of for-profit markets, professional and commercial competition is desirable because the process yields beneficial goods and services, which advances the welfare of private consumers. Yet in the context of government-led imperialism, the nature of professional and bureaucratic competition is dramatically different. The "customers" are those in positions of power and influence in the empire. Those tasked with carrying out interventions will satisfy their customers by going above and beyond their bureaucratic duty to complete the mission. This involves controlling foreign populations to secure cooperation—and to dampen, suppress, or altogether eradicate any resistance. Therefore, interveners will face the incentive to act entrepreneurially in order to develop, implement, and refine a range of social control techniques, aiming to satisfy their political customers at the expense of the target population. Consider the Abu Ghraib torture scandal, where loose bureaucratic guidelines and mandates—combined with unclear rules regarding the legal definition of torture—led to various forms of prisoner abuse as a means to secure "actionable intelligence" and satiate expansive, ill-defined orders from commanders.[21]

Fourth, there are internal mechanisms, beyond indoctrination techniques, that weed out those who fail to fall in line with the interventionist mindset. Sociologist Robert Merton notes that successful bureaus require "a high degree of reliability of behavior, an unusual degree of conformity with prescribed patterns of action."[22] He goes on to argue that the personalities of those working in the agency will tend to conform to these patterns of action because "there are definite arrangements in the bureaucracy for inculcating and reinforcing these sentiments."[23]

Since there is a tendency for people to leave an organization in which they do not belong (voluntarily or through eventual termination), the illiberal mentality stubbornly persists and grows in government. Those who stay have or soon adopt an interventionist mindset, and they become either leaders or cogs in the imperial machine.

The Illiberal Protective State

Despite what it takes to get to the top and run it, proponents of American liberal empire still view the state as a pro-liberty force everywhere.[24] From their perspective, the awesome powers concentrated in the open hands of the US national security state promote liberal values abroad, while upholding and protecting domestic liberties from external *and* internal threats at home. However, the massive concentration of power required for an empire presents a paradoxical challenge: Can government be simultaneously empowered and constrained?[25] Can it remain a force for liberty?

James Madison's solution to this paradox involved the creation of constitutional constraints, empowering government to engage in beneficial behaviors and constraining its ability to engage in predation. Two centuries later, Nobel laureate economist James Buchanan embraced Madison's vision of constitutional constraints. In doing so, Buchanan developed his theory of the "protective state," which emerges at the constitutional level and protects the core rights of citizens via internal security, contract enforcement, and defense against external threats.[26] But what if the paradox is irreconcilable, and the existence and operation of the protective state actively erodes the freedoms it is intended to protect? Moreover, does the pursuit of empire make this erosion inevitable, and far worse?

It is not an anomaly that a protective state influences domestic life in ways that have permanent, authoritarian effects, a great fear of the American Founders and a reason for the implementation of the US Constitution. It must follow that a vast military empire, one which is often outside constitutional boundaries, poses a lethal threat. Ignoring these realities overemphasizes the liberty-enhancing aspects of liberal empire and deemphasizes its liberty-destroying character.

The greatest potential for the protective state to produce authoritarian outcomes has been realized during war. James Madison knew the dangers and provided the following warning regarding the state's war-making abilities:

> Of all the enemies to public liberty, war is perhaps the most to be dreaded, because it comprises and develops the germ of every other. War is the parent of armies; from these proceed debts and taxes; and

armies, and debts, and taxes are the known instruments for bringing the many under the domination of the few. In war, too, the discretionary power of the Executive is extended; its influence in dealing out offices, honors, and emoluments is multiplied; and all the means of seducing the minds, are added to those of subduing the force, of the people. . . . No nation could preserve its freedom in the midst of continual warfare.[27]

Madison understood that, while the protective state may be used to protect the rights of citizens, these powers will also result in threats to their safety. Some of these threats are obvious, such as the fiscal burden (huge spending on war) that determines the scale or size of the state. Other consequences, such as expansions in the discretionary power of the state, affect the scope or range of government activities. It should be noted that, while bigness and intrusiveness are important aspects of the state, they are not always the same, a fact Buchanan recognized: "[a]n interfering federal judiciary, along with an irresponsible executive, could exist even when budget sizes remain relatively small."[28] Fiscal constraint doesn't guarantee a citizen's rights, and can coexist with authoritarianism on the cheap.

Alexis de Tocqueville also recognized the deleterious effects of war-making powers on domestic political institutions. Like Madison, he warned of the threat war posed to liberty:

War does not always give over democratic communities to military government, but it must invariably and immeasurably increase the powers of civil government; it must almost compulsorily concentrate the direction of all men and the management of all things in the hands of the administration. If it does not lead to despotism by sudden violence, it prepares men for it more gently by their habits. All those who seek to destroy the liberties of a democratic nation ought to know that war is the surest and the shortest means to accomplish it.[29]

Ideally, the protective state would undertake only those activities that uphold and defend its citizens' liberties, including the avoidance of unnecessary wars. Ideally, appropriate constitutional constraints can exist and be enhanced to protect against unforeseen threats to liberty in the future, lessening the concerns shared by Madison and Tocqueville. However, the historical record shows that an ideal protective state rarely(if ever) exists, as "[f]oreign affairs, and its close relation national security, have been a graveyard for civil liberties."[30] Scholars have documented numerous instances from history where state-led security and war activities resulted in significant, and often permanent, expansions in state power and consequently less liberty.[31]

The Nature of Protective State Activities

Two features of the protective state are central to understanding how its activities can produce authoritarian outcomes at home. First, at the core of the state's activities is the threat or use of coercive force, both at home and abroad, by government officials and elected politicians attracted to wielding power for their own advancement and that of the state. As James Buchanan and philosopher Geoffrey Brennan wrote, "[O]f course, in the establishment of the political entity, powers of coercion are granted to governments, powers that are designed to prevent criminal trespass and exploitation of rights by internal and external aggressors."[32] In the present day, this includes state-of-the-art policing, military, and sophisticated surveillance capabilities.

This monopoly on the use of force may produce pro-liberty outcomes, but one cannot assume or predict this, since governments have routinely abused their power throughout history. Brennan and Buchanan recognized this distinct possibility when noting that "[i]n the assignment of these powers [to the state], problems of control may arise, problems that are not amenable to easy solution. Once established as sovereign, government may not willingly remain within the limits of its initially delegated authority."[33]

Second, in practice, the activities of the protective state influence and affect almost all areas of domestic life—economic, political, and social. In its ideal form, the minimal protective state will only enforce contracts, provide internal security to protect rights, and supply national defense against external threats. As economist Robert Higgs emphasizes, however, the state's power to engage in national security policymaking is a "master key" because it "opens all doors, including the doors that might otherwise obstruct the government's invasion of our most cherished rights to life, liberty, and property."[34]

One need only consider the revelations of the US surveillance state in the aftermath of the 9/11 attacks and subsequent "war on terror" to understand how the security-related activities of government can bleed into almost all aspects of private life. These revelations made clear that, among other things, the government was monitoring the communications, financial transactions, and travel of US and non-US persons; surveillance is but one aspect of the overall portfolio of government activities related to its protective function.

The conventional terminology employed when discussing protective state actions neglects the wide range of powers it possesses in the name of guarding citizens' rights. The terms "defense" and "security" purposively suggest passive acts of protection from internal and external threats. However, what constitutes defense and security (weapons, arms, equipment, surveillance, intelligence, and all their related subcomponents, as well as the training to wield them efficiently) are sophisticated technologies and methods which have made it easier for governments to control and harm people at home and abroad.

Throughout most of history, governments have used their monopoly on force less to defend the rights and property of their citizens, and more as a tool of direct and indirect social control.[35] This has occurred under authoritarian regimes and constitutionally constrained states. As political scientist Bruce Porter writes, "[W]ars throughout modern history have fostered authoritarian rule, undermined the civic order of traditional states, perverted consensual political processes within constitutional states, and threatened or destroyed established rights and liberties."[36] This raises an important issue, since certain protective state activities lead to the erosion of domestic liberties (directly or indirectly), cutting against its fundamental purpose for existing.

Direct erosions are obvious, occurring when governments openly use blunt force to control and oppress their citizens. Civil conflicts in Libya (under Mu'ammar al-Gadhafi) and Syria (under Bashar al-Assad) offer two of the most recent and brutal examples, as the governments of these countries deployed blunt, coercive force to suppress uprisings. Under the direct erosion scenario, constitutional constraints demarcating protective state functions are either ineffective or absent. The direct scenario is not surprising, since it indicates that when governments are unconstrained, they will abuse their powers as expected. Indeed, the very purpose of constitutions is, in part, to stop direct erosions from occurring.

A bigger concern, noted by Tocqueville, is the indirect erosion of liberties which occurs when a constitutionally constrained government slowly expands the scope of its powers and thereby oppresses its citizens. Supreme Court Justice William O. Douglas captured the essence of this indirect process when he observed that "[a]s nightfall does not come all at once, neither does oppression. In both instances there is a twilight when everything remains seemingly unchanged. And it is in such twilight that we all must be most aware of change in the air—however slight—lest we become unwitting victims of the dark."[37]

How the Protective State Erodes Liberty at Home

There are five ways in which the activities of political leaders, bureaucrats, police, and the military can erode liberties in a constitutionally constrained protective state.[38] These pathways are inherent in the protective state's operations and do not require nefarious motivations on the part of those charged with eroding liberties. As noted earlier, it comes with their jobs. Instead, these channels reflect the insight of Justice Frank Murphy, who noted that "[f]ew indeed have been the invasions upon essential liberties which have not been accompanied by pleas of urgent necessity advanced in good faith by responsible men."[39]

Interpretation in an Open-Ended System

Constitutions contain significant space for interpreting the appropriate role of the state. As historian Charles A. Beard writes, each word or phrase in the US Constitution

> . . . covers some core of the reality and practice on which a general consensus can be reached. But around this core is a huge shadow in which the good and wise can wander indefinitely without ever coming to any agreement respecting the command made by the "law." Ever since the Constitution was framed or particular amendments added,

dispute has raged among men of strong minds and pure hearts over the meaning of these cloud covered words and phrases.[40]

The need for interpretation arises because constitutional framers had, by nature, limited understanding of what the world would look like in the future.

Constitutions establish rules for an open-ended system characterized by creativity, genuine surprise, and shifting interests.[41] For example, no one at the Constitutional Convention in 1787 could have anticipated the nature of the surveillance and military tools available to the US government today. As a result, constitutional interpretation is needed considering technological advances alone, as well as the power they grant to government. The specific nature of these interpretations, which may be pro- or anti-liberty, are influenced in turn by the beliefs of key decision-makers—e.g., the public, elected officials, judges, and other court officers.

Constitutional interpretation in US history is especially evident during times of national emergencies.[42] Despite the fact that the US Constitution does not contain any specific delineation of emergency powers, the government has undertaken a wide range of crisis-induced activities.[43] Courts have often stepped aside during periods of perceived emergency, virtually granting the other branches of government free reign to do as they please.[44] For example, during World War II, the Supreme Court "gave judicial sanction to whatever powers and actions the President and Congress found necessary to the prosecution of the war. . . ."[45] In general, Robert Higgs argues that "when critical trade-offs must be made, war will override all other concerns, and as the ancient maxim aptly warns us, *inter arma silent leges* [in the midst of arms, the laws are silent]."[46]

The Supreme Court's interpretation of government legality during times of emergency varies greatly.[47] To provide one illustration of how these interpretations can be anti-liberty, consider the internment of Japanese Americans during World War II. During the war, the US government forcibly relocated over 110,000 Japanese Americans, an estimated two-thirds of them US citizens, into internment camps.[48] Absent an explicit provision to carry out this forced relocation, the Supreme Court needed to interpret the constitutionality of the government's actions. It did so in two cases, in 1943 and 1944.

In *Hirabayashi v. United States* (1943), the court upheld the curfew set by General John DeWitt, indicating that restrictions against a group of US citizens were constitutional when the United States was at war with the group's country of origin. In *Korematsu v. United States* (1944), the court heard the case of Fred Korematsu, a US citizen arrested after staying in his home in California despite the government's order compelling Japanese Americans to report to relocation camps.[49] The court upheld the relocation order as constitutional. According to political scientist Clinton Rossiter, "[T]he punishment of this loyal citizen [Korematsu] of the United States was sanctioned by the highest court of the land; his crime: sitting in his own home."[50] He goes on to summarize the broader implications of these two Supreme Court decisions:

> The important lessons for the problem of constitutional dictatorship in the United States are these: that the President's unlimited range of dictatorial crisis power was again exerted without legislative, judicial, or popular contradiction; that the Supreme Court demonstrated its continued unwillingness to get in the way of the war power of the United States; and that the most basic rights of a large group of American citizens were grossly flouted under conditions considerably less than desperate, and can be again.[51]

As this example illustrates, the activities of the protective state can (and have) produced anti-liberty results within the confines of existing constitutional rules. During the war, the government expanded the scope of its control over the lives of Americans, reducing their liberties. The court upheld the government's actions, which institutionalized the widened scope of state power over both current and future Americans. This logic applies to numerous other instances throughout US history.

Institutional Changes within Constitutional Constraints

Rules determined at the constitutional stage frame subsequent postconstitutional activity, including processes for making changes to political institutions. However, given the uncertainty of the future, changes that might make sense at one point in time may lead to unforeseeable outcomes later. Even *if* initial institutional changes are pro-liberty, they can generate an array of possibilities for future authoritarian outcomes.

Considering the long-term implications of the National Security Act of 1947, legal scholar Michael Glennon has identified a "double government" with two distinct sets of institutions.[52] The first set of institutions consists of the "dignified institutions," including the executive, legislative, and judicial branches. These are the institutions most people have in mind when they think of the constitutionally constrained protective state. The foundations of the dignified institutions are the Madisonian structure of dispersed power across the three branches of government, intended to address the paradox of government.

The National Security Act of 1947 eroded these Madisonian checks and balances on the national security state. Centralizing power and granting the security agencies significant independence weakened existing checks, lowering the barriers to expansion in both the scale and scope of government over decades. Ultimately, the reforms created an environment within which the national security institutions could expand, given the significant loosening of constraints on those operating in the state's security organizations.

The result was that the dignified institutions were joined by a new set of government institutions—the "efficient institutions"—that exert significant influence over foreign policy.[53] As discussed in the previous chapter, this deep state consists of a complex network of government agencies and departments—military, intelligence, law enforcement, diplomatic—as well as the private contractors and consultants that constitute the national security state (see the next chapter).[54] They are efficient in that those operating within these institutions are largely relieved of the full burdens created by the original Madisonian checks and balances intended to prevent abuses of power. As a result, those operating within the security state have greater freedom to shape and pursue their own agendas in an unconstrained manner.

The implications of the security state's increased autonomy are troubling. According to Glennon, "Large segments of the public continue to believe that America's constitutionally established, dignified institutions are the locus of governmental power; by promoting that impression, both sets of institutions maintain public support."[55] While the dignified institutions still maintain some control over state activities, the efficient institutions exert significant influence. Each of the three branches constituting the dignified institutions has limited power to constrain the efficient institutions, creating space for expansions in state power over the lives of citizens.[56]

Elected officials—both in the executive branch and in Congress—face several realities limiting their ability to monitor and constrain the deep state. The first is sheer information overload due to the array of issues—both domestic and international—that these officials must understand in order to make policy. There is simply no way to understand or monitor all the activities of the complex security state. This leaves room for those in the efficient institutions to control and influence low-priority aspects of foreign policy. Second, those involved with the efficient institutions can control the information available to elected officials, thereby affording them the opportunity to shape policy. Third, members of Congress are constrained by classified information they cannot access. Even when this classified information is available to members of oversight committees, they typically cannot share it with nonmembers. This limits the efficacy of nonmember representatives as a check on the security state. Fourth, the electorate tends to suffer from ignorance regarding foreign affairs and the complexities of the security state. The result is that people tend not to pressure their representatives to understand and check the activities of the national security state. This lack of voter oversight reinforces the ineffectiveness of monitoring by elected officials.[57]

Similarly, the judiciary is limited as a check on the security state. As political scientist Edward Corwin argued in the wake of World War II, "In total war the [Supreme] Court necessarily loses some part of its normal freedom of decision and becomes assimilated, like the rest of society, to the mechanism of national defense."[58] This alignment and integration of the courts with the other branches of government weakens the checks created by the separation of powers, leaving space for those in the deep state to exert a range of influence over security policy in an unchecked manner.

The US government's abuse of surveillance powers through time is but one example of the slack in constraints on the protective state. Consider, for instance, the six-volume Church Committee report released in the wake of the public revelation of the government's domestic surveillance activities in the 1970s. Among other things, the report indicated that the unchecked surveillance apparatus unleashed an unconstrained leviathan, as "virtually every element of our [US] society has been subjected to excessive government-ordered intelligence inquiries," and that "this extreme breadth of intelligence activity is inconsistent with the principles of our Constitution which protect the rights of speech, political activity, and privacy against unjustified governmental intrusion."[59] Despite the implementation of reforms—e.g., the United States Foreign Intelligence Surveillance Court (FISA Court) established under the Foreign Intelligence Surveillance Act (FISA) of 1978—to check the US government, Edward Snowden's 2013 revelations regarding the activities of the US surveillance state indicate the persistence and expansion of the status quo.[60] The Snowden revelations demonstrate not only the independence of the national security state, but also its tendency to self-perpetuate and grow.

Centralization of State Power

Different levels of government can execute the functions of the protective state. For example, policing activities take place at different levels of government operation. However, the federal government plays a central role in protective state activities, especially as they pertain to the large portfolio of activities falling under the broad category of "national security." Moreover, activities at the national level often spill over and influence governments at lower levels. This has important implications because in carrying out its protective activities, the national government can increase its power relative to citizens and lower levels of government.[61] This shift in relative power occurs because conducting national-level security and defense activities requires that the federal government increase its discretionary decision-making powers, as well as its control over resources. Bruce Porter captures the essence of this dynamic when he notes that "a government at war is a juggernaut of centralization determined to crush any internal opposition that impedes the mobilization of militarily vital resources. This centralizing tendency of war has made the rise of the state throughout much of history a disaster for human liberty and rights."[62]

The consolidation of control and power at the national level takes place through two main avenues. The first is through bureaucratization, whereby existing federal government agencies gain more power and resources while new bureaus emerge simultaneously. Edward Corwin captured this logic when, discussing the effects of World War II on American society in 1947, he argued that "on the plea of war necessity we have assembled the most numerous bureaucracies since the Roman Empire, and now that the war is over, appear to be unable or unwilling to reduce it materially."[63]

Second, national security and defense activities provide a focal point for rallying citizens around a common external cause. This shared focus diverts citizen attention away from the domestic threat of the state to external threats and affairs that supposedly require state protection. For example, during a war, citizens and the government tend to unify in the common effort against an external threat. One result is that national government activities previously considered intolerable become acceptable sacrifices necessary to achieve "the country's" foreign policy goals. Another is that there is an increasing centralization of power in the hands of national government employees, in the name of combatting the external threat. Among the main consequences of centralization is the erosion of federalist checks.

Federalism divides power between a central political unit and subunits, dispersing power and limiting what any unit can do. By doing so, federalism serves as one potential solution to the paradox of government. However, there is no assurance of the pro-liberty benefits of federalism. As economist Richard Wagner argues, "A system of competitive federalism stands in opposition to a system of monopolistic federalism, in which political entities act in cartel-like fashion to promote the interests of their supporters over the interests of the rest of society."[64] As the national government consolidates its power, the activities of the protective state shift the relative balance toward the center of political power, weakening the ability of subunits to serve as a check against potential abuses. This clears the path for expansions in political power and concomitant reductions in individual liberty.

To provide an illustration of this phenomenon, consider Section 1208 of the National Defense Authorization Act of 1990, which authorized the Department of Defense to transfer military equipment to federal, state, and local agencies. In 1997, this initiative became the 1033 Program, allowing the Department of Defense to transfer military equipment such as aircraft, armor, riot gear, surveillance equipment, watercraft, and weapons to state and local police. These programs have had two effects. First, they led to the militarization of police, whereby domestic police forces have increasingly adopted military equipment and tactics.[65] Second, these programs linked lower-level governments to the central government through resource flows, increasing their connection to and dependence on the political center. The result is the erosion of the separation of government units necessary to ensure the pro-liberty aspects of federalism.

Writing in 1816, Thomas Jefferson asked, "What has destroyed liberty and the rights of man in every government which has ever existed under the sun?"[66] His answer: the "generalizing and concentrating all cares and powers into one body, no matter whether of the autocrats of Russia or France, or of the aristocrats of a Venetian Senate."[67] An appreciation for Jefferson's insight highlights a tension regarding the protective state. The activities of the protective state purportedly protect the rights and liberties of the populace. Carrying out these activities, however, leads the national government to increase the scope and scale of its power. This expansion increases the discretionary power of the political center and erodes the checks and balances on the power offered by the subunits of the political periphery. When this shift occurs, the protective state expands as a threat to the very liberties it is supposed to safeguard.

Coercion-Enabling Skills

The operations of the protective state require certain skills. The threat and use of force is the foundation of protective state activities. Thus, as noted above, the protective state requires those it employs to possess coercion-enabling skills in order to operate effectively.[68] For example, members of the military must be willing to follow the directives of superiors in an unquestioning manner, to adopt certain coercive techniques of monitoring, control, and suppression against those deemed threats by decision-makers in government.

Those who enter the employment of the protective state and wish to succeed in this environment possess the requisite skills, or will acquire them quickly if they want to keep their jobs. Returning to the case of the military mentioned earlier, Colonel James Donovan notes that "[i]t takes only a matter of months for each of the services to remold the average young American and turn him into a skilled, indoctrinated and motivated member of the armed forces."[69] The coercion-enabling skills required for success in the protective state may generate pro-liberty outcomes by protecting the rights and liberties of private people. However, this same skill set can just as quickly result in anti-liberty outcomes by changing the fabric of domestic life for the worse.[70]

To understand why, consider that the coercion-enabling skill set required for success in the protective state becomes a fundamental part of the makeup of those involved. After leaving the operations of the protective state, these people often reallocate their talents to other areas of life. In certain cases, people move from the public sector to the private sector—e.g., the move from the Department of Defense to a private defense contractor. In other instances, they move across the functions of the protective state—e.g., the move from active military duty to the domestic police force. In still other cases, people move from the protective state to other areas of public life—e.g., the move from the military to elected office.

In these and many other examples, those involved take their specialized skills and experiences with them, becoming key political leaders, security analysts and consultants, executives at private defense firms, police officers, etc. As this process unfolds, the skills necessary for success in the protective state—a comparative advantage in the use of force—bleed into civilian life, changing the nature of domestic institutions and the relationship between citizens and the state.[71]

Colonel James Donovan captured these dynamics when discussing the effects of World War II on US society, noting that "[t]he indoctrination with military codes and creeds experienced by millions of men and women who move in and out of the services has a continuing and prolonged and even regenerative effect upon the ideas, attitudes, and martial fiber of the nation as a whole."[72] He goes on to add that "[t]he lives, the attitudes, and the beliefs of America's war veterans have been influenced by their military service; and because they represent such a large share of the adult male population their degree of militarism creates a strong imprint on the national character."[73] Thus, the protective state can have anti-liberty effects on domestic political and social institutions by influencing the attitudes, beliefs, and skills of the people staffing and shaping those institutions.

The US surveillance state is one illustration of this reality.[74] The origins of the modern surveillance state can be traced back to the Philippine-American War (1899–1902) and its aftermath. Under the leadership of Ralph Van Deman, an officer in the Army who would later become known as the "father of

American military intelligence," the US occupiers established a cutting-edge surveillance apparatus to control the occupied population and combat insurgency. Van Deman returned home in 1902, bringing his unique skill set with him. Back in the United States, he worked to establish a similar surveillance apparatus domestically.[75] World War I presented an opening for Van Deman, and in May 1917, the Military Intelligence Section was established with Van Deman (now a colonel) in charge. Over the subsequent decades, the US surveillance state evolved and matured, culminating in the establishment of the National Security Agency (NSA) in 1952. As this makes clear, expertise in controlling foreign populations can migrate back to the intervening country, thereby expanding state power and threatening domestic liberty.

Coercion-Enabling Technologies

In order to carry out its operations, the protective state also requires the aid of coercion-enabling technologies—e.g., weapons and surveillance technologies —that allow for the efficient control of the target population. Governments invest a significant number of resources in developing coercion-enabling technologies. For example, in FY 2019, the US Department of Defense spent $95.2 billion on research, development, test and evaluation, and $147.3 billion on procurement.[76] In principle, these investments allow the members of the protective state to project force to neutralize any threats to citizens' liberties. At the same time, however, these innovations can contribute to authoritarian outcomes.

Technological advances are one key factor behind the growth of government because improved technology lowers the cost of operating a larger government.[77] For example, it is easier to collect taxes with electronic banking as compared to a situation where the tax collector must go door to door and collect taxes in person. This same logic extends to the scale and scope of protective state activities; advances in surveillance and weapons technologies (with the aim of efficiently monitoring and killing threats) allow the protective state to uphold the rights of citizens. However, these same technological advances also allow the state to undermine individual liberties in a more efficient manner. Advances in coercion-enabling technologies not only allow governments to project force more efficiently over a greater geographic space, but also to more easily conceal their activities so that citizens are unable to recognize expansions in the scope of state power.

Consider, for example, the use of "Stingrays," or cell tower simulators. This technology allows the user to surreptitiously redirect cell phones into transmitting information, such as location and other identifiers. Originally developed for use by the military and intelligence communities abroad, the availability of Stingrays expanded as part of the US government's war on terror. These devices are now in use within the United States by members of local law enforcement, who can surveil people with little or no oversight.[78] This example highlights how the coercive tools of the protective state can turn inward, threatening the liberties of citizens in the same way that protective state people acquire the skills to defend or abuse others. It also illustrates how technological advances allow the members of the protective state to conceal the true cost of their activities, since citizens are unaware of the extent of the state's surveillance activities.

The Realities of Empire

- Imperialism in the name of liberalism requires the adoption, acceptance, and entrenchment of an illiberal mentality and tactics.
- The industrial organization of empire includes mechanisms that attract, reinforce, and perpetuate an interventionist mind-set at odds with liberal values.
- Empire diverts attention away from the perpetual domestic struggle between state power and individual liberty.
- The operation of empire places severe stress on constitutional constraints, often causing irreparable damage and destruction to restraints on government power.
- Imperialism requires expansions in state power that permanently and perversely affect the liberal fabric of domestic political, social, and economic institutions, in both seen and unseen ways.

3

Liberal Empire as State Capitalism Writ Large

"INVESTIGATOR TRUMAN: A democracy has to keep an eye on itself" read the cover of the March 8, 1943 issue of *Time* magazine. Accompanying this headline were images of then Senator Harry Truman and a spotlight shining down upon the United States Capitol building and an industrial plant. At the time, Truman gained national attention for his leadership of the Senate Special Committee to Investigate the National Defense Program, which investigated defense contracts awarded during World War II.[1] According to estimates, the Special Committee identified $15 billion in waste, fraud, and mismanaged contracts involving government and private contractors.[2] Fast-forward almost seventy years to 2011, when the bipartisan Commission on Wartime Contracting in Iraq and Afghanistan released their final report. The opening lines state that "[a]t least $31 billion, and possibly as much as $60 billion, has been lost to contract waste and fraud in America's contingency operations in Iraq and Afghanistan."[3]

Almost seven decades apart, these two examples illustrate how the US military sector is characterized by persistent and systematic cronyism, which refers to a system in which profit is earned through entanglements between the political and private classes.[4] Cronyism is problematic because it replaces the "economic means" of earning wealth with the "political means."[5] The economic means involve innovation and voluntary exchange in competitive, private markets. This process results in improvements in human welfare through the introduction of superior goods and services at lower prices. In contrast, the political means involves earning wealth via the forceful transfer of resources through politics and the use of political tools to restrict and circumvent competition, preventing competitors from eroding the profits of incumbent producers. This undermines the dynamism of competitive markets, leading to reductions in economic welfare.[6] Kenneth Boulding, an economist and peace scholar, captured the reality of the situation in his testimony before Congress, noting that "The war industry is a cancer within the body of American society. It has its own mode of growth, it represents a system which is virtually independent and indeed objectively inimical to the welfare of the American people, in spite of the fact that it still visualizes itself as their protector."[7]

Government programs and interventions create vested interests and promote cronyism. Empire is no different. Furthermore, given the significant expenditures on military-related activities, it should be no surprise that these perverse features—and their effects—are rampant. Many people across the political spectrum correctly worry about the destructive effects of cronyism and corporate welfare on the vitality of the market economy. Yet when it comes to the national security state, there is a tendency to downplay or ignore these issues, which has deleterious effects on economic freedom, the market economy, and ultimately on human well-being.

Foreign interventions are designed and implemented by numerous, overlapping government bureaucracies. This massive bureaucratic network works with the private sector, sharing people and technologies (as noted in the prior chapter) to produce goods and deliver services abroad (e.g., Halliburton, Blackwater, etc.). Interestingly, those on both sides of the US political spectrum take issue with various aspects of these relationships—including cronyism and corruption—when it comes to domestic issues. Yet, ironically, many of those on the right and the left, Republican and Democrat, often ignore their domestic concerns for cronyism and corruption when it comes to the maintenance, operation, and expansion of empire. Both sides are typically willing to endorse empire-related policies that entrench and extend corporate cronyism in the form of lucrative contracts and salaries, allowing well-connected private parties to benefit at the expense of taxpayers.[8]

The roots of cronyism are the state and its operations.[9] To understand why, consider the idea of a minimal, night-watchman state that serves the core function of protecting person and property. When describing the ideal nature of this minimal protective state, the analogy of a sports referee is often used.[10] The idea is that a referee stands outside of the game, serving purely as an enforcer of existing rules. As an enforcer of the rules, a referee is not an active player in the game and does not intervene to shape outcomes. Those employing this analogy typically conclude that if the state remains limited to purely protective functions—like the hypothetical referee—cronyism will be a nonissue. Under this scenario, players in the game will have no incentive to curry government favor, since the referee can only enforce existing rules and cannot influence outcomes.

However, there are two reasons why real-world governments can *never* be limited to the role of a referee who stands aside and enforces the rules. First, even the minimal protective state requires resources to operate. This necessitates government intervention in private economic life to extract resources. In doing so, the state shapes and manipulates economic life, creating an environment conducive to cronyism by relying on political power to determine resource transfers and allocations. These interventions create profit opportunities for a range of private actors seeking to secure wealth through political means, as compared to the normal economic means of voluntary exchange in markets.

Second, those operating the minimal protective state must also have discretion to deal with circumstances that are unforeseen when its initial powers are granted. As F. A. Hayek notes, a government planning authority "cannot tie itself down in advance to general and formal rules which prevent arbitrariness."[11] Planners require the power to address "circumstances which cannot be foreseen in detail."[12] This applies to the planning done by the national security state, where government exerts influence and authority over specific industries or sectors of the economy to achieve predetermined political outcomes in the name of "national security."[13]

By treating the state as an external referee that remains entirely outside of the capitalist system, proponents of the protective state understate, or entirely neglect, these two realities. Despite the use of the term "minimal" to describe the core functions of the protective state, they create significant space for cronyism in practice. That is, even *if* government were limited solely to providing core protective functions, cronyism would still exist. Moreover, it is reasonable to expect the magnitude of this cronyism to be significant under empire, since it requires an expansive portfolio of activities—managed by a massive public-private bureaucratic apparatus—to carry out the global ambition of bringing order to the world.

Peak Cronyism: The US Military Sector

The US military sector illustrates how cronyism results from the operations of an empire and shapes its activities. This sector influences nearly all aspects of the US economy, and therefore represents peak cronyism. Indeed, one would have a difficult time identifying a sector in the United States that better illuminates the operations of cronyism and its damaging effects.

The Foundations of Cronyism

The current US military sector is a product of the two World Wars. Prior to the US government's entry into these global conflicts, state-led military production ebbed and flowed around emerging conflicts (e.g., conflicts with Britain, Mexico, or Spain). This all changed during the World Wars. The state's massive war effort required private sector participation—whether voluntarily or through the threat of state coercion. This dramatically increased government intervention into the American economy and created the foundations of the cronyism that characterizes the present-day national security state.

Discussing the effects of World War I on the economic system, economist Robert Higgs notes that "[w]hile many viewed the mobilization of the economy [during the war] as having established both the possibility and desirability of extended government control of economic life, hardly anyone came away from the crisis with an enhanced understanding or appreciation of the market system or greater insight into the inherent cost-imposing, cost-concealing character of the command economy."[14] Similarly, World War II "moved the prevailing ideology [of the US citizenry] markedly toward acceptance of an enlarged government presence in the economy."[15] As these passages suggest, it was not merely the establishment of a massive bureaucracy that fostered cronyism, but also the ideological shift that normalized entanglements between the private and public sectors as a regular part of life, viewed as necessary to protect "the nation."

During the Second World War, major changes to defense contracting also contributed to creating the foundations of institutionalized cronyism.[16] Procurement laws were changed to allow for the widespread use of noncompete, cost-plus-fixed-fee contracts (contracts covering project expenses plus a set fee established at the contract's inception), as compared to sealed competitive bids. The purpose of this change was to incentivize businesses to enter the military sector.[17] This led to a change in the relationship between government and private business.

As historian R. Elberton Smith notes, the relationship changed "from an 'arm's length' relationship between two more or less equal parties in a business transaction into an undefined but intimate relationship."[18] According to Higgs, the result was that "deals came to turn not on price, but on technical and scientific capabilities, size, experience, and established reputations as a military supplier—vaguer attributes that are easier to fudge for one's friends."[19] Furthermore, "the newly established 'intimate relationship' opened up a whole new world for wheeling and dealing on both sides [government and private business] of the transaction."[20] This arrangement persisted in the post-World War II period with the creation of a permanent war economy to engage in constant preparation and production for future imperial wars.[21]

Crucial to the establishment of the permanent war economy was National Security Council Report 68 (NSC-68), presented to President Truman in 1950. As historian Ernest May wrote, NSC-68 "provided the blueprint for the militarization of the cold war from 1950 to the collapse of the Soviet Union at the beginning of the 1990s."[22] The report's conclusions involved the following point: "[o]ne of the most significant lessons of our World War II experience was that the American economy, when it operates at a level approaching full efficiency, can provide enormous resources for purposes other than civilian consumption while simultaneously providing a high standard of living."[23] This provided the justification for a policy of "military Keynesianism," which involves the US government using military spending to stimulate economic activity and jobs.[24]

The result was the institutionalization of the idea that military spending was not only a means for defending against genuine violent threats, but also a way for the state to manage and shape domestic economic activity to achieve other social goals—e.g., growth, full employment, and smoothing business cycles. To this day, military Keynesian logic is employed by policymakers, academics, and analysts to argue for and justify the US government's military expenditures. Consider the following two examples:

In 2008, Martin Feldstein, an economics professor and former chairman of the Council of Economic Advisers, wrote an article in the *Wall Street Journal* titled "Defense Spending Would Be Great Stimulus."[25] He argues that "countering a deep economic recession requires an increase in government spending to offset the sharp decline in consumer outlays and business investment that is now under way. Without that rise in government spending, the economic downturn would be deeper and longer." Invoking the logic of military Keynesianism, Feldstein claims that increased military spending is the best way to accomplish this goal because "a substantial short-term rise in spending on defense and intelligence would both stimulate our economy and strengthen our nation's security."

In 2011, after signing a $29.4 billion arms sale by the US government to the government of Saudi Arabia, Andrew Shapiro (then assistant secretary for the Department of State's Bureau of Political-Military Affairs), justified the deal partly on the grounds of military Keynesianism. Specifically, he noted that "this agreement will support more than 50,000 American jobs. It will engage 600 suppliers in 44 states and provide $3.5 billion in annual economic impact to the U.S. economy. This will support jobs not only in the aerospace sector but also in our manufacturing base and support chain, which are all crucial for sustaining our national defense."[26]

Most recently, the US Department of State's Bureau of Political-Military Affairs touted the increase in US arms exports to foreign governments in terms of the economics benefits: "Over the last fiscal year, authorized arms exports (including both commercial and government-managed) rose by 2.8 percent from $170.09 billion to $175.08 billion, adding thousands of jobs to the U.S. economy and sustaining many thousands more."[27]

The permanent war economy, which continues to thrive, epitomizes crony capitalism. The US government has a monopoly on final defense provision at the national level. To deliver defense, the US government purchases a significant number of defense-related inputs and outputs from private firms. This

includes purchases of civilian goods used by the government for military activities (e.g., clothing, housing, and healthcare) and of defense-specific goods
and services that are not legally available to the public (e.g., military technologies and weapons). To secure contracts from the US government, private firms
must participate in and successfully navigate the political and bureaucratic
process that defines the sector. In the pursuit of their own interests, both firms
and political actors attempt to influence and shape this process. The cumulative result is an entanglement of private firms with the federal government,
resulting in the well-known "military-industrial-congressional complex."[28]

This matters in terms of the way we think about the idea of even a minimal
protective state. The language of "minimal" or "limited" government con-
flates the number of general, aggregate functions in which the state engages
with the scope of the activities constituting each of those broad functions. To
many, indicating that the state should be limited to providing "defense" or
"security" from internal and external threats suggests that the state is doing
little. However, this masks the true reach and scope of the state's military
activities in economic life.[29]

Consider, for example, that the US Department of Defense is the country's
largest employer, with 1.4 million men and women on active duty, 850,000
civilian employees, 836,000 Select Reserves, and 245,000 Individual Ready
Reserve forces.[30] These numbers do not include the significant number of
people who work in jobs that supply the US military with various goods and
services, which (according to one estimate) total over 1.5 million.[31] Beyond the
labor market, the US military also influences a wide range of industries.[32] A
review of the top one hundred defense contractors for FY 2020 finds recipients
from the following industries: aerospace, technology, accounting and professional services, courier services, engineering and construction, healthcare,
higher education, and telecommunications.[33] As this shows, the reach of the
American empire into the private economy is anything but "minimal."

Instead, the military sector is a prime example of noncomprehensive
government planning, characterized by a tight relationship between private
firms and a state apparatus that governs the relationship and the profitability
of firms through bureaucratic rules and mandates in order to achieve some
set of political objectives.[34] The US military sector's public-private arrange-

ments are more reminiscent of fascist economic systems than of competitive, private markets, a feature of liberal societies.[35] The fascist economic system has been described as a capitalist economy driven by strict top-down state mandates and control to reign in the undisciplined, inefficient outcomes of competitive markets.[36] The system operates by the state "consolidating and cartelizing entire structures of production"[37] such that "political connections ultimately determined economic success."[38] At the core of this system of state capitalism is a form of nationalism, seeking to advance the interests of "the country" through the design and establishment of order by the political and intellectual elite.

The fascist economic system describes the military sector better than does capitalism, where there is private ownership over the means of production, competitively determined market prices, and profit and loss resulting from the decisions of private consumer—or socialism, where the means of production are nationalized by the state.[39] The US military sector is characterized by private ownership over the means of production. At the same time, the actions of private participants in the sector are dictated by state mandates, established by political authorities in the name of advancing the "national interest."

The various parties involved in the defense sector—both private and public—seek to take advantage of gaps in bureaucratic rules and mandates in the pursuit of their own interests. These gaps are often significant, as illustrated by the dysfunctional internal accountability mechanisms for tracking the location and allocation of military-related resources.[40] According to a report by the Government Accountability Office (GAO), for instance, "[t]he Department of Defense (DOD) is responsible for more than half of the federal government's discretionary spending. Significant financial and related business management systems and control weaknesses have adversely affected DOD's ability to control costs; ensure basic accountability; anticipate future costs and claims on the budget; measure performance; maintain funds control; prevent and detect fraud, waste, and abuse; address pressing management issues; and prepare auditable financial statements."[41]

The inability to produce acceptable financial statements is especially illuminating. According to the Government Management Reform Act of 1994, starting in 1997 the GAO has been legally required to audit the financial statements of executive agencies. Despite this law, the GAO was unable to begin to audit the financial statements of the Department of Defense until 2017 (the Department of Defense failed this first audit, as well as a subsequent audit in 2019). This means that for two decades, the Department of Defense operated illegally, in blatant violation of federal law.

A former Pentagon cost analyst nicely captured the implications of the lack of basic financial accountability, writing that "the combination of loose procurement rules and government acquiescence in rip-offs leaves many a crook untouched."[42] Similarly, retired Air Force Colonel James Burton bluntly summarized the essence of the arrangement when he noted that "[t]he business of buying weapons that takes place in the Pentagon is a corrupt business—ethically and morally corrupt from top to bottom. The process is dominated by advocacy, with few if any checks and balances."[43] This extends beyond the purchase of weapons to the other activities undertaken by the Pentagon, activities which often reek equally of the dangerous effects of cronyism.[44] The associated cronyism manifests itself in the following ways.

Rent Seeking and Rent Extraction

To influence political actors, private firms in the military sector engage in what economists call "rent seeking," which involves the expenditure of resources to build, maintain, and use beneficial connections with government as a means of currying favor and securing profits unavailable through normal market competition.[45] This behavior is predictable, since private-sector defense firms receive income through government contracts that are determined by the political process rather than competitive markets. Along these lines, Seymour Melman, a professor of engineering and operations research, noted that "while military-industry firms compete, often in much the same fashion as division managers under a central corporation, in their Pentagon-dominated world 'competence,' including political clout, is the coin of competition rather than the price-quantity contest that is more characteristic of civilian firms."[46] Rent seeking is one form of establishing and extending this "political clout."

Rent-seeking expenditures are best understood as legal bribes, whereby donors seek to establish or maintain favorable terms with political actors in exchange for future benefits. As Robert Higgs notes, "Both the givers and receivers understand these payments in exactly the same way that they understand illegal forms of bribery, even though they never admit this understanding in public."[47] Payments can be campaign contributions, monetary contributions to the favored charitable organizations of elected representatives, or payments in kind to elected officials or Pentagon bureaucrats.

A report by the Center for Public Integrity documented an instance of direct influence when "[t]he Pentagon's top contractors sent an army of more than 400 lobbyists to Capitol Hill this spring [2015] to press their case for increasing the nation's spending on military hardware, in a massive effort costing tens of millions of dollars."[48] The goal was to remove caps on military spending that were put in place (along with other budget controls) to slow the increase in government debt.

This is not a recent phenomenon; an example of payments in kind was documented in a 1975 report, indicating that "Senate investigators have found evidence that at least 10 major defense contractors, in addition to the Northrop Corp., have operated lush entertainment facilities for Pentagon brass. They include quail and pheasant shooting preserves, yachts and 'recreational' facilities in exotic warm climates."[49] These facilities were used by private firms to build relationships with the political gatekeepers who control access to government funds. These are but a few illustrations of the deep-seated culture of rent seeking that permeates the defense sector.[50]

While private firms engage in rent seeking, political actors who control defense-related resources engage in rent extraction. The underlying idea behind rent extraction is that discretionary control over the enforcement of rules and allocation of resources creates a property right for gatekeepers. Politicians who possess this property right can use it to extract payments from those seeking approval or access to resources.[51] While rent seeking is the expenditure of resources to curry political favor, rent extraction consists of resource expenditures to avoid political disfavor by political enforcers, those who possess the power to impose punishment when dissatisfied. In other words, rent extraction is a way for political enforcers to earn profits associated with the power they possess through their implementation of bureaucratic rules and mandates.

The national government's monopoly over defense provision creates property rights for the political gatekeepers, who control the flow of funds and make decisions regarding contracts with private firms. These gatekeepers can extract rents from private defense firms that are dependent on government funding. For example, the House Subcommittee on Defense—a permanent subcommittee of the United States House Committee on Appropriations—controls the flow of military-related funding and is therefore central to the profitability of private defense firms. As such, the members of this committee can extract rents from private firms for their narrow benefit. As journalist Peter Schweizer notes, the final report of the subcommittee is "the sort of document that can make or break the programs of defense contractors, both large and small."[52] This control over the budget allows the gatekeepers to seek favors from firms that are incentivized to comply.

Together, rent seeking and rent extraction contribute to an understanding of the US military sector. Decisions are not made based on the "national interest," or to provide for the "common defense" of the nation. Instead, the foundation and operation of this industry are based on political relationships, favors, and privileges. The result is a system of state capitalism and the associated cronyism.

The Revolving Door

The revolving door "refers to the back-and-forth movement of personnel between the government and private sector,"[53] the logical result of the defense sector's structure. On the private-sector side, firms have an incentive to hire experts who understand the bureaucracy—namely, the organizational structure and procedural rules—associated with the government's defense operations. Based on their experience and connections, former government employees are likely to possess the necessary knowledge. When discussing the revolving door in the military sector, international relations scholar Gordon Adams notes that former government employees "are knowledgeable in the ways of Government, aerospace technology, and procurement strategies. . . .The expertise brought by these individuals is not only technical but political."[54] As one investigative journalist observed, "When a general-turned-businessman arrives at the Pentagon, he is often treated with extraordinary deference—as if still in uniform—which can greatly increase his effectiveness as a rainmaker for industry. The military even has name [sic] for it—the 'bobblehead effect'."[55] This enhances the ability of private firms to secure profits through political means.

The revolving door dynamic is prevalent in the US defense sector. According to one study, "[f]rom 2004 through 2008, 80 percent of retiring three- and four-star officers went to work as consultants or defense executives."[56] A separate report revealed a "mentorship program" in which retired officers—many of whom now worked for defense contractors—were hired by the military as "consultants" to serve as advisers and guides to active duty officers.[57] This program allows these mentors insider access to represent the interests of their current private employers. Yet another report by the Project on Government Oversight identified "645 instances of the top 20 defense contractors . . . hiring former senior government officials, military officers, Members of Congress, and senior legislative staff as lobbyists, board members, or senior executives in 2018."[58]

The revolving door also operates in the other direction, with people flowing from private industry to government agencies. Government bureaus need people to create and enforce regulations, and to make decisions regarding resource allocations to private firms. Those who have gained experience in the private defense sector are well suited for this role, since they have firsthand knowledge of the operations and capabilities of private firms, as well as an understanding of the broader interplay between the private and public actors in the sector. The concern, of course, is that prior private connections can result in government employees showing bias to their former colleagues and employer, even though they are supposed to be pursuing the "public interest."

To provide one example of this dynamic, consider the case of William Lynn. He was confirmed as the top deputy for the Department of Defense in 2010, despite serious concerns about his close connections to top defense contractor Raytheon. Lynn had spent the prior decade working as a lobbyist for the company.[59] His experience in the private defense sector prepared him well for the government role, which is based on entanglements with the private defense industry.[60]

Local Politics vs. the "National Interest"

In the ideal model of democratic politics, elected representatives work together to provide common defense and security for the entire nation. Reality deviates sharply from this ideal, with elected representatives pursuing their own narrow interests as dictated by local politics. This is entirely predictable because it is local politics that determines whether the representative will be reelected. The pursuit of local political interests is evident in elected officials' efforts to channel military funds to private firms and labor unions in their home states. This often leads to the production of goods and services that are pure waste, unnecessary for defense against genuine threats. Elected officials pursue these resource allocations because this delivers funds and resources— much of which are paid for by other taxpayers—to their constituents.

To provide one illustration, in 2009 then Secretary of Defense Robert Gates informed Congress that additional C-17 cargo jets were not needed, as the planned order of 205 jets for the Air Force was enough to meet the branch's needs. Overruling Gates, members of Congress ordered a further expansion of the fleet in order to direct benefits to their constituencies. Boeing, the company that manufactured the C-17, estimated that the program supported 650 suppliers and over 30,000 jobs across forty-four states.[61]

While undertaken in the name of contributing to "national security," the reality was that the production of the C-17 became a "welfare program, offering profits for companies, jobs for workers and unions, and political support for cooperative lawmakers. Planes the Pentagon has not thought necessary have been built to promote the reelection of congressman and senators."[62] Numerous other activities in the military sector follow a similar pattern.

Private firms are aware of the incentives facing elected officials and actively structure their operations accordingly. One example of this is Lockheed Martin's F-35 Joint Strike Fighter, whose production is spread over forty-five states.[63] This means that elected officials in those states have a shared interest in continuing to fund the program, ensuring that resources are channeled to their local constituents even when the project has been plagued by numerous cost overruns and failures. By strategically locating the production of the aircraft across geographic space, Lockheed Martin has created a too-big-to-fail scenario where elected officials have a vested interest in the continuation of the project, irrespective of its feasibility and performance relating to national security.[64]

In general, elected representatives are highly unlikely to vote against a defense project that brings jobs and money to their constituents, even if that project contributes little or nothing to the security of the country. The late

Mississippi Representative Jamie L. Whitten summed it up nicely during congressional testimony, when he stated, "I am convinced that defense is only one of the factors that enter into our [Congress's] determination for defense spending. The others are pump priming, spreading the immediate benefits of defense spending, taking care of all of the services, giving defense contractors a fair share, spreading the military bases to include all sections."[65] As this quote suggests, vested interests and cronyism—not some mythical concept of advancing the "national interest"—drives the provision of what falls under the overly broad category of defense.

The Realities of Empire

- Imperialism is connected to the growth of an active and paternalistic government involved in economic affairs at home.
- Imperialism produces an "iron triangle" consisting of entanglements between congressional committees, bureaucracy, and special interest groups who press for further expansions and interventions, fostering cronyism.
- Imperialism undermines the desirable, dynamic aspects of a market system based on voluntary exchange and productive entrepreneurship.
- The cronyism inherent in the operation of empire encourages pervasive waste, fraud, and abuse, all of which have immediate and long-term consequences in reducing economic welfare under the false pretense of providing for national security.

4

The Limits of Liberal Imperialism

IN DECEMBER 2019, the *Washington Post* released the "Afghan-istan Papers," a collection of over 600 documents from the Special Inspector General for Afghanistan Reconstruction (SIGAR) that provides insight into the realities of the US government's occupation of Afghanistan since October 2001.[1] The documents, which include numerous interviews with policymak-ers and practitioners involved in the occupation, revealed a shocking lack of knowledge of Afghan society. As Dr. Thomas Johnson, a professor at the Naval Postgraduate School and an Afghanistan specialist, declared, "the num-ber one lesson" to take away from the Afghanistan intervention is that US policymakers and forces "just did not understand the environment."[2] Another US official noted that the US government "should have built our assistance and government based on tribal structures," emphasizing that "Afghanistan has never had a tradition of governance by democracy" and that the US gov-ernment "cannot export democracy" to a country that lacks the underlying traditions required for the operation of political institutions.[3]

The Afghanistan Papers also revealed the perverse incentives and lack of coordination involved in the US military occupation. David Marsden, former deputy director at the United States Agency for International Development (USAID), stated that "there were too many organizations so it was very con-fusing. . . . There were strategies all over the place."[4] Another interviewee noted, "There were too many people, with too many agendas, and they were not talking to each other."[5] Others recalled how "[t]he priorities shift con-stantly based on the person in charge,"[6] resulting in "a multiple prioritization of policies and conflicting priorities."[7] Retired US Army Brigadier General

Brian Copes discussed an environment ripe for waste, fraud, and abuse, saying, "Congress gives us money to spend and expects us to spend all of it." He continued, "No one in the military is going to go back and say we really don't need all this money, we only need *x* amount of money. The attitude became we don't care what you do with the money as long as you spend it."[8]

How is it that a lavishly funded and staffed occupation, motivated by supposedly humanitarian ideals, failed so badly?[9] To answer this question, we need to focus on the constraints facing those operating the levers of empire. Where proponents of American empire argue that it is necessary to design and maintain global order and stability, the Herculean burden is on them to demonstrate that policymakers possess the requisite knowledge and incentives to achieve their preferred outcome without creating greater instability.[10] Therefore, a thorough consideration of empire requires an appreciation of the constraints facing imperialists, and what these constraints imply when powerful, flawed, less-than-ideal people are in charge.[11]

Knowledge Problems

Absent government control and planning, the interventionist sees disorder and chaos everywhere in the world. Moreover, it is not simply control by any government that is required for order, but control by the "right" government, as determined by interventionists' preferences. This mentality has a long history in the United States, and can certainly be traced back to the early twentieth century (though some argue earlier), when President Theodore Roosevelt famously declared (see Chapter 1) that "chronic wrongdoing" in other societies requires intervention by a "civilized nation."[12] From the perspective of many US policymakers and pundits, this "civilized nation" is always and everywhere America.

The interventionist believes he possesses the superior knowledge, resources, and morality necessary to carry out foreign interventions.[13] The entrenched belief that order is contingent on government design and control neglects the importance of spontaneous orders—the emergent orders that result when people pursue their diverse ends in lieu of conscious, centralized planning. Instead of viewing societies as complex, constantly evolving entities consisting of individuals who contribute to broader emergent phenomena in the pursuit of their personal goals, the interventionist treats society and the world as a grand project, one which can be rationalized and improved by enlightened, well-intentioned technocrats.

This neglects the long tradition of spontaneous order thinkers, who emphasize that vital parts of the world in which we live—i.e., economic, legal, and social arrangements—are not the result of human design or planning but emerge through the actions of decentralized and disparate individuals. Their complexities are beyond the grasp of human reason and cannot be recreated in other settings.[14] The very idea of a single "global order" that can be known, designed, and achieved for the world through expert rule is a fallacy.[15]

Kenneth Boulding noted that there is a tendency to focus on observable quantities and behaviors and infer order and disorder in matters of international relations. According to this way of thinking, where disorder is observed, it can be fixed by expertly adjusting controllable behaviors and resources. This belief misclassifies the international system, Boulding argues, which is "not unlike the system of the earth's atmosphere, in which certain probabilities develop but the actual course of the weather depends on largely random circumstances at any point in time."[16] Likewise, political scientist Robert Jervis states that in international affairs, a "common misconception is to see the behavior of others as more centralized, planned, and coordinated than it is. This is a manifestation of the drive to squeeze complex and unrelated events into a coherent pattern."[17] The risk is overemphasizing the centrally observable and controllable, misclassifying the nature of order, and concluding that the world can be designed according to the desires of enlightened experts. This can have disastrous consequences for human welfare.

One of the implications of treating the world as a simple linear system (one in which there is a single path to a single outcome that can be grasped using human reason), as opposed to a complex adaptive system, is that the interventionist downplays or completely ignores the high probability that their actions will create unintended, perverse consequences. This ignorance was evident in the 2011 NATO military intervention in Libya, the example which opened this book. Since the operation violently deposed Mu'ammar al-Gadhafi without any so-called boots on the ground, it was touted as a model of limited foreign intervention with the objective of removing a dictator and avoiding a humanitarian disaster. However, the reality was chaos, instability, and a humanitarian crisis, both in Libya and in the broader region. Quite the contrary from bringing peace and stability to the Middle East, the US empire has created most of the terrorist groups that are currently targeting it—for example, al Qaeda by aiding the Islamist Mujahideen in Afghanistan in the 1980s, and ISIS arose during the US invasion and occupation of Iraq (2003–2011).[18]

When intervening in other countries, policymakers may know *what* outcomes they want to bring about, but that does not mean they know *how* to achieve them, despite powerful military weapons and lavish resources. Knowledge of observable variables is distinct from the dispersed, local, and tacit knowledge that is not observable, and which is not subject to quantification or aggregation. F. A. Hayek described this local knowledge as "the knowledge of the particular circumstances of time and place" that cannot be fully comprehended or articulated by the human mind.[19] Foreign interventions encounter many types of these peculiar knowledge problems.[20]

The Knowledge Problem over Institutions

US imperialism often purports to create (or help with the creation of) liberal democratic institutions. Institutions are the formal and informal rules governing interactions on a variety of levels (international, national, intranational). A key issue facing interveners is the basic knowledge problem of how to establish the democratic institutional foundations of a liberal society.[21] Many agree on the general characteristics of a free society—protection of individual and property rights, freedom of speech, rule of law, etc.—but the knowledge of how to design and implement these institutions in specific settings is lacking. This shortcoming is captured in a list of propositions detailing what scholars understand and (more importantly) do not understand about democratic institutions:

1. There are few preconditions for the emergence of democracy.
2. No single factor is sufficient or necessary to the emergence of democracy.
3. The emergence of democracy in a country is the result of a combination of causes.

4. The causes responsible for the emergence of democracy are not the same as those promoting its consolidation.

5. The combination of causes promoting democratic transition and consolidation varies from country to country.

6. The combination of causes generally responsible for one wave of democratization differs from those responsible for other waves.[22]

Clearly, this list shows that success in foreign interventions is not simply a matter of taking what works in one society and imposing it on another society.[23] The ability to transport rules between societies is constrained by the fact that underlying belief systems, values, and ideals often differ across societies. What works in the United States will not work in, say, Middle Eastern countries; similarly, what worked in Japan and West Germany following World War II would be an extremely poor guide for current and future foreign interventions.[24]

Discussing the situation in the Middle East, Steven Cook, a senior fellow at the Council on Foreign Relations, notes that "[t]he Middle East is caught up in a broader struggle. . . . Until Arabs figure out who they are and what kind of countries they want to live in, there is little Washington can do to help."[25] As this suggests, internal belief structures and buy-in from those subject to intervention place hard limits on the ability of interveners to impose institutions. Moreover, belief systems are not a type of technological knowledge that can be acquired easily with the investment of more resources.

Treatments of liberal foreign intervention often focus on the amount of "effort," in the form of time spent planning, monetary and physical aid, troop levels, the timing of new democratic elections, and exit strategy. This effort is framed in terms of simple cause-and-effect relationships in what is often implicitly assumed to be a simple system. Unfortunately, this overlooks the deeper issue—whether interveners have the requisite knowledge to achieve their desired ends. More broadly, to the extent that the knowledge over the institutions of any society is lacking, it places hard constraints on what an empire can accomplish.

The Knowledge Problem within Institutions

In addition to attempting to reform or create institutions, foreign interventions often seek to achieve a variety of goals within institutions. However, even in seemingly simple situations, such as in the delivery of humanitarian goods, an intervener's efforts can be frustrated by ignorance.

For example, in areas that lack lifesaving medical devices, the solution to the problem would seem to be the transference of medical devices from wealthy countries to those in need. Such a solution was attempted at Uganda's Mulago National Referral Hospital and Bwindi Community Hospital, with foreigners donating the incubators and anesthesia machines needed by both hospitals.[26] However, some shipped with instructions in a language the recipients did not understand, making them inoperable. Additionally, a majority of the incubators broke in short order, and the donors failed to anticipate the need for spare parts, repair services, or support staff for these machines. Without these necessary, complementary goods and services, the donated machines were worthless.

Further compounding the problem is the dynamic nature of tacit knowledge and expectations. Knowledge and expectations are not static; they are constantly subject to potential change and evolution. Outsiders often lack local knowledge due to their knowledge distance, which refers not to geographic remoteness, but instead to the distance between local, "on the ground" knowledge and the knowledge possessed by interveners.[27] As interventions become more complex, so do the knowledge problems involved. For example, economists Lant Pritchett and Michael Woolcock have noted that "valuable local 'practices'—idiosyncratic knowledge of variables crucial to the welfare of the poor (e.g., soil conditions, weather patterns, water flows)—get squeezed out, even lost completely, in large centralized development programs."[28] Similar problems plagued the US occupation of Afghanistan, where both foreign and domestic bureaucrats failed to respect local institutions. In many cases, the issue was not that Afghans were entirely excluded from the process, but that those who were included lacked the knowledge—based on local customary and self-governing associations—to accurately represent the interests of the populace.[29]

Beyond the loss of knowledge regarding local practices, there is an even more fundamental issue, namely that interveners lack the knowledge necessary to create genuine development. Economic development requires the ongoing reallocation of scarce resources to their highest valued uses.[30] The knowledge necessary to resolve the core economic problem (such that scarce resources are continually reallocated to their highest valued uses) does not exist outside of private markets owing to the absence of economic calculation, which refers to the ability of economic decision-makers to gauge the added value of alternative uses for scarce resources.[31] For example, should scarce metals be used to construct buildings (if so, which ones?) or railways? Or should they be directed to an alternative use, including the option of sitting idle? Answering these types of questions requires a means of gauging the potential added value of alternative uses for scarce resources.

Economic calculation is a tool that allows people to sort through technologically feasible projects and select the highest-valued alternative. Outside markets, there exists no knowledge of market prices or profit-and-loss accounting whereby decision-makers can allocate scarce resources according to the expected added value of alternative uses. Absent these fundamental economic calculations, decision-makers have no way of knowing the best way to utilize scarce resources.

Appreciating this basic knowledge problem has important implications for understanding the limits of foreign interventions. Because planning outside markets cannot solve the economic problem, such planning cannot replicate the ability of markets to foster societal economic progress either, a key liberal intervention objective. This places hard constraints on what liberal empires, in particular, can hope to achieve in terms of economic development.[32] Economic development itself is the outcome of a process of entrepreneurial discovery and innovation that occurs in the context of economic freedom, where people can experiment and interact voluntarily.[33]

Knowledge Problems in Executing Interventions

Interveners face an additional knowledge problem because people "on the ground" are not passive. This is not a matter of simply understanding local conditions, but also of accepting the dynamic and changing nature of those conditions. Interveners may believe they have an effective strategic plan, but as conditions change due to local responses by the target population, so too does the usefulness of that strategy. This dynamic is more evident in military operations associated with foreign interventions.

For example, economist Garrett Wood analyzed the effects of substitution in improvised explosive devices (IEDs) by the Afghan and Iraqi insurgencies.[34] US occupiers were initially unprepared for IEDs, and would attach scrap metal and compromised ballistic glass from landfills to their vehicles for any extra degree of protection.[35] Billions of dollars were spent on creating and updating counter-IED technologies and techniques. Despite this investment, the number of effective IED incidents continued uninterrupted, increasing dramatically over the course of the war in Afghanistan between 2002 and 2010, and in Iraq between 2003 and the Sunni Awakening in 2007.[36]

This is explained by the insurgency's response to changes in US military strategy, whereby they changed their methods and techniques for developing and deploying IEDs against occupiers. For example, in 2007 the Joint Improvised Explosive Device Defeat Organization (JIEDDO) declared that existing jamming technologies had mostly stopped insurgents from detonating their bombs remotely. Yet by 2009, this was no longer the case as insurgents had devised new ways to overcome the existing jamming technologies.[37] Not only had no one anticipated IEDs being a problem prior to engaging in these armed interventions, no one had planned around them becoming a persistent and adaptive problem fueled by the local knowledge of substitute weapons.

Due to uncertainty in an open-ended system, planners cannot entirely foresee how those being intervened upon will respond. This limited knowledge of future behavior will always curb the effectiveness of interveners and force them to adapt, resulting in significant losses of money and lives.

Political Economy Problems

Because they are designed and implemented by governments, the foreign interventions of an empire are fundamentally political in nature. Politics—both within the intervening country and in the society subject to intervention—shape and influence what is feasible, as well as the outcome of said interventions. Political factors also influence the adaptability of interveners facing various knowledge problems. There are four categories of political economy issues that are relevant to the foreign interventions of empire.

The Credible Commitment Problem

For reforms to be effective, interveners must have the incentive to follow through with their committed course of action, and this incentive must be evident to those living under the reform. This requires finding solutions to the credible commitment problem, which can be understood as follows: without a binding and credible commitment to engaging in a specific course of action, those involved in foreign interventions may have an incentive to renege on the announced course of action in the future.[38]

For example, if citizens expect interveners to capriciously change their policies in future periods, they will not believe announcements made in the present. These types of credible commitment problems have hindered efforts in Afghanistan, where interveners' constant changes to policy have led to fundamental, widespread uncertainty among Afghan leaders and citizens. As Rory Stewart, a diplomat and former member of the UK Parliament, explains, "Frustrated by a lack of progress, the U.S. and its allies have oscillated giddily between contradictory policies. The British government that once championed more generous budgetary support for the Kabul government now portrays it as corrupt, semi-criminal, ineffective, and illegitimate."[39] This lack of commitment to a particular policy hinders the credibility of interveners and contributes to "regime uncertainty," which refers to general instability in the rules of the game, making it difficult for people on the ground to accurately plan for the future.[40]

The credible commitment problem can manifest itself in other ways during foreign interventions. For example, certain groups may consent to power-sharing agreements while occupiers are present, only to renege once the occupiers have left. In this case, the absence of a credible commitment leads to the unraveling of previous agreements and the potential breakdown of the intervention. Alternatively, leaders of the intervening country may express their commitment to democratic ideals, only to support more authoritarian leaders who can be more easily controlled and influenced by the occupiers. If the populace under occupation anticipates this outcome, they are more likely to view the occupiers as an alien ruler set on exploitation.

Solutions to the credible commitment problem require finding ways to signal a commitment to fulfilling promised policies, reforms, and actions, while also establishing binding constraints on future behavior. This can be difficult, if not impossible, because of the knowledge problems over the design of institutions. Further complicating matters are the subjective perceptions of credibility by those who must live under interveners and the reforms they seek to impose.[41] For example, if the populace views the interveners as exploitative occupiers seeking to impose their will, it will be difficult for interveners to establish credibility regarding claims of a commitment to liberal values (such as self-determination, free expression, and individual freedom). Likewise, if there is a long history of violence or hatred between indigenous groups, it will be difficult for outsiders to impose legitimate arrangements.

The Conflict between Political and Nonpolitical Goals

Foreign interventions tend to assume that political and nonpolitical—i.e., economic, legal, and social—goals are fully compatible and aligned, with no tradeoff between the desired ends. This view underemphasizes the potential difficulties democracy can create with regard to achieving the interveners' other goals. While interveners typically develop a comprehensive list of targets and goals related to the establishment of democratic political systems, the reality is that the implementation of plans for political reform often undermines other goals.[42]

According to one study, "countries that undergo extensive democratization in the immediate post-conflict period recover more slowly than countries that do not."[43] This may be because "typically early elections in a highly polarized society empower elites, senior military leaders, and organized criminal elements."[44] Without effective constraints, democracy can produce illiberal outcomes—political, economic, social, and legal—that can do significant harm to the society in question. To understand the potential conflict between political and nonpolitical goals, consider the following possible outcomes under foreign intervention intended to foster institutional change: "(1) the rule of law can degenerate into the rule of lawyers—litigious, costly, and dilatory; (2) economic efficiency can turn into profligacy—piratical and predatory; (3) free speech can reward superficiality and extremism; (4) the demand for unfulfilled rights can invite invidious reverse discrimination; (5) checked-and-balanced governmental institutions can yield policy stasis."[45]

These perverse possibilities, of which there are many, highlight the necessity of establishing effective constraints in order to ensure that reform efforts result in stable political and economic orders. Yet creating these checks and balances is no simple task; social scientists and practitioners lack the knowledge of how to construct and implement effective liberal constitutional rules that will last in the long run. Formal institutions (such as liberal constitutions) must be grounded in informal customs and belief systems, which are largely beyond the reach of interveners and their policies. This places a hard constraint on the ability of interveners to design institutions and establish "order" in accordance with their desires.

Bureaucratic Pathologies

Government bureaus play a central role in foreign interventions. These agencies face a range of issues relating to information, incentives, and knowledge.[46] These factors produce predictable patterns of behavior that are relevant to understanding the limits of empire in intervening abroad.[47]

Bureaus involved in foreign interventions will often attempt to secure the largest possible share of financial resources—and the associated influence over policy—related to the intervention. This typically involves the agency's investment of scarce resources, signaling the relative importance of their bureau over others. It also involves downplaying the relevance of other bureaus involved, although they may be important for overall success. This competition over scarce resources creates tension in the design and execution of foreign interventions. Ideally, government agencies should be united in the common goals of the intervention, yet they compete with one another for funds and control over policy instead. Each bureau has its own agenda, which may clash with the agenda of other agencies, as well as with the overarching goal of the requirements for overall success.

Consider the case of the US government's invasion of Iraq, beginning in 2003. Political sociologist Larry Diamond notes that "a number of U.S. government agencies had a variety of visions of how political authority would be reestablished in Iraq. In the bitter, relentless infighting among U.S. government agencies in advance of the war, none of these preferences clearly prevailed."[48] Others involved in the occupation indicated that "relations between the Office of the Secretary of Defense (OSD) and the State Department became increasingly acrimonious. U.S officials vied for control over the Iraq policy."[49] This infighting had the consequence of undermining the intervention, and had nothing to do with staffing, resources, or effort.

Another tendency is for bureaus to exhaust their entire budgets while continually seeking financial appropriations to increase their size and scope. The failure of a bureau to spend its allocated budget typically leads to budget reductions in subsequent periods. This creates the incentive to ensure that budgets are exhausted, even if wasteful expenditures are necessary to achieve this outcome. There are four factors that contribute to this bureaucratic waste.

First, the absence of economic calculation in government agencies means that bureaucrats are unable to gauge the effective allocation (and reallocation) of resources in terms of the return on investment.[50] Even the most well-intentioned bureaucrats lack access to the economic knowledge needed to maximize the value of scarce resources, leading to the inefficient use of these resources. Second, bureaucratic rules tend to be rigid in nature, which often limits adaptability to rapidly changing conditions. This can contribute to the persistence of waste; due to binding administrative mandates, bureaucrats are limited in their ability to change their behavior. The third factor is the challenge of long information chains—from lower to higher levels—within bureaus.[51] The longer the information chain, the more likely that noise will be introduced into the process of information transmission, decreasing the likelihood that higher-level bureaucrats will receive the necessary information. Fourth, weak lines of accountability provide a disincentive to change behaviors despite waste or ineffectiveness.

To provide a concrete example of some of these dynamics, consider the case of the $544 million "Community Stabilization Program" (CSP) in Iraq; this program was meant to contribute to economic rebuilding, while undermining the insurgency by winning the hearts and minds of Iraqi citizens. A 2008 audit by the USAID's inspector general noted that the review was "unable to determine if the Community Stabilization Program was achieving its intended result," and added that "the audit found evidence of potential fraud occurring in projects."[52] Most disturbingly, the audit found that some funds—which were intended to weaken the insurgency by providing alternative livelihoods to potential recruits—instead went to insurgents and corrupt community leaders.[53] This is just one of many examples. As Peter van Buren— a former member of the State Department, who served as a team leader for two Provincial Reconstruction Teams (PRTs)—indicates, the occupation of Iraq was ". . . lavishly funded, yet, as government inspectors found, the efforts were characterized from the beginning by pervasive waste and inefficiency, mistaken judgements, flawed policies, and structural weaknesses."[54]

Together, these bureaucratic pathologies undermine the broader goals of foreign interventions. Poor information flow, inertia, and perverse incentives are inherent in the industrial organization of government agencies. These pathologies are magnified by large-scale interventions in foreign societies and contribute to the limits of what empire can hope to achieve abroad.

Self-Interested Elected Officials and Special Interests

Two other political factors influence the viability of empire's foreign interventions. The first is domestic democratic politics within the empire. Elected officials respond to the incentives generated by domestic political institutions (which create some predictable behaviors)—these officials will seek policies benefiting their constituency, even if they are short-sighted or at odds with the goals of the intervention. This dynamic was evident in the experience of former Secretary of Defense Robert Gates, who recounted:

> I did not just have to wage war in Afghanistan and Iraq and against al-Qaeda; I also had to battle the bureaucratic inertia of the Pentagon, surmount internal conflicts within both administrations, avoid the partisan abyss in Congress, evade the single-minded parochial self-interest of so many members of Congress and resist the magnetic pull exercised by the White House, especially in the Obama administration, to bring everything under its control and micromanagement. Over time, the broad dysfunction of today's Washington wore me down, especially as I tried to maintain a public posture of nonpartisan calm, reason and conciliation.[55]

Gates succinctly captures how domestic politics, in conjunction with the political economy of bureaucracy, can adversely affect foreign interventions.

The second factor is special interests, referring to a group of people who come together to work toward a joint goal. Through the use of taxpayer dollars, foreign interventions are well funded. The result is that special interests—domestic and foreign, private, public, and nonprofit—will actively scramble to secure as much funding as possible, as quickly as possible. Special interest groups seek to concentrate benefits on their members, while dispersing the associated costs on others. In the context of foreign intervention, these "others" may be taxpayers in the intervening county, or those living in the society subject to intervention. The result of special interest lobbying is often waste and fraud, as well as activities that contribute nothing to accomplishing the goals of the foreign intervention or advancing liberalism.

To understand how special interests can influence foreign interventions, recall that the US military sector incentivizes unproductive entrepreneurship—entrepreneurship that is zero-sum and wealth-destroying—during times of peace, as special interests seek to secure portions of the military budget.[56] The military budget can be seen as a common pool resource, and various private parties seek to influence the gatekeepers (see Chapter 3) in order to secure as much of the commons as possible for their own benefit, at the taxpayers' expense.[57]

These tendencies are intensified during military interventions due to an injection of significant funds, along with highly imperfect monitoring and accountability processes.[58] These realities were well documented during US interventions in both Afghanistan and Iraq, as well as in numerous other foreign interventions.[59] This undermines foreign interventions by diverting resources and effort toward negative-sum activities that contribute nothing to the achievement of the desired goals.

An appreciation of domestic politics also poses a challenge to the common argument that empire is necessary for the maintenance of ocean trading routes. From this perspective, waterways are a type of commons lacking security.[60] Many argue that a liberal hegemon is necessary to fill this gap, by providing the public good of security to facilitate economic trade.

This argument neglects the reality that proactive state involvement in trade will open the door for cronyism, as special interests influence and manipulate government for their own benefit. Decisions need to be made about what type of security (i.e., the quantity and quality) to supply, where it will be supplied, and how far governments will extend security to protect private interests. At each step, there are opportunities for self-serving special interests to influence government policy.

Historically, special interests have been a central driver of military imperialism.[61] Discussing the British Empire and her colonies, Adam Smith wrote, "To found a great empire for the sole purpose of raising up a people of customers may at first sight appear a project fit only for a nation of shopkeepers. It is, however, a project altogether unfit for a nation of shopkeepers; but extremely fit for a nation whose government is influenced by shopkeepers."[62] Similarly, economist Wilhelm Röpke argued that an "aggressive foreign policy" often results "when private pressure groups understand how to make use of their national government for their own purposes, or the true economic interests of the nation as a whole are falsely depicted."[63] There is no reason to believe that the provision of security for trading routes somehow stands outside of crony capitalist politics and avoids the perils of state capitalism at the core of empire. In stark contrast, as discussed in the previous chapter, the operation of an empire exacerbates the scale and scope of cronyism, as an array of private interests seek to secure the profits created by government power and continue the interventions justified on the grounds of providing a public good in the "national" and "global" interest.

Together, the knowledge and incentive constraints involved in foreign intervention place underappreciated limits on what empire can hope to achieve. In general, when considering whether to empower empire, it is best to follow David Hume's famous political maxim that "in contriving any system of government, and fixing the several checks and controls of the constitution, every man ought to be supposed a *knave*, and to have no other end, in all his actions, than private interest."[64]

The Realities of Empire

- Imperialism faces a variety of constraints that limit the effectiveness of empire as a viable top-down solution to create global order and stability while spreading liberal values.

- While political, economic, and social failures in other countries are indeed grave and tragic, the failures generated by US imperialism can be even greater.

- The knowledge and political economy constraints facing empire indicate that the first-best (and often second- and third-best) imagined policies will often not be possible in practice.

- When examining empire, considering less-than-ideal scenarios is crucial for the appreciation of potential bads and the identification of ways to avoid them.

- While the actions of an empire are often justified in terms of a moral obligation to help others, appreciating what empire can accomplish allows for the understanding of whether those obligations can be met without violating the humane credo of "first, do no harm."

5

Illustrating Public Bads: The War on Drugs in Afghanistan

THE AFGHANISTAN PAPERS pulled back the curtain on the causes of the disastrous US occupation. Among other issues, the interviews noted the dismal performance of the US government's effort to eradicate drugs in Afghanistan. In a 2015 interview, Michael Flynn—retired US Army lieutenant general, former national security adviser, and former director of Defense Intelligence Agency—noted, "The narcotics today, is the worst it has ever been. I don't think that there was a year that has gone by in our time in Afghanistan where the narcotics industry has had a bad year."[1]

How is it that Afghanistan experienced record opium harvests and terror activities despite the US government's unprecedented investment of resources intended to accomplish the opposite?[2] Efforts by US occupiers to curtail the drug trade in Afghanistan created opportunities for terrorist groups to form, strengthen, and impede the US government from achieving their policies' stated goals. The Afghanistan experience illustrates the limits of imperialism in general, as well as the negative consequences resulting from military intervention.

The Failed War on Drugs and War on Terror

From the start of the occupation, US government and allied leaders repeatedly asserted that winning the war on drugs in Afghanistan was crucial to winning the war on terror.[3] In 2002, less than a year after the start of the US invasion, Afghanistan produced more than three-quarters of the world's opium.[4] Since that time, the US government spent at least $8.6 billion on a variety of counternarcotics initiatives.[5] The US government also "exported" many elements of its domestic drug interdiction efforts to help fight the Afghan drug war. For example, the Drug Enforcement Agency (DEA) opened thirteen offices in Afghanistan in 2003. By 2013, ninety-five offices were in operation. Over that same period, the DEA increased the operating budget for its Afghanistan initiative by $6 million per year.[6]

Two decades have passed since the US launched its ambitious wars on drugs and terror in Afghanistan. The results are an abject failure, as illustrated by Figure 1, which shows the annual growth of the area under opium poppy production in the pre- and post-invasion periods (with the 2001 US government invasion marked by the bold vertical line).[7]

The United Nations Office on Drugs and Crime (UNODC) reports that the estimated area under opium poppy cultivation in Afghanistan *quadrupled* from 74,000 hectares in 2002 to a record 328,000 hectares in 2017, with the majority of production (69 percent) occurring in the country's southern provinces—namely, the Helmand and Kandahar provinces.[8] The drop in estimated area under cultivation in 2018 was due to drought, not to government eradication efforts.[9] The estimated area under cultivation fell by 38 percent in 2019 (163,000 hectares in 2019 versus 263,000 hectares in 2018), driven by a fall in opium prices due to the bumper harvests in the prior two years.[10] Despite the decrease in land under cultivation, the opium yield per acre increased as a result of favorable weather, meaning that total output did not fall year on year.[11] Significantly, government eradication efforts played no substantial role in the area under cultivation, as the number of hectares eradicated fell by 95 percent from 2018 to 2019.[12] According to estimates, Afghanistan now produces 80 percent[13] of the world's illicit opium. As opposed to observing a shift in the Afghan economy—away from opium and toward alternative, legal products—UNODC Executive Director Yury Fedotov stated that Afghanistan is on the verge of becoming a "fully-fledged narco-state."[14]

The war on terror in Afghanistan produced similarly abysmal results. According to the Global Terrorism Index, "Total deaths from terrorism in Afghanistan have increased by 631 per cent since 2008."[15] In 2019, the Taliban reclaimed the title as the world's deadliest terror group (overtaking the Islamic State of Iraq and the Levant, or ISIL), with Afghanistan designated the world's deadliest country for terrorism.[16]

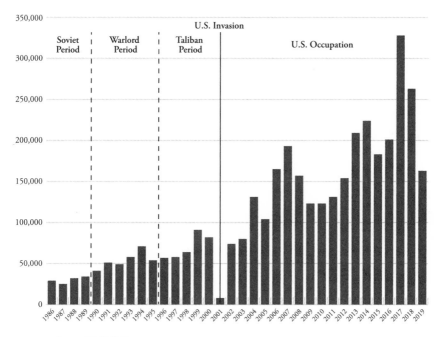

Source: UNODC 2004: 3, 2013: 5, 2021: 7.

Figure 1. Estimated Area under Opium Poppy Cultivation by Year (in Hectares)

The History of US Drug Policy in Afghanistan

Following the launch of Operation Enduring Freedom in 2001, the US government pursued several different strategies in its joint wars on drugs and terror in Afghanistan. These strategies are best understood as three distinct phases. Before considering each phase, it is important to understand the pre-occupation situation for context.

Pre–US Occupation

For most of its history, Afghanistan played a relatively minor role in global opium production. This changed in the 1970s, following opium bans in Turkey, Iran, and Pakistan. By the end of the decade, opium poppy cultivation had spread to more than half of Afghanistan's twenty-eight provinces, though total production remained only a fraction of global output.[17] Starting in the late 1970s, the decade-long Soviet war in Afghanistan destroyed the country's legal agricultural trade network, leading many rural farmers to farm opium in order to sustain their livelihood. By 1989, opium had become one of Afghanistan's leading exports, and roughly a third of the world's opium was produced in Afghanistan.[18]

The Taliban, which took control of the country in the mid-1990s, allowed local warlords to maintain opium production and illicit arms trading in return for their allegiance.[19] It is estimated that the Taliban collected millions of dollars annually from taxing the economy during their initial years in power.[20] In 2000, Taliban leaders issued a religious decree, or *fatwa*, banning opium cultivation and declaring it "un-Islamic." There is no consensus on the exact reason for this reversal, although one explanation is that the ban was issued to gain international credibility and foreign assistance.[21] Farmers who violated the prohibition often suffered public beatings, and were paraded through the streets with blackened faces on "walks of shame" before being sentenced to prison terms.[22] The ban and the significant punishments for violating the decree had the intended effect, resulting in an unprecedented 95 percent reduction in Afghan opium production the following year[23] and a 99 percent reduction in areas under Taliban control.[24] Globally, the result of the Taliban's opium ban was a 65 percent reduction in potential illicit heroin supply.[25] This dramatic year-over-year decrease in output was the situation facing US occupiers when they invaded in 2001.

The Hands-Off Approach: 2001–2002

On October 7, 2001, the US military invaded Afghanistan with the goal of overthrowing the Taliban.[26] The fall of the Taliban resulted in the end of their short-lived ban on opium production. Once established, Afghanistan's interim government, led by Hamid Karzai, implemented its own national ban on opium production to combat the drug trade.

Occupying coalition forces did not initially seek to eliminate the market outright. Rather than actively prohibiting production and trade, the US government sought to use the opium producers' interests to their advantage. Specifically, coalition forces attempted to establish military alliances with regional warlords to help defeat the Taliban. In return for their allegiance, the US government essentially agreed to turn a blind eye to opium trafficking.[27]

At least thirty-five warlords are known to have received millions of dollars from the US government in exchange for their assistance.[28] The US government also formed an agreement with the Northern Alliance (whose regional area under opium poppy cultivation had nearly tripled to 6,342 hectares) to fight the Taliban.[29] Hoping to avoid any direct involvement, US forces relied on the Afghan government to lead limited counternarcotics efforts so that they could focus on counterterrorism. Toward this end, the Afghan Interim Authority (AIA) was formed in 2001—with US government support—to "combat international terrorism, cultivation and trafficking of illicit drugs."[30] Though the war on terror was the top priority, many US policymakers were optimistic that drugs could be eliminated over time, with the proper planning and coordinated action facilitated by the new Afghan government.[31]

This was not the case, however, as President Hamid Karzai and the new Afghan government's ban on opium production was largely ineffective. The area under opium poppy cultivation increased 8 percent—from 74,000 hectares in 2002 to 80,000 hectares in 2003—rivaling the highest levels of opium cultivation in the preinvasion era.[32] Farm gate prices for opium (the price received by farmers for their crop) rose from $28 per kilogram in 2000 to $301 per kilogram in 2001, and to $350 per kilogram in 2002.[33]

The Hands-On Approach: 2003–2009

After three consecutive years of record opium harvests, the US government pivoted to a zero-tolerance policy toward opium. Emphasizing complete eradication, US forces became directly involved in combating opium in Afghanistan. Seeking to align the goals of counternarcotics with counterinsurgency, military equipment and personnel were mobilized to assist in US government–led eradication programs. Christopher Blanchard, an analyst in Middle Eastern Affairs, summarizes the "hands-on" period when he notes that "[f]rom 2002 through 2009, Congress and the Bush administration gradually expanded the role for U.S. military forces in training, equipping, and providing intelligence and airlift support for Afghan counternarcotics teams."[34]

In May 2003, the US government prepared its first official National Drug Control Strategy for Afghanistan. It aimed to achieve a 70 percent reduction in opium cultivation by 2008, and complete abolition by 2013, through a combination of the physical eradication of poppy fields and the interdiction of trafficked drugs.[35] The US government also established a variety of new task forces involving the Afghan government and provided equipment and training to engage in counternarcotic operations.[36]

In December 2004, Lieutenant General David W. Barno, then the top US commander in Afghanistan, renewed the US commitment to drug eradication, claiming that the war on drugs was one of three wars crucial to winning the war on terror.[37] The three wars included the ongoing battle against al-Qaeda and Taliban insurgents, the search for the top-ranking leaders of these organizations, and the war against warlords and drug trafficking. Other policymakers agreed. Thomas Schweich, then the US State Department's coordinator for counternarcotics in Afghanistan, stated that "[i]t's all one issue. It's no longer just a drug problem. It's an economic problem, a political problem and a security problem."[38]

However, these renewed commitments did nothing to reduce opium production. For the first time in its history, Afghanistan surpassed the cultivation of 100,000 hectares of opium poppy during this period. In fact, Afghans grew some 131,000 hectares of opium poppy in 2004, representing a nearly two-thirds increase over the previous year.[39]

In the face of increased production, attempts to further refine the counternarcotics policy continued. In 2005, the US government announced a "Five Pillar" counternarcotics strategy to combat the opium industry on a variety of levels.[40] A central part of this strategy was the mass mobilization of US personnel and monetary resources, intended to counter drug production on a national scale.

The State Department escalated its International Narcotics and Law Enforcement (INCLE) funding from zero in 2003 to $220 million in 2004, and to $710 million in 2005, using a significant portion to bankroll the Central Poppy Eradication Force (CPEF) and other enhanced eradication efforts.[41] The State Department and Justice Department also cofounded an $8 million Counter Narcotics Justice Center (CNJC), an Afghan-based facility intended to serve as a "one-stop shop" for all drug cases.[42]

At the same time, the role of the US military was significantly altered to align counternarcotics initiatives with counterinsurgency efforts. The Department of Defense more than tripled its operating budget dedicated to counternarcotics between 2004 and 2005, from $72 million to $225 million. Most of these funds were used to support joint Afghan and American antidrug efforts directly.[43] The Pentagon altered its rules of engagement, permitting US troops to provide support in the search for drug traffickers and to assist with counternarcotics raids by accompanying and protecting counternarcotics forces.[44] The battlefield shifted from the mountains to the agrarian countryside, as US soldiers began patrolling flower-laden poppy fields and monitoring key drug trafficking routes.

In addition to the Department of Justice, the Department of State, and the Department of Defense, the Drug Enforcement Agency (DEA) also dramatically escalated its role in Afghanistan. After reopening its Kabul office in 2003, the agency steadily expanded its presence from thirteen to ninety-five offices.[45] DEA advisers were flown in from Colombia and other key regions to train local drug investigators and Special Forces.[46] The DEA's operating budget in Afghanistan quadrupled from $3.7 million in 2004 to $16.8 million in 2005, and would increase still further—to $40.6 million in 2008. At this point, more US resources were devoted to eradication than ever before.[47]

US government officials credited these policy changes for the decline in the area under opium poppy production—from 131,000 hectares in 2004 to 104,000 hectares in 2005. Whatever gains were made, however, were fleeting. A year later (in 2006), a record 165,000 hectares of opium poppy were cultivated, a 60 percent increase over 2005 levels.[48] This increase in cultivation occurred despite a tripling in the amount of eradicated opium poppy. Over 5,100 hectares were destroyed in 2005. This amount increased in 2006 and 2007 to 15,300 and 19,000 eradicated hectares, respectively.[49] Despite significant US resources and effort, Afghanistan remained the world's dominant opium producer.[50]

The US government kept eradication at the center of its counternarcotics strategy throughout the remainder of the Bush administration. The area under opium poppy cultivation did fall to 157,000 hectares in 2008, and to 123,000 hectares in 2009; yet, these declines should not be interpreted as an indicator of effective counternarcotics policy. Instead, they are better explained by the poor agricultural conditions—i.e., drought and disease—

responsible for killing up to one-third of the opium poppy in the region during this period.[51]

After five years and nearly $5 billion spent on intense eradication, US policymakers acknowledged that their efforts had largely failed.[52] According to US Special Representative Richard Holbrooke, the US government "wasted hundreds and hundreds of millions of dollars" on efforts to combat opium production, with no positive results to show for it.[53]

The Alternative Livelihoods Approach: 2009–2021

In response to these failures, the US government again restructured its nationwide eradication policies, starting in 2009. The new approach focused on regional efforts and the provision of legal "alternative livelihoods" for Afghan farmers. Through programs of crop replacement and economic assistance, the US government hoped to win the hearts and minds of Afghan citizens. Such efforts, it was argued, would foster a connection between citizens and the new government, resulting in the elimination of opium and the weakening of the Taliban.[54] The US military distanced itself from direct participation in the physical destruction of crops. Instead, the State Department paid provincial governors to carry out targeted eradication and interdiction campaigns against high-level producers and traffickers.[55]

The "alternative livelihoods" approach, which garnered the support of both General David Petraeus and General McChrystal, became the centerpiece of newly elected President Obama's renewed counterinsurgency strategy in Afghanistan. Combined with the "troop surge" beginning in 2009, these aid programs were intended to be an integral part of eliminating the drug trade and, ultimately, the terrorist networks in Afghanistan. The largest of these direct aid programs—the Economic Support Fund (ESF), administered through USAID—increased its support from $2.08 billion in 2009 to $3.34 billion in 2010.[56] The increase in resources was intended to encourage provincial governors to provide local farmers with economic alternatives to opium cultivation. To provide further incentive, the American Embassy and State Department both announced performance awards for "poppy-free provinces," paid directly to local governors who successfully eradicated opium poppy by providing for alternative livelihoods.[57]

Despite the shift in policy, poppy cultivation continued to rise. As farm-gate prices rose some 300 percent, farmers increased the amount of cultivated land from 123,000 hectares in 2011 to a record 209,000 hectares in 2013.[58] Since then, land under cultivation has continued to increase, hitting a record high of 328,000 hectares in 2017.[59]

Critics have noted that the aid programs associated with the alternative livelihoods programs were implemented by injecting large sums of money into short-term, observable projects focused on achieving output targets rather than contributing to actual value-added development.[60] In other cases, invest-ments in infrastructure (such as irrigation) were successful, but were used to produce additional opium rather than grow alternative crops.[61]

The alternative livelihood approach continued, but the US government also reintroduced a new, air-based eradication program in the wake of the record land under cultivation in 2017. This program involved the use of US and Afghan military aircraft to target Taliban production facilities in the Helmand Province.[62] The area under opium poppy cultivation did fall, from 328,000 hectares in 2017 to 263,000 hectares in 2018. However, this fall can also be attributed to the severe drought in Afghanistan (especially in the northern and western regions) in 2017, rather than to US eradication efforts alone.[63] The long-term impact of this new eradication program is unclear, but skepticism and legitimate concerns have been raised, given the consistent failure of prior eradication programs.[64] Moreover, with the withdrawal of ground troops from Afghanistan in August 2021, the US government's future role in interdiction and eradication remains unclear.

The Economics of the Failed Experiment with Interdiction

After two decades of fighting the war on drugs in Afghanistan, the opium economy is stronger and more concentrated in Taliban hands than at any time before or during the invasion. In his 2014 testimony before Congress, John F. Sopko, Special Inspector General for Afghan Reconstruction, stated, "Afghan farmers are growing more opium today than at any time in their modern history."[65] Four years later, a subsequent report by Sopko concluded that, despite the US government's significant investment, "drug production and trafficking remain entrenched. Afghanistan is the world's largest opium producer, and opium poppy is the country's largest cash crop."[66]

The economic issues behind this failure are straightforward. As economist Jeffrey Clemens notes, drug efforts in "source countries" focus on reducing the quantity of drugs by shifting the supply curve.[67] The effectiveness of such efforts, in turn, depends on two key factors. The first is the ability of governments to reduce supply. Ultimately, widespread and permanent crop eradication would be necessary in order to do so. However, for the reasons discussed in the previous subsections, coalition forces and the Afghan government were unable to achieve significant eradication.

The second factor is the elasticity of the demand curve. The term "elasticity" refers to the responsiveness of quantity demanded by consumers to a change in price. In his research, Clemens finds that the demand curve is relatively inelastic; this refers to a situation in which a change in price leads to a relatively small change in the quantity demanded. This means that reductions in income accruing to drug suppliers (due to seizing or eradicating opium poppy) will be minimal compared to the increase in the value of the remaining stock.[68] That is, the gain from the increase in price per unit (due to the decrease in supply) more than offsets the loss due to the decrease in quantity demanded. Together, these economic insights help us explain the failure of eradication efforts.

Five Perverse Consequences of the US War on Drugs in Afghanistan

The US government's various interventions in Afghanistan's opium market were intended to not only eliminate the opium economy, but also disrupt and dismantle the insurgency. However, these policies generated a series of perverse consequences that produced outcomes contrary to the stated ends of the US government.

Regime Uncertainty and Credible Commitment Problems

Stable, predictable policies and rules reduce uncertainty and allow people to plan because they can have some confidence in what actions the government will and will not undertake. In contrast, unstable policies and rules make planning difficult, as people cannot accurately gauge future government behavior. Economist Robert Higgs emphasizes the role of "regime uncertainty," which refers to vagueness regarding future policies and activities of the government, in preventing economic recovery in the United States in the wake of the Great Depression.[69] He argues that uncertainty regarding property rights in capital and future returns disincentivized investment on the part of private entrepreneurs. This, in turn, hampered economic recovery. The same logic of regime uncertainty can be extended to efforts to foster institutional change in foreign societies through military imperialism.

If citizens of the occupied country experience uncertainty regarding the future policies and activities of occupiers and the new government, they will not feel confident in supporting reforms or making costly investments. Instead, they will reject, if not openly combat, attempts at reform. The US government's policies toward opium in Afghanistan created significant regime uncertainty. This uncertainty was the result of contradictory policies at different levels of governance—e.g., local versus national—and dramatic policy swings concerning the acceptability of opium production. Significant uncertainty emerged both within each policy period and across policy periods.

To illustrate the uncertainty created within a specific policy period, consider the "hands-off approach" adopted for the first two years of the occupation. During this period, the Karzai government imposed a national ban on opium, but the US government decided not to engage in direct eradication efforts. This strategy was plagued with contradictions from the outset.

While attempting to ally with local warlords, the US government simultaneously supported strict antidrug programs at the national level. Though the US government initially avoided any direct involvement in Afghanistan's drug war, it heavily financed many of the Afghan government's early drug eradication efforts. In effect, the US government was endorsing the national ban—going so far as to fund Afghan-led eradication initiatives—while contemporaneously partnering with and empowering local warlords who were deeply embedded participants in the opium economy.

As a result of this inconsistency, the US government actively undermined its stated objective of establishing a strong, secure central government in Kabul.[70] Bankrolled by the US government and shielded from legal repercussions, local warlords began offering protection services to opium traffickers as a means of raising additional revenues.[71] The cumulative effect was to strengthen the warlords as autonomous economic and governance units, thus incentivizing even greater opium poppy cultivation and undermining proclamations that the US government was committed to establishing a stable national government.

Major policy shifts toward opium every few years also created widespread regime uncertainty, as illustrated by the following summary of events:

> We [the US-led coalition of forces] armed militias in 2001, disarmed them through a demobilization program in 2003, and rearmed them again in 2006 as community defense forces. We allowed local autonomy in 2001, pushed for a strong central government in 2003, and returned to decentralization in 2006. First we tolerated opium crops; then we proposed to eradicate them through aerial spraying; now we expect to live with opium production for decades.[72]

Significant changes in policies across time made it extremely difficult for occupied Afghans to determine where the US government truly stood at any point in time, and to predict how it would act in the future. Regime uncertainty occurred in two areas—security and economic activity—that were central to the lives of Afghan citizens. These policy swings not only created credibility issues for the US government, but further strengthened the Taliban, as Afghan citizens turned to local warlords for the stability and predictability the US government and Afghan central government were unable to offer.

Cartelization

The US government's war on drugs in Afghanistan was intended to disrupt and eliminate larger drug-producing enterprises. The underlying idea was that destabilizing or eradicating the major producers would significantly reduce the production of opium. This, in turn, would reinforce the broader war on terror, given that opium was a source of funds for insurgent and terrorist groups. However, the outcome was the exact opposite. Smaller opium producers gave way to large producers, which became centralized under the control of the Taliban.

US government drug policy in Afghanistan contributed to cartelization in two ways. First, eradication efforts acted as a tax on opium producers by imposing additional costs of doing business—e.g., imprisonment or death. This tax effectively increased the production costs of opium such that smaller producers—who could not incur the additional costs (either the risks or costs of avoidance)—chose to exit the market. The exit of these small producers meant that larger producers, who could afford the additional costs, were left to dominate the market.

Second, once the US government adopted a "hands-on" approach of active eradication, many local Afghan leaders had an incentive to manipulate eradication efforts to target smaller producers (as opposed to larger producers).[73] Absent the appropriate resources and connections to avoid eradication, smaller producers made easy targets for those involved in executing interdiction policies.[74] By pursuing small producers, local leaders and other officials could show that they were "doing something" to combat opium production without having to combat the larger, more organized producers. The result was that the large producers thrived. These same producers became increasingly integrated with the Taliban, who developed a cartel over the country's opium production.

This integration was driven by the Taliban's entrepreneurial alertness. Seeing the significant profit opportunities resulting from US-led eradication efforts and the national ban on opium, the Taliban became a one-stop shop for all the needs of local farmers. According to one report, the Taliban became "increasingly engrossed in both the upstream and downstream sides of the heroin and opium trade—encouraging farmers to plant poppies, lending them seed money, buying the crop of sticky opium paste in the field, refining it into exportable opium and heroin, and finally transporting it to Pakistan and Iran, often in old Toyotas to avoid detection."[75] Additionally, the Taliban began to offer protection in exchange for a portion of farmers' crops or revenues.[76] In fulfilling these roles, the Taliban became the most powerful and violent cartel in the region, controlling or influencing almost all aspects of the opium economy.[77]

In discussing the domestic war on drugs in the United States, Nobel laureate economist Milton Friedman once said, "If you look at the drug war from a purely economic point of view, the role of the government is to protect the drug cartel."[78] This is precisely what happened in Afghanistan, where the opium economy remains a source of revenue for the Taliban.[79] Captured Taliban fighters have stated that opium poppy production is the primary source of operational funding for their organization—including personnel salaries, weapons, fuel, food, and explosives.[80] Thus, US government interdiction policies had the counterproductive effect of increasing the income of the Taliban, as opposed to reducing it.

Criminalization of Ordinary Life

The opium economy is a main source of income for many Afghan citizens. According to estimates, the opium economy provides between 400,000 and 600,000 full-time jobs to Afghans.[81] This figure does not include those involved in the opium economy on a part-time, seasonal basis. Another perverse consequence of the US government's opium policy was the criminalization of hundreds of thousands of Afghan citizens, whose livelihoods were severely jeopardized. As a result, these citizens faced a substantial incentive to align with the Taliban, who offered protection from—and proactive retaliation against—US eradication efforts.[82]

Further strengthening this incentive was the fact that Taliban commanders often received revenues even at the village level, collected as payments from farmers and smugglers involved in the opium economy.[83] The potential income opportunities prompted many to join the organization in the hopes of improving their own livelihoods.[84] To provide some context, consider that NATO researchers estimate contracted Taliban soldiers to receive as much as $150 a month, $30 more than official Afghan police. In a country where the average annual income is less than $500, such a relatively high-paying position has obvious appeal, especially for those already categorized as criminals by the Afghan government and coalition forces.[85]

For many Afghan citizens, participation in the opium economy is the only means of earning a sufficient income.[86] Respondents to a 2013 survey by the United Nations Office on Drugs and Crime indicated that the main reasons they cultivated opium (despite the ban) were the high price of opium, increased income, improved living conditions, and that the crop allowed them to afford basic food and shelter.[87] Interviews with individual Afghan farmers support these survey results.

For example, one farmer explained that growing opium poppy was the only way to make ends meet. "[F]or the rest of our product [corn, cotton, potatoes, etc.] we have no market. We can't export [other crops] and get a good price. We can't even sustain our families."[88] Another farmer echoed his sentiments, saying, "[W]e have to do this in order to have a better life."[89] The criminalization of opium poppy production led many farmers to turn to the Taliban for protection of their livelihoods, making them much less likely to support or cooperate with coalition forces or the new Afghan government. In stark contrast, the occupiers and national government were viewed by many Afghans as direct threats to their well-being.

Reflecting on the eradication efforts of the US government, Special Representative Richard Holbrooke explicitly recognized these perverse consequences when he noted, "Western policies against the opium crop have been a failure. They did not result in any damage to the Taliban, but they put farmers out of work and they alienated people and drove them into the arms of the Taliban."[90] It was this realization that led to the shift in the US government's policy toward the "alternative livelihoods" approach, starting in 2009. Yet in strengthening the insurgency and undermining the US government's stated counterterrorism goals, the damage had already been done.

Corruption

A report by the United Nations Office on Drugs and Crime captured the extent of corruption in Afghanistan: "While corruption is seen by Afghans as one of the most urgent challenges facing their country, it seems to be increasingly embedded in social practices, with patronage and bribery being an acceptable part of day-to-day life."[91] In testimony on Afghanistan before the US Senate, retired General John Allen stated, "[F]or too long we [the US government] focused our attention solely on the Taliban as the existential threat to Afghanistan," noting that, compared to the problems caused by corruption, the Taliban "are an annoyance."[92] However, the policies undertaken by the US government as part of its war on drugs contributed to the perpetuation and entrenchment of corruption.

Making products and services illegal is a source of corruption, because "prohibition creates illicit profit opportunities that would not exist in its absence."[93] In Afghanistan, the national ban on opium—combined with the US government's eradication efforts—meant that both farmers and members of the Taliban needed to find ways to circumvent the law. In general, the extranormal profits caused by prohibition incentivize those in the industry to bribe an array of public actors—police, military, elected officials, judges, etc.—involved in combatting black market activity.[94] This is precisely what happened in Afghanistan, where the prevalence of existing networks of corruption, and the importance of opium to the Afghan economy incentivized bribery at all levels of society. According to Thomas Schweich, a special ambassador to Afghanistan during the Bush administration, many top Afghan officials were intimately involved in the narcotics trade. He notes:

> Narco-traffickers were buying off hundreds of police chiefs, judges, and other officials. Narco-corruption went to the top of the Afghan government. The attorney general [of Afghanistan] . . . told me and other American officials that he had a list of more than 20 senior Afghan officials who were deeply corrupt—some tied to the narcotics trade. He added that President Karzai . . . had directed him, for political reasons, not to prosecute any of these people. . . . Around the same time, the United States released photos of industrial-sized poppy farms—many owned by pro-government opportunists, others owned by Taliban sympathizers. Farmers were . . . diverting U.S.-built irrigation canals to poppy fields.[95]

Local eradication efforts were also riddled with corruption. Among other initiatives, the US government offered one-time financial payments to local political leaders for eradicating opium poppy in their provinces. There were numerous reported instances of local officials receiving rewards for eradication efforts, only to use the money to fund their drug businesses elsewhere in Afghanistan.[96] In many cases, the success of eradication efforts was short-lived because local governors—after receiving the one-time payout for their assistance—would turn a blind eye toward opium poppy production in future years, in exchange for payoffs from farmers.

In 2007, President Karzai appointed Izzatullah Wasifi, a convicted heroin dealer, to the head of Afghanistan's anticorruption commission. Wasifi, in turn, appointed several known corrupt politicians as local police chiefs.[97]

Reports state that Karzai's half-brother, Ahmed Wali Karzai, who was responsible for overseeing the poppy-laden province of Kandahar, was deeply involved in the drug trade.[98] In 2004, Afghan security forces uncovered a large stash of heroin in Kandahar, seizing drugs and the truck in which they were being transported. The commander soon received a phone call from Ahmed Wali Karzai, asking that the vehicle and drugs be released. After another phone call from an aide to President Karzai, the commander complied.[99]

Two years later, another truck was apprehended near Kabul, carrying 110 pounds of heroin. Investigators linked the shipment to one of Ahmed Wali Karzai's bodyguards, who was believed to be acting as an intermediary. In discussing these issues regarding the president's half-brother, Afghan informant Hajji Aman Kheri stated, "[I]t's no secret about Wali Karzai and drugs. A lot of people in the Afghan government are involved in drug trafficking."[100]

Other examples of public corruption related to the opium industry abound. In 2005, for example, British forces uncovered 20,000 pounds of opium in the office of Helmand governor Sher Mohammed Akhundzada, a close ally of President Karzai. Akhundzada was forced out of public office, but Karzai later appointed him to the Senate.[101] In 2006, heroin was found in a car belonging to Hajji Zaher Qadir, President Karzai's nominee for the head of border police protection. Although his appointment was abandoned, Qadir became a prominent representative in the Afghan Parliament.[102]

Political corruption not only strengthened the Taliban's cartel in the short run, but also undermined US government attempts to establish a strong central government and foster long-run economic development. Afghan citizens largely distrust the new national government for a variety of reasons, including the perceived corruption of the political elite.[103] This has important implications for development, as indicated by scholarship examining the impact of trust and corruption on economic growth.[104] The main finding of this research is that low-trust and high-corruption environments impede economic growth. By contributing to corruption and distrust, US government policies toward opium poppy helped foster an environment conducive to economic stagnation, while simultaneously empowering the very groups coalition forces were tasked with defeating.

Violent Conflict

The cartelization of the drug industry, combined with the strengthened insurgency, contributed to increased violence against coalition forces. Unfortunately, there are no data on violence or fatalities due solely to drug-related activities. There is, however, data available on the number of hostile fatalities of coalition troops in Afghanistan by month. Care must be used in interpreting this data, given that drug activity is by no means the only cause of violence or hostile casualties. Nonetheless, there is a reason to believe in a connection between drug activity and violence against coalition forces.

According to the US Department of State, the "opium trade and the insurgency are closely related. Poppy cultivation and insurgent violence are correlated geographically."[105] The agency also states that "UNODC [United Nations Office on Drugs and Crime] and other major international stakeholders all acknowledge that the Taliban-led insurgency and the Afghan drugs trade are increasingly linked."[106] Similarly, a separate empirical study of the relationship between the opium trade and domestic terrorist activity in Afghanistan, between 1996 and 2008, found that "provinces that produce more opium feature higher levels of terrorist attacks and casualties due to terrorism, and that opium production is a more robust predictor of terrorism than nearly all other province features."[107]

Jeffrey Clemens, an economist, argues that the coalition forces' efforts to reduce poppy cultivation led to an increase in resources flowing to the Taliban.[108] The reason is that eradication efforts were most successful in cases where the government—namely, the Afghan government and coalition forces—already had strong control. In contrast, efforts were least successful when the government had weak control. Through their interdiction efforts in Taliban-controlled areas, the Afghan government and coalition forces reduced competition and increased the market power of the Taliban. In doing so, they gave the Taliban a stronger incentive to maintain control over its territories—using violence where necessary—while unintentionally providing increased resources to do so.[109]

While drug activity is not the only factor behind Afghan violence, the evidence shows a strong link. The data in Figure 2 for the 2001–2019 period can be used to provide some insight (albeit indirect) into the effects of US government interdiction policies in Afghanistan.

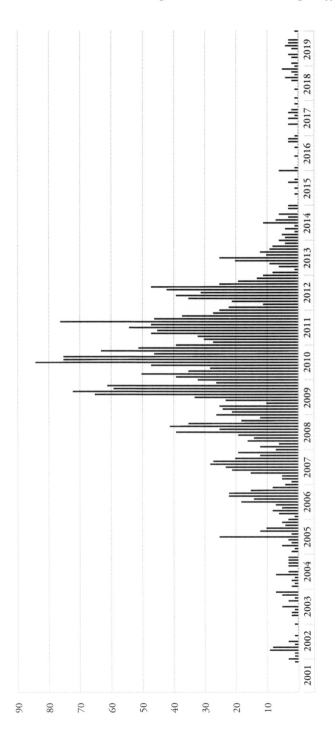

Source: http://icasualties.org/App/AfghanFatalities?

Figure 2. Hostile Coalition Fatalities in Afghanistan by Month, 2001–2019

We would expect the use of violence to protect the significant profits associated with control over opium production. Since April and May are the peak months for harvesting opium poppy, it follows that we should expect to see increases in violence then, as those involved in the opium trade attempt to combat eradication efforts by coalition and Afghan forces that threaten the season's crop. Furthermore, there have been historical increases in insurgent violence against coalition forces in the summer months, immediately following the peak harvest.[110] One reason for this increase is the more favorable weather, which makes it easier to carry out attacks. Another important factor is that, as the peak harvesting reaches an end, opium farmers can reallocate their labor away from cultivation and toward supporting efforts (often led by the Taliban) to actively combat the eradication forces they see as a threat.

For fourteen of the nineteen years shown in Figure 2, the highest annual hostile-fatality month fell in the April to August period. Moreover, the number of hostile fatalities slowly increased over time—in line with the adoption of the "hands-on approach"—and peaked in 2010, when the US government eased its hands-on eradication efforts against Afghan farmers engaged in opium production. The increase in hostile fatalities in the period of the peak opium harvest and summer months suggests that Afghanistan's insurgency remained strong and effective, causing violent harm despite the significant efforts of the US government. This insurgency relied on revenue from the drug trade to fund its activities, meaning that a healthy insurgency implied a healthy drug trade.

The Realities of Empire

- Imperialism produces a wide range of perverse consequences, both seen and unseen, that run counter to liberalism while generating a backlash against the invader and the liberal values they purport to represent.

- Imperialism is often associated with the growth of organized crime.

- Imperialism by a hegemonic power tends to create and reinforce brutal, corrupt, and incompetent client-state ruling elites.

- Client elites created by imperialism do not have an interest in promoting liberal values or sustained economic development, as these will create rivals to their power.

- Even if a foreign power is benevolently distributing liberal public goods, it remains invasive and alien despite providing military aid and training, foreign aid, and the like to a client-state.

- Imperialistic interventions freeze and sustain dysfunctional political structures and arrangements.

6

Illustrating Public Bads:
Drones as Mechanized Terror

TECHNOLOGICAL ADVANCES CHANGE the strategies of empire and the character of imperialism, but not the results. Drones—unmanned aerial vehicles (Uavs) controlled remotely or autonomously via computer—are a good example. Drones have become justifiably associated with American imperialism and the government's transnational war on terror.[1] Since 2001, the use of drones has shifted from instruments of training and surveillance to tools for conducting offensive strikes. Over the years, the US government's covert drone program has become institutionalized—a defining aspect of its militaristic foreign policy, broadcasting control and terror over foreign populations.[2]

The liberal values and ideology supposedly upheld by the US government are undermined by the fundamental tension in the strategy of fighting terror with mechanized terror. This irony is only intensified by US officials' public statements, such as the following made by Mary McLeod, legal adviser to the US Department of State, in front of a UN panel: "The United States is proud of its record as a leader in respecting, promoting and defending human rights and the rule of law, both at home and around the world."[3] The disconnect between such public rhetoric and the actions of US government officials—using drones to execute people outside a formal battlefield—is not lost on many key international constituencies, whose support is ultimately necessary to reduce the threat of terrorism. By adopting and endorsing the use of terror-creating technology to fight terrorist threats, the leaders of the US government have, in the eyes of many, failed to differentiate themselves from the very evil they seek to destroy—a classic bad of empire.

Drone institutionalization raises numerous issues related to their use, including potential violations of international law and state sovereignty, ethical issues concerning the use of robotics in warfare, the lack of transparency by the US government regarding its drone program, appropriate checks on the US government's use of drones as a tool for waging war, adverse psychological effects on drone pilots, and the precedent established by the US government for other governments' future use of robotics to engage in surveillance and warfare.[4] Therefore, drones are at the intersection of many of the bads of empire outlined in this book. To highlight this, this chapter explores the hypocritical use of terror to fight terror despite liberal justifications and rhetoric.[5]

The targets of drone strikes are often embedded in communities that include innocent civilians. Even when drone strikes are successful in annihilating a target identified by the American government, they simultaneously produce negative spillover effects that impose significant costs on the surrounding populace. These negative effects can be physical (bodily injury or death) or psychological (anxiety and terror) and contribute both to individual harms and to broader economic and social degradation by disturbing—if not outright destroying—social networks and communities.[6]

Furthermore, the intelligence associated with drone strikes is imperfect. Government decision-makers often rely on patterns of behavior determined as terrorists' "general signatures." Subsequent "signature strikes" occur when a drone is used to target a person or group of people based not on their known identity, but instead on their geographic location and behaviors observed from afar. In many instances, these pattern-of-behavior analyses are inaccurate, meaning that innocent people are injured or killed by signature strikes.

An associated issue is determining what constitutes an "accurate target." In many instances, the category of "target" is defined by the US government in broad, abstract terms that include significant portions of a population. For example, absent clear evidence demonstrating that a person killed in a strike was either not a military-aged male, or was a military-aged male but not an unlawful combatant, they are automatically counted as an "enemy combatant" by the US government.[7] This methodology obfuscates the true costs imposed by drones because it can easily classify ordinary, innocent civilians as enemies by default, based on a small number of general characteristics (e.g., age and gender).

Together, these factors contribute to a fundamental tension regarding the use of drones as a tool of imperialism and counterterrorism. The leaders of the US government justify their use of drones as an efficient method for weakening—and ultimately ending—the threat of international terrorism, while protecting members of the American military. However, the use of drones creates and perpetuates terror among foreign populations. These terror-creating aspects of drones are typically neglected, which understates their net effect on global terror and downplays the broader bads of empire and its imperial activities.

A central reason for this neglect is that the use and efficacy of drones are typically evaluated from the perspective of those in control. This framing emphasizes categories such as "valid targets" and "collateral damage"—as defined by members of the US government—while minimizing, if not altogether ignoring, the views of those experiencing the presence of drones in their everyday lives. From the perspective of the target population, the damage done by drones is not "collateral"; rather, it is blunt, brutal, and devastating harm caused by the violent intervention of a foreign state. Understanding this alternative perspective is crucial, because what the intervening government perceives as "combating terrorism" may simultaneously be viewed as an act of state terrorism by the target population.

"Collateral Damage," or the Maiming and Killing of Innocents

Nearly every argument for the expansion of the US government's use of drones stems from the claim that they are a more efficient means of achieving foreign-policy goals, as compared to alternatives.[8] It is argued that drones minimize the potential harm to members of the US military while accurately targeting terrorists. When in office, President Obama explicitly stated that drones are better at targeting and killing foreign adversaries. After noting that drones "are effective," he went on to say, "[D]ozens of highly skilled al-Qaeda commanders, trainers, bomb makers and operatives have been taken off the battlefield. . . . [T]he primary alternative to [drones] would be the use of conventional military options. . . . Conventional airpower or missiles are far less precise than drones."[9] As this quote illustrates, the use of drones is typically compared and contrasted with conventional bombings, which are assumed to be the relevant alternative (note that the inevitability of some form of government intervention is a given).

A related argument is that drones reduce the costs of conflict in terms of reduced civilian casualties, or "collateral damage." Former CIA Director John Brennan, for example, stated that drones have "surgical precision—the ability with laser-like focus to eliminate the cancerous tumor called al Qa'ida, while limiting the damage to the tissue around it."[10] At another point, Brennan stated, "[T]here hasn't been a single collateral death [in a year] because of the exceptional proficiency, precision of the [drone] capabilities we've been able to develop."[11] Harold Koh, former legal adviser to the State Department, stated that "[b]ecause drone technology is highly precise, if properly controlled, it could be more lawful and more consistent with human rights and humanitarian law than the alternatives."[12] As these policymakers argue, the US government can intervene in other societies and exterminate confirmed threats with precision, because drones are more effective than certain alternative military interventions (e.g., bombing). This is a flawed argument.

For one, *if* we accept the claim that drones are more accurate than conventional bombing (seen as the appropriate comparison), it is not clear ex ante that the adoption of drones will result in fewer deaths of innocent people. In economic terms, drones may reduce the "price" of offensive attacks (deaths), which allows the military to move down the demand curve, increasing the quantity of drone strikes demanded.[13] While the use of drones might reduce deaths in a single strike by providing a substitution for other, more deadly alternatives (e.g., conventional bombing), this very well might be offset by an increase in total innocents' deaths due to "cheaper," more frequent drone attacks.

Moreover, presenting conventional bombing as an alternative to drone bombing is an artificial, narrow dichotomy. If the foreign policy goal of the US government is to eliminate individual enemy targets, it isn't clear that conventional bombing is the appropriate alternative to drone bombing. Instead, the appropriate alternative might be something akin to special operations missions against specific targets.[14] Of course, a complete assessment would weigh these alternatives against the number of innocent people who would be maimed or killed absent US government intervention, rather than taking US intervention as inevitable, which tends to be the default position.

Despite their public rhetoric, members of the US government are cognizant of the fact that drones are not as accurate as publicly claimed.[15] In June 2016, the Obama administration released information regarding the deaths of combatants and noncombatants outside formal war zones (Afghanistan, Iraq, and Syria) from January 2009–December 2015. According to their calculations, 473 strikes (this includes all airstrikes—both drones and conventional airstrikes—as the government failed to provide more precise details on strike types) took place during that period, outside areas of active hostilities. The administration estimated that between 2,372 and 2,581 combatants were killed in the strikes, while between 64 and 116 noncombatants were killed.[16] The government's public reporting on noncombatant deaths was short lived, as President Trump ended the practice via executive order in 2019.

At a minimum, the reporting by the Obama administration clarifies that strikes are not as accurate as proponents claim. Irrespective of whether one considers their range of "noncombatants" to be a high or low number, the fact is that innocent human beings are killed by US government strikes. Moreover, it is likely that the government's accounting understates the number of civilians killed by drone strikes, for two reasons.[17]

The first is the US government's commitment to using signature strikes against targets.[18] The reliance on general behaviors means that the government cannot be sure exactly who is being killed by drone strikes. Intended targets (who are assumed to be worthy of execution) may be killed by signature strikes, but the same could be said for innocent civilians. There is no way to obtain accurate numbers for these two categories, both because of the lack of specific reporting in areas where drone strikes take place and due to the general secrecy surrounding the US government's drone program.[19]

The second is the methodology of counting enemy combatants. Absent evidence to the contrary, military-aged males are categorized by default as enemies killed in combat.[20] By broadly defining who is counted as an enemy combatant, this methodology allows the members of the US government to understate, and therefore downplay, the death of innocent civilians due to drone strikes. People are categorized as combatants based on broad characteristics, rather than a careful assessment of individual actions and a broader commitment to respect for human dignity.

There have been efforts by independent sources to estimate the number of civilian casualties resulting from drone strikes.[21] For instance, the Bureau of Investigative Journalism—a nonprofit organization focused on public interest investigations—tracked the consequences of US drone strikes and covert military actions in Pakistan, Afghanistan, Yemen, and Somalia for the 2010–2020 period. According to their data, an estimated 14,040 total strikes during this period resulted in total deaths ranging from 8,858 to 16,901, including civilian deaths ranging from 990 to 2,200.[22]

Other efforts have focused on estimating the number of civilian injuries and deaths from specific drone strikes. For example, a report by Human Rights Watch reviewed the effects of six targeted killings via drone strikes by the US government in Yemen over the 2009–2012 period. The report concluded:

Two [of] these attacks were in clear violation of international humanitarian law—the laws of war—because they struck only civilians or used indiscriminate weapons. The other four cases may have violated the laws of war because the individual attacked was not a lawful military target or the attack caused disproportionate civilian harm, determinations that require further investigation. In several of these cases the US also did not take all feasible precautions to minimize harm to civilians, as the laws of war require.[23]

A report by Amnesty International reviewed nine drone strikes in Pakistan during the January 2012–August 2013 period.[24] The report detailed each strike and traces some of the harm—ranging from injury to death—incurred by innocent civilians. The authors concluded "that the cases in this report raise serious concerns that the USA has unlawfully killed people in drone strikes, and that such killings may amount in some cases to extrajudicial executions or war crimes and other violations of international humanitarian law."[25]

Another study by Human Rights Watch analyzed a 2013 drone strike in Yemen that "killed at least 12 men and wounded at least 15 others, 6 of them seriously."[26] The US government declared that the victims were militants, but Human Rights Watch confirmed that the target was a wedding procession, and that at least some of those killed were civilians. A 2017 report summarizing a selection of airstrikes investigated by nongovernmental organizations in Yemen and Pakistan between January 2009 and April 2014 identified 52 strikes, with estimated civilian deaths ranging from 161 to 183.[27] Finally, a 2019 report by Amnesty International "investigates five incidents in Lower Shabelle, Somalia, in which 14 civilians were killed and eight injured." The authors provide "credible evidence that US air strikes were responsible for four of these incidents and that the fifth was most plausibly caused by a US air strike."[28] Equally troubling is the possibility that the drone attacks "may have violated international humanitarian law (IHL) and could, in some cases, constitute war crimes."[29]

Further insight into the harm caused to civilians by drone strikes is provided by US government documents on Operation Haymaker, which targeted members of the Taliban and al-Qaeda along Afghanistan's northeast border with Pakistan.[30] Haymaker involved a combination of special operations forces and other members of the intelligence community on the ground, using drone strikes from above to carry out targeted killings. Among other things, the government documents revealed that "during a five-month stretch of the campaign, nearly nine out of ten people who died in airstrikes were not the Americans' direct target."[31] Furthermore, the documents include "a chart revealing that airstrikes killed 219 people over a fourteen-month period in 2012 and 2013, resulting in at least thirty-five jackpots [the killing of intended targets]."[32] This means that the 184 other casualties—84 percent of the total people killed during this period—may not have been the intended targets of US airstrikes.

As this review of the existing public evidence (which is limited and incomplete, due to US government secrecy and obfuscation) indicates, there are numerous sources indicating that drone strikes cause injury and death to innocent civilians.[33] At a minimum, this suggests that drones lack scalpel-like precision, often claimed by proponents as a defining feature of this technology. Appreciating drones' lack of precision in offensive strikes is important for two related reasons.

First, innocent civilians are often maimed or killed as a result of drone strikes. This is a significant bad, one that must be considered when discussing the efficacy of drones as a tool of imperialism. Second, given drones' potential to cause significant damage to innocent civilians, their use creates terror among the populace in targeted areas. This sense of terror can exist among targeted individuals, but it also spills over on to the broader populace who recognize that they (and members of their community) may also be surveilled, maimed, or killed by drone strikes. The implication is that even a full appreciation of the civilian injuries and deaths caused by US drones still understates the true cost of this technology's use.

Mechanized Terror from Above

Terror is an emotional state caused by some extreme threat, whether real or perceived. Public terror involves shared fear of an extreme perceived threat to the collective well-being of a group. Public fear can often lead to widespread support for strong responses by the state, in order to combat the cause of fear.[34] For example, the public terror caused by the 9/11 attacks on American soil—and the fear of potential future attacks—led to public support for the US government's global war on terror, which aims to eradicate terrorist threats.[35] Given their supposed efficiency in killing terrorists, drones are a central component of this war. However, the use of drones to combat terrorism creates tension because drones, which are intended to kill terrorists to reduce the terrorist threat, also create terror among the populace living in the targeted area. To the extent that drones alleviate the fears of Americans, they do so by exporting fear to others, calling into question whether American empire produces *global* public goods.

The US government documents associated with Operation Haymaker offer some insight into the psychological effects of drones on the members of targeted terrorist organizations. According to a Taliban detainee identified only as "Ahmad" in the documents, "Hands down the scariest/most intimidating message for the Taliban, at any level, from fighter to Taliban senior leadership, is anything to do with drones or aerial bombings. The Taliban," he continues, "has no way to defend against them and they are certain to end in absolute destruction of whatever their target is."[36] Similarly, David Rohde, a journalist who was a prisoner of the Taliban for seven months, notes that "for months the drones had been a terrifying presence. Remotely piloted, propeller-driven airplanes, they could easily be heard as they circled overhead for hours. To the naked eye, they were small dots in the sky. But their missiles had a range of several miles. We knew we could be immolated without warning."[37]

From the perspective of US government leaders, this "target terror" is desirable. It disrupts the operations of targeted individuals and organizations, creating a constant sense of uncertainty and fear.[38] Moreover, living under the constant threat of drone strikes may deter some people from joining the target organization. From this perspective, drone-created terror extends beyond the current members of the organization to potential members, who realize they too will be subject to surveillance and potential strikes if they join the target organization.

However, terror is not limited solely to the segment of the population consisting of target organizations and potential recruits. Targets are typically embedded in broader communities populated by innocent civilians. The civilian segment of the population is not immune from drone-created terror; they also suffer the psychological costs of living in constant fear of surveillance, injury, or death. The following thought experiment illustrates these negative spillover effects:

> Imagine that you are living somewhere in Pakistan, Yemen, or Gaza where the United States and its allies suspect a terrorist presence. Day and night, you hear a constant buzzing in the sky. Like a lawnmower. You know that this flying robot is watching everything you do. You can always hear it. Sometimes, it fires missiles into your village. You are told the robot is targeting extremists, but its missiles have killed family, friends, and neighbours. So, your behaviour changes: you stop going out, you stop congregating in public, and you likely start hating the country that controls the flying robot. And you probably start to sympathize a bit more with the people these robots, called drones, are monitoring.[39]

There is ample evidence to suggest that the negative externality aspects of drone-created terror are not merely a hypothetical thought experiment. Indeed, the generalized terror created by drones has been well documented in a variety of geographic contexts.

Based on his firsthand experience as a prisoner of the Taliban, David Rohde captures the widespread sense of terror created by drones: "The drones were terrifying. From the ground, it is impossible to determine who or what they are tracking as they circle overhead. The buzz of a distant propeller is a constant reminder of imminent death."⁴⁰ This terror was experienced not only by the Taliban, but also by the broader community living under the constant presence of drones overhead.

In a joint report, the International Human Rights and Conflict Resolution Clinic (located at Stanford University) and the Global Justice Clinic (located at New York University) detail the effects of drone strikes in northwest Pakistan on the civilian populace. The content of the report was based on over 130 interviews with "victims and witnesses of drone activity, their family members, current and former Pakistani government officials, representatives from five major Pakistani political parties, subject matter experts, lawyers, medical professionals, development and humanitarian workers, members of civil society, academics, and journalists."⁴¹ The report concludes that "US drone strike policies cause considerable and under-accounted for harm to the daily lives of ordinary civilians, beyond death and physical injury."⁴² One interviewee, a humanitarian worker in Pakistan, captured the general climate of drone-created terror that will resonate with many Americans:

> Do you remember 9/11? Do you remember what it felt like right after? I was in New York on 9/11. I remember people crying in the streets. People were afraid about what might happen next. People didn't know if there would be another attack. There was tension in the air. This is what it is like. It is a continuous tension, a feeling of continuous uneasiness. We are scared. You wake up with a start to every noise.⁴³

The report also discusses the US government's tendency to carry out repeated drone strikes in the same area, as well as the perverse consequences of these secondary strikes:

> The US practice of striking one area multiple times, and evidence that it has killed rescuers, makes both community members and humanitarian workers afraid or unwilling to assist injured victims. Some community members shy away from gathering in groups, including important tribal dispute-resolution bodies, out of fear that they may attract the attention of drone operators. Some parents choose to keep their children home, and children injured or traumatized by strikes have dropped out of school.⁴⁴

As this suggests, secondary drone strikes in the same area create systematic terror among the general populace, severely and adversely affecting the well-being of citizens. For these very reasons, the use of secondary strikes—which often end up harming first responders and innocent civilians responding to the initial attack—is a hallmark of terrorist organizations, as recognized by the US government in the past.[45]

In 2013, the family of Momina Bibi appeared before the US Congress to testify about a US drone strike in North Waziristan, Pakistan, which resulted in her death. According to Bibi's 13-year-old grandson,

> Now I prefer cloudy days when the drones don't fly. When the sky brightens and becomes blue, the drones return and so does the fear. Children don't play so often now, and have stopped going to school. Education isn't possible as long as the drones circle overhead.[46]

This testimony illustrates some key negative spillovers of drone strikes, and how they may affect children and the broader community. It also highlights the fact that, from the perspective of the target population, the harm from drones is not some overly broad notion of "collateral damage," but rather the fear of blunt destruction; this does not merely involve potential injury and death, but also social and economic degradation on numerous margins.

More recently, *The Guardian* conducted a series of interviews with six people in Pakistan and Yemen who have lost family members to drone strikes. The common themes across the interviews can be summarized as follows:

> The people [subject to drone strikes] are left impoverished, anguished and infuriated. Justice, let alone apologies, never arrives, even as a modest amount of blood money flows from the local governments. The United States, which styles itself a force for justice in the world, is to them the remote force that introduced death into their lives and treats them like they are subhuman, fit only to be targeted. At any moment, they fear, another drone could come for them.[47]

Mohammed Tuaiman, a 13-year-old boy living in Yemen, stated, "[A] lot of the kids in this area wake up from sleeping because of nightmares from them [drones] and some now have mental problems. They turned our area into hell and continuous horror, day and night, we even dream of them in our sleep."[48]

Tuaiman was killed by a subsequent US drone strike, six months after being interviewed.

The negative spillover effects produced by drones can be far-reaching, extending well beyond the local communities where immediate surveillance and strikes occur. In Pakistan, for example, "public outrage at the strikes is hardly limited to the region in which they take place—areas of northwestern Pakistan where ethnic Pashtuns predominate. Rather, the strikes are now exciting visceral opposition across a broad spectrum of Pakistani opinion in Punjab and Sindh, the nation's two most populous provinces."[49] Human Rights Watch notes that, based on their interviews, many Yemenis fear US drone strikes more than they do al-Qaeda.[50] A similar dynamic is at work in Pakistan, where "[w]hile violent extremists may be unpopular, for a frightened population they seem less ominous than a faceless enemy that wages war from afar and often kills more civilians than militants."[51]

Drone-created fear is often used by organizations targeted by the US government to bolster their support and recruit new members. This runs counter to the purported purpose of drone strikes, which is to weaken these very organizations and thereby combat terrorism. In response to drone strikes, "terrorists and ordinary people are drawn closer to each other out of sympathy, whereas a critical function of any successful counter-terrorism policy is to win over public confidence so that they join in the campaign against the perpetrators of terror."[52] David Rohde notes that, during his time as a prisoner of the Taliban, "[t]he drones killed many senior commanders and hindered their operations. Yet the Taliban were able to garner recruits in their aftermath by exaggerating the number of civilian casualties."[53] This implies that even when drone strikes do kill intended targets, the benefit may be at least partially (if not altogether) offset by the strengthening of the targeted organization through increased sympathy, support, and recruitment, due to the public perception that the US government is the true terrorist threat.[54] The negative consequences of drones do not end here.

The use of drones by the US government normalizes this technology as a tool of international relations.[55] The associated negative risk is significant.[56] If the world is viewed as a battlefield—as in the US government's war on terror—and if drones are perceived as a legitimate means of resolving conflict, the net result may very well be greater instability and illiberalism, both of which are at odds with the purported goals of liberal empire. Other states have already begun to follow the US government's lead by adopting drone technology for military purposes. If the leaders of these states decide to follow the US government's approach to deploying these technologies—declaring the right to kill enemies around the globe at their discretion, based on secret criteria and with few (if any) constraints—the result will likely be increased global disorder and the further entrenchment of violence as the primary means of resolving conflict.[57]

The Realities of Empire

- Interventions can never do just one thing, and where interveners are successful on one margin, they will often generate significant costs and failures on other margins.

- The range of seen and unseen costs resulting from imperialism often fall on innocent people in the target country, those who are vulnerable and unable to avoid harm.

- The costs of imperialism are understated, due to political incentives in the intervening country and the tendency to view imperialism from the perspective of the intervener.

- Empires invest significant resources in technological innovations that make the imperial power more efficient, covertly projecting its power while hiding the illiberal nature of its actions.

- The expansive activities of liberal empires often violate—and therefore erode—the international laws of war, while setting the precedent for other governments to justify grossly illiberal behaviors in the name of liberalism.

7

Rethinking Empire

MY SKEPTICISM, AND critique, of empire is based on the study of constraints and incentives facing imperialists, as well as a recognition of the negative, illiberal consequences of foreign interventions—including, paradoxically, this real possibility: less freedom and security at home. The failure of government applies to imperialism just as much as it applies to domestic programs and schemes of economic and social control—more so, in fact. Policy is not designed and implemented in a vacuum. Just because policymakers know *what* they want to achieve abroad does not mean that they know *how* to do it.[1] Moreover, even a well-formulated initial conception of the *what* does not guarantee success, given the often perverse frictions in democratic politics—elected officials and vested interests seeking to design and influence policy for their own narrow gains, bureaucratic inertia and waste, and voters who typically lack the necessary information or the ability to discipline government actors. The messy international part of foreign policy further means that these political dynamics do not operate solely within a country, but across the globe. Therefore, government failures on such a global scale are likely to be epic, leading to worldwide instability.

The reasons are clear. Many skeptics of domestic government programs (e.g., social programs, healthcare, education, and so on) and of centralized economic and political power held by private people and organizations (e.g., corporate welfare, regulatory capture, monopoly power) are entirely comfortable embracing grandiose government programs if they fall under the purview of "national security" and "defense." However, differences between domestic government programs and empire are of degree rather than kind. Both involve the same state apparatus and numerous pathologies and realities, which limit what government can achieve while generating significant harm.[2] In fact, all the problems identified by those on both sides of the political spectrum regarding domestic government programs are magnified in the operation of a nation-state empire.

Of course, opposition to empire should never naively ignore the existence of conflict and threats to individual security. It recognizes instead that a culture of imperialistic militarism elevates violence as the primary means of human interaction, with brutal and unintended results, as we saw in the chapters on the Afghan drug war and the use of drones to combat terrorism. The cost of placing militarism on such a pedestal is evident everywhere: "Everyone can see the immense harm the state causes day in and day out, not to mention its periodic orgies of mass death and destruction."[3] Beyond the costs in treasure and blood, US military imperialism threatens and destroys many of the liberal values it claims to advance, including the comity among nations that governments purport to desire.[4] The resulting damage is difficult, if not impossible, to reverse. Given the realities of empire, such illiberal outcomes must be presumed as the most likely result, absent overwhelming new evidence to the contrary.

The precautionary principle is often adopted in the formulation of government regulatory policy. It "holds that if an action or policy might cause great, irreparable harm, then, notwithstanding a lack of scientific consensus, those who support the action or policy should shoulder the burden of proof."[5] The precautionary principle is typically applied in regulating the environment, as well as scientific and technological innovations. Given what is at stake in the operation of an empire, I suggest that we also direct the precautionary principle to the operations of an empire.

What are the implications of this shift in assumptions regarding empire and its relation to liberal outcomes and genuine security? First, the view that military imperialism is the primary means of engaging in international relations must be removed from its current pedestal.[6] Second, retrenchment—taking steps to pull back America's forward deployments (military personnel and hardware) around the world—should be elevated in importance relative to entrenching and expanding an empire.[7] Third, we should then look to peaceful interaction between private, nonstate actors living in different geographic spaces.[8]

Paradoxically, this shift in perspective regarding foreign policy involves looking internally, within our borders, to remove the barriers that prevent peaceful interaction—not only between Americans, but also with those in other countries, regions, and cultures. This approach stands in contrast, for example, to "war by other means," which involves the US government's aggressive use of geoeconomic tools such as sanctions, trade and investment policy, monetary policy, and aid to force other governments and peoples to bend to its will.[9]

My position, then, is inherently nonisolationist and liberal. It is not a retreat from the world, but a call for global engagement by means other than militaristic imperialism and the associated hubris which assumes the world can be controlled by Western government elites.[10] It involves a commitment to people, goods, and services moving across borders, all of which are important contributors to peace, toleration, and human well-being.[11] It embraces peaceful dealmaking as a means of resolving differences.[12] It is grounded in cultures of peace (which is intentionally plural because of the wide diversity of peaceful means), in contrast to a culture of militarism. Furthermore, it is grounded in values, beliefs, and behaviors promoting mutual caring, respect, and human well-being.[13] Cultures of peace do not deny conflict; rather, they recognize that conflict is a social constant that must be navigated by discovering and exercising arrangements, particularly with the aim of minimizing violence.

And let me also underscore—the shift from a culture of militarism to cultures of peace requires shedding the belief that the military operations of the nation-state are the central source of security and liberty in a free society. Contrary to this belief, the primary source of order is civilian-based people power—the power possessed by dispersed, self-governing individuals—rather than political power exercised in the name of the nation-state (which is, frankly, something of an abstraction) by highly centralized elites, who often preemptively project that power overseas, thus spawning empire. By stark contrast, Alexis de Tocqueville emphasized the importance of association, or civil society, for freedom.[14] Associations allow people to come together to solve common problems without relying on the government at home or, by extension, on its imperial practices in foreign lands. If thick enough, these associations offer the opportunity for self-governing people to solve collective action problems, while providing an important check on arbitrary rule and the abuse of power by political actors. Self-governance, by definition, limits state power—both here and overseas. However, effectively associating with others is not an innate skill, but an art that requires ongoing practice by a citizenry dedicated to self-governing ideals—and also dedicated to peace with that citizenry's neighbors, both proximate and far-flung.[15]

Therefore, thinking imaginatively about alternatives to the state provision of defense is crucial to constraining various abuses of power and maintaining liberty in as many places as possible. By necessity, this entails an entirely different view of foreign policy, one that does not lead to imperialism—and there is real urgency in our getting this right. One negative consequence of clinging to the belief in the state as the primary source of security is the atrophying of creative citizens' ability to address conflicts and security dilemmas. Another is that the present view of the nation-state and its empires necessarily implies the nonreturnable transfer of control to the state (political power) at the expense of people power; these consequences threaten cherished freedoms in the name of protecting them.[16]

What might such alternatives look like? While there is no set answer to this question—after all, a key idea of this book is that there is no single successful blueprint from on high for micro-organizing society—we can certainly envision and observe diverse ways of providing security for a society's residents. The remainder of this chapter does just that. It is suggestive and nonprescriptive; its purpose is to move beyond typical treatments of the international affairs of nation-states, which overwhelmingly embrace a top-down, monocentric view of security and take state-provided defense as a given necessity.

Polycentric Defense: Moving beyond the Nation-State

From a young age, people are conditioned to view the national government as *the* source of a country's security. The first step in ending this habituation is to recognize alternatives to the nation-state providing security. After all, people are the final caretakers of the country, not trapped in a helpless situation where political power is given and fixed, and where violent conflict is constant. They possess significant agency over their own lives, including how much authority to grant to the rulers of the nation-state and whether to practice "peaceableness." As sociologist and peace scholar Elise Boulding noted, peaceableness refers to "a constant shaping and reshaping of understandings, situations, and behaviors, in a constantly changing lifeworld" in the ongoing pursuit of peaceful means to resolving ever-present conflict, both domestically and internationally.[17]

Peaceableness involves people recognizing their individual capacity to shape the world for the better. Exercising this capability is central to maintaining and extending the liberal values underpinning self-governance, freedom, and humane relations with other peoples across the globe. A polycentric system empowers citizens to exercise individual agency, creativity, and collective problem solving, all of which are at the foundation of a peaceful, self-governing society.[18]

A polycentric system is one involving numerous decision-making units—each with autonomy in action—operating within a shared set of rules.[19] A polycentric order stands in contrast to a monocentric order, where there is only one centralized decision-making unit. A monocentric order relies on centralized coordination and conflict resolution in order to function. A polycentric system does not; it utilizes noncentral mechanisms of coordination and conflict resolution. The nation-state's monopoly on violent force within a geographic space in the name of "national defense" is monocentric.

The economic logic underpinning the national provision of defense is as follows. Economists traditionally divided goods into two types: private goods and public goods.[20] Private goods are excludable; public goods are nonexcludable. A good is excludable if nonpayers can be prevented or excluded from consuming the good. A cup of coffee is an excludable private good; once purchased, nonpayers can be excluded from drinking the coffee. The opposite applies to public goods—other people can consume them whether or not they pay, which encourages free riding off the contributions of others.

Social scientists consider the defense of the nation-state as the quintessential case of a public good.[21] To understand why, consider the standard example of a missile defense shield, intended to protect a country from missile attacks. In this example, defense is asserted to be nonexcludable, as it is exceedingly difficult to defend me from a missile strike without also defending my neighbor. This makes it difficult to exclude nonpayers—those who refuse to pay for the service voluntarily. The resultant free riding—"I will refrain from paying for the defense service because I still benefit when you pay"—suggests that security will be severely underprovided without state intervention to fill the gap.

Over time, however, social scientists have introduced various nuances to the theory of the provision of goods that go beyond the simple public-private dichotomy.[22] These developments require rethinking defense provision. Security should not be assumed prima facie to be a public good; even when it has public characteristics, this does not automatically imply the requirement of state provision.[23] Contrary to the view that "defense" is the sole purview of the nation-state, there is no one-size-fits-all approach to security provision. People can gather creatively to solve collective action problems and provide goods that generate widespread community benefits while serving as a check on potentially abusive state power.[24]

The Benefits of Polycentric Defense

Relative to monocentric defense, polycentricity offers several distinct benefits. First, decentralized decision-making allows actors to take advantage of local, context-specific information in a rapid manner.[25] A key aspect of security is that it requires coproduction to be supplied effectively. Coproduction refers to direct input and participation by consumers who are actively involved in the supply of a good.[26] Many goods do not require coproduction. For example, the production of an iPhone does not require any direct input from consumers. For these goods, there is a clear separation between production and consumption. For others, however, coproduction is essential. Education is one example—a student will learn little from a class if that student (along with the instructor) does not put in the required work to coproduce the desired outcome.

Likewise, effective security requires active coproduction—this time, on the part of the citizenry. Citizens cannot entirely outsource security provision to specialized professionals in the military, police forces, or private security firms. They contribute to security provision in a variety of ways, including locking their doors, possessing arms to deter security threats, and reinforcing social norms that deter violence, among many other activities.[27] As urbanist Jane Jacobs noted, citizens walking around communities while going about their daily business often deter violence simply by serving as "eyes on the street."[28] Polycentric governance encourages citizen coproduction by aligning governance with community norms, incorporating local knowledge, and promoting social trust within the community.

Examples were evident during the 9/11 attacks in the United States, as well as in their aftermath. As the attacks unfolded, the monocentric federal government's national security state struggled to mobilize resources in an effective and timely manner. In contrast, the private citizens on Flight 93 were heroically able to coordinate and mobilize to stop the terrorists from striking their intended target.[29] In the post-9/11 period, private citizens successfully resisted and thwarted the "Shoe Bomber" (Richard Reid) in 2001 and the "Underwear Bomber" (Umar Farouk Abdulmutallab) in 2009. In each of these cases, the proximity of private citizens to the would-be attackers gave them specific knowledge of the situation and the ability to respond quickly, relative to the monocentric alternative provided by the lavishly funded and well-staffed (but highly fallible) national security state.

Second, polycentric defense permits greater competition, experimentation, and flexibility compared to monocentric control. A polycentric environment introduces multiple margins of competition, and therefore creates incentives for entrepreneurs to serve the desires of those who consume collective goods.[30] As a result, polycentric orders are better able to meet—and satisfy—a diversity of preferences. A monocentric order necessarily offers a "one-size-fits-all" solution. Polycentricity, in contrast, allows for a range of different outcomes across decision-making units. And because polycentricity allows for the use of local knowledge and experimentation, there is a greater likelihood that diverse preferences will be satisfied.[31] This is especially important when the monocentric order fails to provide security to certain segments of the population, either through dysfunction or choice.

During the civil rights movement, African American activists could not reliably expect monocentric, state-provided defense to protect them from racial violence. In response, entrepreneurs within the African American community organized armed self-defense to safeguard activists from violence.[32] From the perspective of these activists, defense provided through a top-down, monocentric order was ineffective at best and, at worst, directly threatened their personal safety. Given the context-specific challenges facing activists, the type of security they desired was unique to their local circumstances and often could not be effectively delivered by the state.

Third, polycentric defense disperses risk and produces a more reliable, robust system that can better withstand strain. Under a monocentric system, there is a single point of failure. If the central mechanism of coordination and conflict resolution fails, then the system does not operate as intended. Because polycentric systems involve numerous, overlapping decision-making units engaged in competition and experimentation, failure by any one unit does not undermine the overall stability of the system. Returning to the citizen-based response in the United States during and after the 9/11 attacks, sole reliance on the monocentric order—i.e., the US national security state—would have led to a larger number of successful terrorist attacks compared to relying on dispersed citizens, who proved effective in stopping certain attacks from occurring when the government failed to do so.

Finally, polycentric defense disperses power within a society, as compared to a monocentric system, which concentrates power in the hands of a small group of elites. This monocentric power can be (and is!) abused under the cloak of advancing the "public interest." Polycentric defense offers a means of mitigating the harm by dispersing power across multiple decision-making units, limiting political-power monopolies.

For example, the US national security state invests significant resources in cybersecurity, surveillance, and cryptography, mainly through the National Security Agency (NSA). In principle, the fruits of this investment are used to protect US persons from foreign threats. At the same time, however, these advances have been used by the US government to surveil and control people domestically and internationally.[33] In addition to monitoring the communications of citizens, the US government has proposed restrictions on encryption and has demanded backdoor access to encryption from private firms as a means of accessing information.[34]

This has prompted civil liberties groups—such as the American Civil Liberties Union, Electronic Frontier Foundation, and Human Rights Watch—to encourage internet users to engage in self-defense by adopting encryption technologies to protect their communications from state surveillance.[35] Given the inherent, pervasive problems engendered by secrecy within a highly centralized national security state, any decentralized innovations reducing these problems are a potential source of greater individual freedom.[36]

Pervasive Polycentric Defense

Polycentric defense is not just academic or utopian. It already exists in two areas. The first is within the global international space, in which nation-states exercise autonomy in decision-making. Power and influence vary across nation-states, but there is no formal world government, and states act as the main decision-making units in international affairs. This nation-state level of defense is the typical focus of most treatments of foreign affairs and empire.

The second—and unfortunately neglected—area of polycentric defense operation is at the individual level, where private people are the autonomous decision-making units. In practice, ordinary civilians engage in a broad, diverse range of real-world security activities. Let's explore this overlooked aspect of polycentric defense in more detail.

The polycentric approach appreciates that defense is not a single good, but rather a bundle of diverse goods depending on the specific context.[37] It recognizes that there is no one-size-fits-all approach when it comes to the provision of security. Instead, effective security is best provided by individuals operating within a diverse network of enterprises, including households, private firms, nonprofit organizations, civic associations, and public economies of various scale. This wide range of defense activities fall along a spectrum, ranging from local defense to scaled-up defense (which serves far larger collective consumption units).[38]

At the most local level, individuals and households act to secure themselves against various forms of violence and plunder. People lock their doors, protecting their property from external threats to their security. Many people invest in more advanced technologies, such as elaborate home security systems. Whether they protect their home with locks, alarms, or cameras, these forms of defense rely on technologies sold by private entrepreneurs on the market, all to create an architecture of security that helps enforce the protection of people and their property.

Technological advancements alter individuals' available means for protecting their property. For example, Lojack is a car retrieval system that relies on a radio transmitter hidden in an automobile. This radio transmitter can be remotely activated after the car is reported stolen, allowing police to track the car. Economists Ian Ayres and Steven Levitt argue that this technology creates positive externalities because criminals cannot easily discern whether a car has Lojack, and therefore the technology's prevalence deters car theft generally, protecting Lojack users and nonusers alike.[39] Despite the positive spillovers for drivers who do not purchase cars with Lojack, there are sufficient private benefits such that some people purchase cars with Lojack installed. Similar logic applies to other security-enhancing technologies.

Private gun ownership is another form of defense that occurs at the individual and household levels (with profound consequences, throughout history, for an effective polycentric defense of the country). Individuals use their firearms to ward off criminal assailants in diverse social contexts. Gun owners are typically aware of crime attempts far before state police, and can use their local knowledge of time and place to defend themselves from assaults, home invasions, and robbery attempts. This can be particularly important for marginalized individuals, who believe they will not be effectively protected by state-provided security.

In some instances, gun owners have organized to defend social movements from violent political opponents and state repression. During the civil rights movement, African American activists organized through groups like the Deacons for Defense and Justice to engage in armed defense of civil rights activists.[40] Depending on the context, the same good—in this case, a gun—can be used both for individual or household-level self-defense, and coordinated as part of the collective provision of defense against internal or external threats.

Collective provision of defense also occurs at the neighborhood level, through organizations such as Neighborhood Watch groups. In practice, these groups can vary in scale from "just a few households . . . [to] many thousand households."[41] These groups deter crime by surveilling the neighborhood and creating "signs of occupancy . . . [by] removing newspapers and milk from outside neighbors' homes when they are away, mowing the lawn, and filling up trash cans."[42] These actions might seem mundane and minute, but they make prospective invaders anticipate that they are more likely to be caught by residents if they engage in crime.[43]

One specific example is the Guardian Angels, a volunteer organization of unarmed individuals committed to crime prevention. Founded in New

York City in 1979, the organization now has close to one hundred chapters, located in over twenty countries around the world.[44] The organization has rules for screening and training members, as well as for the structure of safety patrols. Community-watch activities are a form of coproduction, in which citizens help produce the security they consume through safety patrols and communication with private security producers and state employees.

Security threats do not only arise in physical space. Commerce, community, and civic life increasingly occur online. Irrespective of their geographic location, invaders can cause grave harm if they acquire access to sensitive information about an individual's bank accounts, credit cards, or private communications. To respond to these concerns, individuals and firms rely on encryption to defend against attacks. There is a robust for-profit cybersecurity industry. Additionally, there are voluntary associations that collaboratively produce open-source cybersecurity software with publicly accessible source code.[45] And just as there are on-the-ground safety patrols, so too are there cybersafety patrols by nonprofit groups, monitoring chat groups and offering education and assistance to citizens in the name of enhancing cybersecurity. Overall, cybersecurity reflects a polycentric system of security, within which competitive private markets coexist with an independent voluntary sector.

Polycentric defense involving private people is pervasive. It is easy to overlook innovative civilian-based solutions to real-world challenges because of the association of security with the large-scale actions of monocentric nation-states. This overly narrow focus not only biases treatments of foreign affairs towards grandiose military force by states, but also neglects the creative power of private civilians to effectively provide security. One powerful example of this civilian-level creativity is nonviolent action, which has been employed historically to combat both domestic and foreign threats.

Nonviolent Action as One Form of Polycentric Defense

People tend to think about defense as involving weapons and violence, but this view is too narrow. Security also includes polycentric nonviolent action, which involves individuals exerting social power to defend against threats, bringing about change through means that avoid the use of physical force.[46] There are many historical examples of citizens employing nonviolent methods, both to combat domestic and foreign threats and to protect their freedoms.[47]

At the foundation of nonviolent action is the idea that political power is derived from the consent of the people living under that government.[48] In this view, power is not intrinsic to the political elite—rather, it is the result of several sources, including (1) voluntary acceptance of authority; (2) the skills and knowledge of those who accept the ruler's authority; (3) ideological factors, such as tolerance for obedience and submission; (4) material resources, such as the ruler's control of wealth and infrastructure; and (5) sanctions that include the tools of state control over citizens and other governments.[49] These sources of power ultimately depend on the consent of the populace, meaning that people can choose to obey the power of the political authority while possessing the power to withdraw their consent. The realization that citizen consent can be withdrawn creates the possibility of nonviolent action.

A key challenge facing nonviolent action is that states typically possess a relative advantage in commanding obedience by the populace. There are several factors underpinning this obedience, including (1) habituation of consent to political authority; (2) fear of sanctions by authorities; (3) a sense of moral obligation to obey one's political masters; (4) self-interest with regard to such things as income and prestige bestowed by the political elite; (5) an emotional or psychological connection with political leaders (the belief that they provide indispensable leadership); and (6) indifference, which creates a range of tolerance regarding the exertion of political power.[50]

Nonviolent action requires members of the populace to overcome these factors in order to remove their obedience to political authorities, whether native or foreign.[51] If they can do so, they can weaken or remove the five sources of political power and defend themselves against a threat, even if that threat has the advantage of physical force. The specific manifestations of nonviolent action vary, and may include some combination of acts of omission—i.e., refraining from doing what one would typically do, based on norms, custom, or formal laws—and acts of commission—i.e., engaging in legal or illegal acts in which one would not normally partake (such as participating in protests).

An obvious concern with nonviolent action is that it may very well be met with violence from the source of the threat. Perhaps counterintuitively, Gene Sharp—a political scientist and one of the world's foremost experts on nonviolence—argued that often the best response to violent repression is continuing to engage in nonviolent resistance. The underlying logic is that the stark contrast between the perpetrator's violent acts of repression and the nonviolent actions of the populace can be used to delegitimize the threat by revealing its true tyrannical nature. This type of "political jiu-jitsu" entails using the power of the perpetrator against those who wield it, undermining their legitimacy.[52]

There are three types of success associated with nonviolent action.[53] The first is "conversion," whereby the enemy genuinely shifts their position and willingly wants to bring about the changes desired by nonviolent forces. The second is "accommodation," which refers to situations in which the opposition does not desire to change, but nonetheless acquiesces due to the success of nonviolent actors and the implications for maintaining the status quo. Finally, "nonviolent coercion" refers to situations where the perpetrator wishes to continue the fight but is unable to do so, because nonviolent actors have successfully undermined their authority and sufficiently reduced their power.

The idea of nonviolent action as a form of defense may seem unrealistic and romantic, but this view would be at odds with the empirical record. As Sharp noted, "Most people are unaware that . . . nonviolent forms of struggle have also been used as a major means of defense against foreign invaders or internal usurpers."[54] They have also been employed by marginalized groups to protect and expand their individual rights and liberties. Over the past several decades, one can see examples of large-scale nonviolent action in the Baltics, Burma, Egypt, Ukraine, and the Arab Spring. A 2012 article in the *Financial Times* highlighted "the wildfire spread of systematically non-violent insurgency" around the world, noting that this "owes a great deal to the strategic thinking of Gene Sharp, an American academic whose how-to-topple-your-tyrant manual, *From Dictatorship to Democracy*, is the bible of activists from Belgrade to Rangoon."[55] Audrius Butkevičius, a former Lithuanian defense minister, succinctly captures the power and potential of nonviolence as a means of citizen-based defense when he noted, "I would rather have this book [Gene Sharp's book, *Civilian-Based Defense*] than the nuclear bomb."[56]

More recent scholarship has focused on systematically examining the effectiveness of nonviolence. Political scientists Erica Chenoweth and Maria Stephan examine a dataset of 323 violent and nonviolent resistance campaigns that occurred between 1900 and 2006. They find that "nonviolent resistance campaigns were nearly twice as likely to achieve full or partial success as their violent counterparts."[57] They attribute this success to the lower cost of participating in nonviolent campaigns, which creates a larger pool of participants. The source of these lower costs is twofold. First, the use of nonviolent tactics removes the need for the physical strength associated with violence. Second, the wide range of nonviolent methods employed—e.g., noncooperation, strikes, civil disobedience, boycotts, etc.—creates an opportunity for a larger number of participants, as compared to violence.

Of course, nonviolent action is not always effective in providing security, but neither is the monocentric nation-state and its reliance on centralized military force. The US government's experience with the Bay of Pigs Invasion (1961), the Vietnam War (1962–1975), the invasion of Somalia (1992), the 9/11 attacks (2001) within US borders, and the invasions of Afghanistan (2001–2021) and Iraq (2003–2011 and 2013–2017) are just a few examples illustrating this point. In a variety of context-specific settings, people come together to provide defense and security against both internal and external threats. At a minimum, the existence and success of nonviolent movements—across both time and geography—serves as proof that people can provide security without reliance on the monocentric nation-state. In fact, in many cases, nonviolent action is a response to threats posed by the state itself. Nonviolent action is just one illustration of the many potential forms of civilian-based polycentric defense that exist, or which may emerge in the future. It demonstrates how a broader, more open-minded notion of defense provision offers an array of options—some known, some yet to be discovered—which do not rely on the monocentric monopoly of the nation-state.

Of course, for civilian-based defense to operate, people must hold a certain set of ideological beliefs about the appropriate role of the citizen and the state (as it pertains to security). American diplomat and historian George Kennan captures this point, noting that the system of civilian-based defense requires

a rather basic change in the view hundreds of millions of people have been taught to take of the sources of national security and of the means by which it may be usefully promoted. The new view would be one that looks primarily inward—to the quality of the respective society, to the character of its institutions, to its social discipline and civic morale, rather than outward to the effectiveness of its armed forces—for the true sources of its strength and its security.[58]

The need for these ideological commitments might make civilian-based polycentric defense seem unfeasible. Note, however, that the operation of any system requires certain ideological commitments on the part of citizens.[59] Even when the state is viewed as the sole provider of defense, citizens must hold certain beliefs about the appropriate scale and scope of the state in this role. Furthermore, alternatives to the status quo, such as a grand strategy of restraint—which holds that the American government should be more limited in its military engagements around the world—similarly require certain ideological commitments regarding a revised role of the state in providing security.[60] If the ideology necessary for such alternatives is viewed as possible, so too is the ideology necessary for civilian-based polycentric defense.

Hope for a Stable Peace

The question remains—how far can the logic of civilian-based polycentric defense be extended into American life? The answer is unknowable today, but not unfathomable. We know for certain that the status quo is defined by imperialism and a culture of militarism, which has perverse and unintended consequences everywhere. Perpetual liberal war for perpetual liberal peace fails due to internal contradictions, intentionally or unintentionally eroding liberal values and creating enemies abroad in the process. Instead, creative thinking is needed to empower people to achieve a stable peace—defined by arrangements of sufficient strength that, in the face of strain on the system, minimize the likelihood of violence—in a manner consistent with liberal values.[61] Stable peace, Kenneth Boulding notes, refers to "a situation in which the probability of war is so small that it does not really enter into the calculations of any of the people involved."[62] One of the salutary consequences of a stable peace is a culture of friendship in the international arena.

The good news is the search for a stable peace is an ongoing project, entailing self-governing individuals engaged in an active process of discovery, experimentation, and practice to navigate conflicts without resorting to violence. This view of peace is expansive—including all people, not only foreign policy elites. After all, national security involves "the nation," ultimately a collection of individuals who reside in a geographic space and possess the power to be peace activists in their daily lives. The framing of peace as an open-ended project is "a far cry from stereotyped notions of peace as a dull, unchanging end state. A static image of peace, as reflecting human inactivity, is dramatically opposed to the characterization of peace as a process, of peacebuilding as adventure, exploration, and willingness to venture into the unknown."[63]

Even better news is that cultures of peace already exist within and across societies, examples we wrongly take for granted. They exist when we navigate conflicts in our families, in our places of work, and in our local communities. Peace also exists between the peoples of many nations (Americans today tend *not* to view Canada as a threat, even though it was once a major source of conflict with the British). In discussing historical peace between societies, Kenneth Boulding presented "Boulding's first law," which states, "Anything that exists must be possible."[64] His point is that much peace exists in the world, and therefore a stable peace is possible and can be accelerated by the choices made by people—including the choice to emphasize cultures of peace over the culture of militarism associated with empire.

This requires a fundamental shift in perspective, from the idea that military violence through empire is the source of order to the appreciation that peaceful behavior exists in all societies. "Underneath the layers of violence," Elise Boulding noted, "each society, without exception, has its peace behaviors, precious resources that can be available to help bring about a new and gentler form of governance locally and on a larger scale."[65] The culture of militarism associated with empire elevates force as a primary means of social relations and, in the process, not only neglects these peace behaviors but also contributes to their erosion. In contrast, the polycentric approach to defense offers an opportunity to unlock the potential of cultures of peace by empowering people to discover sources of nonviolent conflict resolution.

In discussing the possibility of peace, Kenneth Boulding noted that hope rests on the ability to imagine futures previously unimagined, and to engage in the learning process of testing these possibilities.[66] Imagining alternatives to empire offers a path to a potential stable peace. These alternatives offer neither utopia nor the certainty of peace. What they do offer is the possibility of a stable peace grounded in the liberal values of individual freedom and dignity, tolerance, cosmopolitanism, voluntary association, and a commitment to peacefully resolving interpersonal conflicts. While conflict is an ever-present part of life, the way we respond is a choice. Each of us possesses the power to throw off the shackles of militarism in the search for stable peace. Whether you choose to exercise this power is ultimately up to you.

Epilogue: The Siren Song of Empire

THE SIREN SONG of empire remains powerful. In the wake of the US government's chaotic exit from Afghanistan in August 2021, there was little self-reflection regarding the realities and limits of American military imperialism. The window for introspection closed with the Russian government's invasion of Ukraine in February 2022, which led to renewed calls for the reassertion of American empire.

Michael Beckley and Hal Brands argued in "The Return of Pax Americana?" that Putin's invasion of Ukraine offers a golden opportunity for the US government to reassert its global dominance by reestablishing the US-led international order. In their telling, success in this enterprise requires "massive investments in military forces geared for high-intensity combat, sustained diplomacy to enlist and retain allies, and a willingness to confront adversaries and even risk war."[1]

Robert Kagan, a leading advocate for US military imperialism, asserted that Putin's invasion of Ukraine is partially due to the passivity of past American policymakers who failed to wield their military and economic might to contain Russia effectively. The implication, he argues, is that it "is better for the United States to risk confrontation with belligerent powers when they are in the early stages of ambition and expansion, not after they have already consolidated substantial gains."[2] What exactly this entails is left unsaid, but from Kagan's past writings it likely involves major military investments and proactive, preventive wars to subdue threats identified by the US government.

The foundation for these renewed calls for American empire was established several years ago. The 2018 National Defense Strategy (NDS)—a cornerstone document for Department of Defense planning—argued that the US government needed to shift away from terrorism and toward the great power competition with China and Russia.[3] More recently, Elbridge Colby, who played a central role in developing the 2018 NDS, argued that the US government must adopt a strategy to deny the Chinese government influence in Asia.[4] To accomplish this goal, he proposes the formation of an "anti-hegemonic coalition," with the US government as the "cornerstone balancer," to ensure the effective projection of power to counter the influence of China.[5] This arrangement, which in Colby's vision would include Australia, India, Japan, the Philippines, South Korea, Taiwan, and Vietnam, would allow the US government to effectively balance China's power without directly engaging in the region or posing a direct threat to China.

These renewed calls for American empire are exercises in speculative, first-best theorizing about international relations. They are speculative because they are based on conjectures regarding what the Chinese and Russian governments might do to expand or leverage their influence. They involve first-best theorizing because they fail to consider deviations from first-best assumptions about the US government's ability to design, implement, and execute the optimal strategy to balance global power.

Consider the case of China and the idea of a coalition operated by the US government. What if the proposed coalition members choose not to pick sides between China and the United States? If this occurs, the proposed coalition strategy with minimal direct US involvement begins to unravel. The US government must then either limit its involvement in the region—unlikely given the incentives inherent in empire, the 2018 NDS, and the aforementioned calls for more intervention—or engage in more direct involvement to counter China's influence, which increases the chance of violent confrontation.

First-best theorizing offers one approach to engaging in thought experiments and may produce some benchmark against which to compare the actual world. But at some point, we need to consider the real world—especially when discussing nuclear powers engaging each other in a power competition that could potentially devolve into violent conflict. Policies are not designed and implemented in an institutional vacuum. Instead, specific (fallible) people with decision-making rights are embedded in specific institutional contexts that yield constraints and incentives which shape their behaviors for better or worse.

The result is that real-world outcomes deviate from ideal visions, often dramatically. Earlier (see Chapter 4), I discussed "The Afghanistan Papers," consisting of interviews conducted by the Special Inspector General for Afghanistan Reconstruction (SIGAR).[6] These documents paint a startling picture of systematic incompetence, waste, fraud, and dysfunction in US foreign policy. These realities were dramatically different from both the initial vision set forth by those in the US national security state, and from the picture presented by US elected officials to the public about the state of the occupation.

What has changed that gives proponents of American empire confidence that their first-best strategy will be implemented as they imagine it? Why shouldn't we assume variants of the Afghanistan experience are the likely outcome of future military adventures?

Proponents of empire tend to treat the US government as a defense brain, a supercomputer that can design, implement, and execute first-best plans to manage the world through optimal responses to well-defined threats.[7] The "state" is assumed to advance the national interest through its actions, but the actual operations of government are not subject to analysis. By assumption, there is no space for political frictions—e.g., voter ignorance, special-interest groups' influence, bureaucratic dysfunction—or government failure. As the previous chapters have documented, this is not the reality of the matter.

This approach is especially problematic in the realm of perverse consequences, which are part and parcel of military imperialism. Consider, for instance, the "security dilemma," a well-known issue among international relations scholars. The dilemma is as follows: When one state moves to increase its security, it makes other states relatively less secure. Other states will respond by taking steps to increase their security, which makes the initial-acting state less secure. The resulting escalation can be a source of tension and potentially violent conflict.

In one illustration of defense-brain reasoning, Elbridge Colby, in his proposed strategy to deny China's influence, recognizes this possibility but quickly dismisses it: "But so long as US efforts are clearly directed at denying Beijing hegemony rather than dismembering China, occupying it, or forcibly changing its government, the security dilemma should be manageable."[8] The phrase "should be" is doing enormous work here and raises many questions.

What does effective management of the security dilemma look like in practice? Who is doing the managing? What are the knowledge and incentive requirements for effective management? What reason do we have to believe that these requirements exist in reality? What mechanisms are in place for the relevant choosers to adapt if they cannot engage in effective management or if perverse or unanticipated consequences arise? As the previous chapters make clear, these are the types of questions that are relevant and required to understand and judge the feasibility of empire as a means to achieve the desired ends of its proponents.

Underlying renewed calls for American empire is the assumption that flexing military might is the only way for the US government to respond to China and Russia's existence and influence. This approach has costs—both monetary and nonmonetary—which must be considered. As the US government's experience with the war on terror indicates, extensive reliance on the military instrument has a high monetary price tag, with one estimate placing the total cost of post-9/11 wars at $8 trillion.[9] These costs far exceeded initial government projections based on strategies of a similar sort to those proposed by current proponents of American empire to confront China and Russia—i.e., straightforward plans based on an array of favorable assumptions about interveners with promises of grandiose outcomes.

By assuming the best of the US government and the worst of other governments, proponents of empire bias their analysis in favor of proactive, militaristic US-government intervention. This conceals a significant cost of this strategy—the elevation of militarism as the primary means of international relations crowds out other, nonmilitary ways of interacting and discovering ways of living peacefully together. From the perspective of empire, the only pathway to peace is through military might. But what if militarism begets militarism both at home and abroad? Failure to consider this possibility means ignoring the full range of consequences of a proactive, military-driven foreign policy and the damage it might cause to human well-being and liberal values.

The siren song of empire is strong, especially when violent conflict is front-page news. My skepticism regarding American empire as a solution to the world's ills, as well as my suggested alternative paths to peace, may appear naive. Isn't my vision of human nature and the possibility of non-American "others" as potential partners in a stable peace unrealistically benign and misguided, if not dangerous? Just the opposite.

The bedrock of my analysis of empire is the recognition that there are people in the world who are cruel, violent, and vainglorious. I differ from many proponents of empire because I appreciate that people with these undesirable characteristics exist across geographic boundaries. American citizens, as well as those outside of America's borders, are not immune to wicked behaviors from US actors; in fact, the illiberal nature of liberal empire attracts and rewards these types of behaviors (see Chapter 2). The threats—to domestic and international life—posed by nefarious people are greatly magnified in the operation of a proactive empire.

We, the people, are told that American empire is necessary to protect our person and values at home while promoting order and peace abroad. But who will tame Leviathan? If we are helpless to protect ourselves against the supposed threats of the world, what leads us to think we can protect ourselves against the extraordinary and expansive powers of a mighty empire strong enough to bring the belligerent actors and nations of the world to heel?

We must resist the siren song of empire.

Notes

Prologue: American Global Interventionism Buried in the Graveyard of Empires

1. Crawford 2021: 16.
2. Barfield 2010: 2, 255.
3. Crawford and Lutz 2021.
4. Quoted in Matthews 2021.
5. Schmitt 2021.
6. Aikins 2021; Seligman 2021.
7. See Gopal (2021) and Graham-Harrison (2021) for a discussion of the implications of civilian deaths.
8. Crawford and Lutz 2021.
9. Vine et al. 2021.
10. Source: https://watson.brown.edu/costsofwar/figures/2021/human-and-budgetary -costs-date-us-war-afghanistan-2001-2022. This total includes Defense Department Overseas Contingency Operations (OCO) War Budget ($1,055bn), State Department OCO War Budget ($60bn), Defense Department Base Budget War-Related Increases ($433bn), Veterans Care for Afghan War Veterans to Date ($233bn), and Estimated Interest on War Borrowing ($532bn).
11. Source: https://watson.brown.edu/costsofwar/figures/2021/BudgetaryCosts.
12. Matthews 2021.
13. Bush 2001.
14. See Mueller and Stewart 2011, 2012, 2016, 2021.
15. See Mueller and Stewart 2021.
16. See Matthews 2021.
17. See Gopal 2021.
18. Allen and Felbab-Brown 2020.

Chapter 1: The American Empire

1. Quoted in Goldberg 2016: n.p.

2. Mises 1996: v.

3. McCloskey 2019: 10, emphasis original. See also Kukathas 2003; Aligica 2018; Boettke 2021.

4. Ferguson 2004. On the academic debate over whether America is an empire, see Hanson 2002; Pagden 2005; Maier 2007; Hexon and Wright 2007; Hopkins 2007.

5. See Ikenberry 2012; Posen 2014.

6. See Posen 2014: 5–6.

7. Posen 2014: 5.

8. On the difference between imperialism and colonialism, see Gilmartin 2009, Young 2015. Imperialism refers to an ideology and policies, while colonialism refers to the physical taking and control of an area. Imperialism can result in colonization but is not defined by taking control of a geographic space. Former US Secretary of Defense Robert Gates 2020 discusses the perverse consequences of what he terms the "overmilitarization of American foreign policy."

9. Hobbes 1904: 84.

10. For a critique of the common assumption of anarchy in international relations, see Milner 1991.

11. Kagan 1998, 2012, 2018, 2021; Boot 2001, 2002, 2003; Ferguson 2003, 2004; E. Cohen 2004; Lal 2004; Mitchener and Weidenmier 2005; Ferguson and Schularick 2006. In economics, the term "public good" has a specific technical definition. A public good is nonexcludable, meaning nonpayers cannot be prevented from consuming the good, and nonrivalrous, meaning one person's consumption does not reduce the amount available for others to consume. Conceptually, the combination results in the good being underprovided relative to its optimal amount. For more on this in the context of defense, including some issues with treating defense as a public good, see Coyne 2015.

12. Fukuyama 2005; Dobbins et al. 2003; Ferguson 2003, especially ch. 4.

13. See, for instance, Kindleberger 1981; Lal 2001, 2004; Ferguson 2003, 2004; Lieber 2005, 2016; Mitchener and Weidenmier 2005; Ferguson and Schularick 2006; Jones and Kane 2012; Kane 2012.

14. In political science, one notable exception is Hendrickson (2018: 105–136), who recognizes the real possibility of public bads in the context of American imperialism.

15. For various treatments of these three phases of American empire, see Williams 1969, 1980; LaFeber 1998; Bacevich 2002; Johnson 2004; Maier 2007; Nugent 2008; Atwood 2010; Maurer 2013; Kinzer 2007, 2017; Bulmer-Thomas 2018; Hopkins 2018; Immerwahr 2019; Vine 2020.

16. It should be noted that manifest destiny and westward expansion were politically controversial during this period (see Howe 2007: 705).

17. The discussion of phase two of American empire draws on Coyne and Davies 2007.

18. I thank Ivan Eland for pointing out how the Spanish-American War, although not technically falling under the Monroe Doctrine, had a more lasting effect than Roosevelt's Corollary to the doctrine.

19. For a history of the Monroe Doctrine, as well as an analysis of the doctrine's impact, see Gilderhus 2006; Sexton 2011.

20. Roosevelt 1910: 176–177.

21. On US interventions in Latin America prior to the Roosevelt Corollary, see Williams 1980: 102–110; Healy 1991.

22. For the debt crisis, the blockade, and in particular the German role, see Forbes 1978; Anderson 1995; Mitchell 1996; Morris 2002.

23. See Ricard 2006: 19–20. This should be contrasted with the response of Grover Cleveland to the earlier Venezuelan debt crisis of 1895 and his withdrawing of a treaty for a Nicaraguan isthmian canal in 1885 as "coercive and expansionist" (Kelley 1990: 342; Tompkins 1970).

24. Ricard 2006: 20–21.

25. Powell 2006: 68–69, 76.

26. LaFeber 1986.

27. Mitchener and Weidenmier 2005.

28. On US intervention in the Dominican Republic and the perverse consequences, see Castor 1974; Millet and Gaddy 1976; Calder 1984; Hanson 1994.

29. In Cuba, the constitution written under American supervision contained the Platt Amendment, which provided for control of sovereign debt and for intervention by the United States government. For more on the Platt Amendment and its consequences, see Perez 1978, 1979, 1984, 1986a, b. For the historiography of the amendment and its origins, see Hitchman 1967; Cummins 1967. See Staten 2005 and Perez 1995 for a more general account of Cuban history, including the way US intervention led to the rise of Batista.

30. See Howlett 1988; Salisbury 1997; Harrison 1995. For a discussion of the numerous interventions (and their consequences) in Central America, see Grieb 1967; Baloyra-Herp 1983; Woodward 1984; Mahoney 2001.

31. In Venezuela, the outcome was the dictatorship of Juan Vicente Gómez from 1909–1935. See Ellner 1995 and Yarrington 2003a, b.

32. In Colombia, the years between 1904 and 1921 saw repeated but unsuccessful attempts to stabilize the public finances and the consolidation of the division between Liberals and Conservatives that would burst into open war in 1948. For a survey of the way this division played out between the later 1880s and the *violencia* after 1948, see Ruiz 2001: 31–58.

33. See Reich and Lebow 2014.

34. LaFeber 1984.

35. See Glasgow 1987; Langley and Schoonover 1995; Langley 2002.

36. Lafeber 1984: 14.

37. Langley 1988.

38. Moya Pons 1998: 337.

39. For more on the history of the Guardia Nacional de Nicaragua, see Grossmann 2005.

40. Quoted in Winn 1999: 517.

41. Wertheim 2020: 7.

42. Hogan 1998: 14.

43. On the history and evolution of the National Security Council, see Gans 2019; Bessner 2019.

44. Unger 2012: 74–75.

45. Stuart 2008: 1.

46. On the history of the term "deep state," see Gingeras 2010. For a discussion of the deep state in the context of the US security state, see Glennon 2015 and Koppl 2018. On the history and erosion of civilian-military relations in the US military, see Brooks, Golby, and Urben 2021.

47. See Powell 2006: 76.

48. Ricard 2006: 17.

49. Wilson used this motivation in his request for a Declaration of War against Germany by the US Congress on April 2, 1917.

50. Bush 2005: n.p. Existing scholarship is clear that efforts to establish democratic political institutions via military-led regime change fails to do so in any kind of consistent and systematic manner (See Enterline and Greig 2005, 2008; Bueno de Mesquita and Downs 2004, 2006; Payne 2006; Pickering and Peceny 2006; Coyne 2008a; Berger, Corvalan, Easterly, and Satyanath 2013; Downes and Monten 2013; Denison 2020).

51. See Unger 2012 for a discussion of the operation and evolution of the US emergency state.

52. See Beard 1946, 1948; Appleman 1969, 1980; Schlesinger 2004; Irons 2005; Fisher 2013; Edelson 2016; Burns 2019; Eland 2019.

53. Schlesinger 2004: xxiv.

54. Priest and Arkin 2011.

55. For one illustration of the operations of the deep state, see Gans 2019 on the history of the National Security Council.

56. On the information asymmetries in the US national security state, see Coyne, Goodman, and Hall 2019; Coyne and Hall 2021.

57. Fisher 2013: 302.

58. Jablonsky 2002–2003: 9. Sherry 1995 traces the widespread militarization of American society to the 1930s, when President Franklin D. Roosevelt employed war analogies during the New Deal. In his telling, the onset of the Cold War fully institutionalized the military mentality in American domestic life.

59. See Johnson 2004; Bacevich 2005, 2009; Hendrickson 2018.

60. Bacevich 2005: 19.

61. Vagts 1937: 15.

62. Ekirch 2010.

63. Shoup 1969: 53.

64. Donovan 1970: 1.

65. Bacevich 2005: 1.

66. See Fulbright 1970; Coyne and Hall 2021.

67. See Higgs 1987 on the role of ideology in growth of government and what is perceived as the appropriate relationship between the citizen and the state.

68. Melman 1970, 1985; Duncan and Coyne 2013a.

69. This includes (in billions) Department of Defense (DOD) base budget ($554.1), Overseas Contingency Operations ($173.8), Department of Energy nuclear programs ($24.8), defense-related activities ($9), Veterans Affairs ($216), Homeland Security ($69.2), Interna-

tional Affairs ($51), Intelligence ($80), and the defense-related share of interest on federal debt ($156.3). Source: Hartung and Smithberger 2019.

70. Source of all figures on global military expenditures is Tian et al. 2020. Note that these figures are for military expenditures only, and exclude spending on other military-related activities.

71. See Coyne and Hall 2019a.

72. See Melman 1970, 1985; McCartney 2015; Sorensen 2020; Cockburn 2021.

73. See Duncan and Coyne 2013b.

74. Fitzgerald 1972, 1989.

75. See Coyne, Michaluk, and Reese 2016.

76. Quoted in Lindorff 2018: n.p.

77. Quoted in Lindorff 2018: n.p.

78. Department of Defense 2019: 7. The report defines a "site" as "[a] specific geographic location that has individual land parcels or facilities assigned to it. Physical (geographic) location that is, or was owned by, leased to, or otherwise under the jurisdiction of a DOD Component on behalf of the United States. A site may be contiguous to another site, but cannot geographically overlap or be within another site. A site may exist in one of three forms: land only—where no facilities are present; facility or facilities only—where there the underlying land is neither owned nor controlled by the government; and land with facilities—where both are present" (Department of Defense 2019: 4).

79. Vine 2015: 3.

80. Department of Defense 2019: 2.

81. See Glaser 2017.

82. Mason 2012: 3.

83. International Security Advisory Board 2015: 40.

84. Turse 2021: n.p.

85. Stockholm International Peace Research Institute 2020: n.p.

86. Stockholm International Peace Research Institute 2020: n.p.

87. Lawson and Morgenstern 2020: 1. Foreign aid can be bilateral—government-to-government transfers—or multilateral—government transfers to organizations that pool contributions from multiple government donors and then disperse the funds. Aid is typically categorized by donor intent—economic development (which includes political and strategic economic assistance), military and security assistance, humanitarian assistance, and the support of multilateral organizations.

88. Organisation for Economic Co-operation and Development (OECD) n.d.: n.p.

89. See Coyne 2013.

90. See Blackwell and Harris 2016.

Chapter 2: Illiberal Foundations of a Liberal Empire

1. See Tirman 2011, 2015; Connah 2020.

2. Carpenter and Innocent 2015; Hendrickson 2017; P. Porter 2018, 2020; Carpenter 2019; Bevins 2020.

3. See Brenner 2014; Coyne and Hall 2016.

4. Reich and Lebow 2014: 23.

5. See McCoy 2006, 2009; Tirman 2011, 2015; Slahi 2015; Physicians for Social Responsibility et al. 2015; Scahill 2016.

6. Quoted in Tirman 2015: n.p.

7. Quoted in Oppel Jr. 2010: n.p.

8. See Tirman 2015.

9. See Easterly 2014; Carpenter and Innocent 2015; Carpenter 2019; Bevins 2020.

10. Coyne and Hall 2016, 2018a: 30–40.

11. Knight 1938: 868–869.

12. Knight 1938: 869.

13. Hayek 1944: 135.

14. Willers 1977: 45.

15. Donovan 1970: 39.

16. Willers 1977: 45.

17. Kissinger 1969: 18.

18. See Shoup 1969.

19. Shoup 1969: 54.

20. Donovan 1970: 80.

21. See Coyne and Coyne 2013.

22. Merton 1940: 562.

23. Merton 1940: 562–563.

24. The discussion of the illiberal protective state draws on Coyne 2018.

25. This question is central to the field of constitutional political economy. See Buchanan 1975; Brennan and Buchanan 1985; Weingast 1995; Gordon 2002; Coyne 2018.

26. Buchanan 1975: 95–97.

27. Madison 1865: 491.

28. Buchanan 1975: 163. See also Higgs 1987; Coyne and Hall 2018a.

29. Tocqueville 1840: 285.

30. Dorsen 1989: 840.

31. See Corwin 1947; Higgs 1987, 2004, 2007, 2012; Linfield 1990; Porter 1994; Rehnquist 1998; Stone 2003; Cole and Dempsey 2006; Cole 2008; Cole and Lobel 2009; Herman 2011; Walker 2012; Coyne and Hall 2018a.

32. Brennan and Buchanan 1985: 31.

33. Brennan and Buchanan 1985: 31.

34. Higgs 2015: 276.

35. See Oppenheimer 1922; Nock 1935.

36. Porter 1994: 10.

37. Douglas 1987: 162.

38. The discussion in this section draws on Coyne 2018; Coyne and Hall 2018a: 54–60.

39. Murphy 1943: n.p.

40. Beard 1936: 30.

41. See Devins et al. 2015.

42. See Higgs 1987, 2004, 2007; Congleton 2005; Coyne 2011.

43. Higgs 1987, 2004.

44. See Fraenkel 1946; Dorsen 1989; Rehnquist 1998.

45. Rossiter 2009: 265.

46. Higgs 2015: 276.

47. See Higgs 2004: 201–218; Rossiter 2009.

48. Higgs 2004: 203.

49. The Supreme Court officially repudiated the Korematsu decision in *Trump v. Hawaii* (2018).

50. Rossiter 2009: 282.

51. Rossiter 2009: 283.

52. Glennon 2015.

53. Glennon 2015: 6–7.

54. For more on the "deep state" and associated "elite theory," see Mills 1956; Dye 2001, 2014; Lofgren 2016.

55. Glennon 2015: 6.

56. See Bamford 1983, 2008; Higgs 1987, 2004, 2007, 2012; Cole and Dempsey 2006; Cole 2008; Cole and Lobel 2009; Herman 2011; Priest and Arkin 2011; Risen 2014; Greenwald 2014; Coyne and Hall 2018a; Coyne and Yatsyshina 2021 for examples of expansions in state power in a variety of contexts.

57. See Coyne and Hall 2018a: 57–60; Coyne, Goodman, and Hall 2019; Coyne and Hall 2021.

58. Corwin 1947: 177.

59. Senate Select Committee to Study Governmental Operations with Respect to Intelligence Activities 1976: 169.

60. See Greenwald 2014.

61. Coyne and Hall 2018a: 25–30.

62. Porter 1994: xv.

63. Corwin 1947: 181.

64. Wagner 2014: 3. See also Greve 2012.

65. See Balko 2013; Hall and Coyne 2013; Boettke, Lemke, and Palagashvili 2016; Coyne and Hall 2018a: 96–119; Schrader 2019.

66. Jefferson 1854: 543.

67. Jefferson 1854: 543.

68. See Coyne and Hall 2014: 170–171, 2018a: 30–36.

69. Donovan 1970: 33.

70. For a discussion of the moral and social costs of militarization, see Dobos 2020.

71. See Coyne and Hall 2014, 2018a: 19–52.

72. Donovan 1970: 32.

73. Donovan 1970: 37.

74. Coyne and Hall 2014: 175–179, 2018a: 71–95.

75. See McCoy 2009; Coyne and Hall 2014, 2018a.

76. Office of the Under Secretary of Defense (Comptroller) 2019: 7.

77. See Cowen 2011, 2021.

78. See Wessler 2014; Waddell 2015; Bates 2016; American Civil Liberties Union 2018.

Chapter 3: Liberal Empire as State Capitalism Writ Large

1. Riddle 1964.

2. Hamilton 2009: 301.

3. Commission on Wartime Contracting in Iraq and Afghanistan 2011: 1.

4. For a comprehensive analysis of the foundations and operation of political capitalism, see Holcombe 2013, 2018. For a discussion of the tensions between capitalism and cronyism, see Munger 2019.

5. See Oppenheimer 1922; Buchanan 1980.

6. See Olson 1965; Baumol 1990; Coyne and Leeson 2004; Choi and Storr 2019.

7. Quoted in Joint Economic Committee 1969: 140.

8. See Coyne 2008a; Duncan and Coyne 2015a; Coyne, Michaluk, and Reese 2016.

9. The core arguments in this chapter draw on Coyne and Hall 2019b.

10. See, for instance, Buchanan 1975: 95–97.

11. Hayek 1944: 82.

12. Hayek 1944: 83.

13. See Coyne and Hall 2019a, b.

14. Higgs 1987: 156.

15. Higgs 1987: 236.

16. See Higgs 2012: 214–218.

17. Higgs 2006a: 36–40.

18. Smith 1959 [1991]: 312.

19. Higgs 2012: 217–218.

20. Higgs 2012: 217.

21. See Melman 1970, 1985; Duncan and Coyne 2013a, b.

22. May 1993: vii.

23. National Security Council 1950: n.p.

24. See Johnson 2004: 32–33. For an overview and assessment of the theoretical and empirical academic literature on this topic, see Dunne 2013.

25. Feldstein 2008: n.p.

26. US Department of State 2011: n.p.

27. US Department of State 2020: n.p.

28. See Higgs 2012: 204–224; Duncan and Coyne 2013a, b; Coyne, Michaluk, and Reese 2016. On the nuances of the military budgeting process, see Thorpe 2014.

29. See Higgs 1987, 2012: 204–224; Duncan and Coyne 2013b; Coyne and Hall 2018a.

30. Department of Defense 2015: 6.

31. Reich 2010.

32. Coyne and Hall 2019a.

33. For a list of the top one hundred defense contractors for FY 2020, see http://www .fi-aeroweb.com/Top-100-Defense-Contractors.html.

34. See Melman 1970, 1985; Lavoie 1985b; Coyne and Hall 2019a.

35. See Flynn 1944; Twight 1975; Higgs 2012.

36. Holcombe and Castillo 2013: 39, 46.

37. Holcombe and Castillo 2013: 46.

38. Holcombe and Castillo 2013: 39.

39. Holcombe and Castillo 2013: 15, 19.

40. See Paltrow 2013; Coyne, Michaluk, and Reese 2016: 229–230.

41. Government Accountability Office 2015: 172.

42. Fitzgerald 1989: 290.

43. Burton 1993: 232.

44. See Fitzgerald 1972, 1989; Burton 1993; McCartney 2015.

45. See Tullock 1967; Buchanan 1980; Tollison 1982.

46. Melman 1985: 35.

47. Higgs 2012: 214.

48. A. Cohen 2015: n.p.

49. McCartney 1975: 13.

50. For a general theory of the culture of rent seeking, see Choi and Storr 2019.

51. See McChesney 1987, 1997.

52. Schweizer 2013: 37.

53. Duncan and Coyne 2015a: 391.

54. Adams 1981: 79.

55. Bender 2010: n.p.

56. Bender 2010: n.p.

57. Vanden Brook, Dilanian, and Locker 2009.

58. Project on Government Oversight 2018: 9.

59. Griffin and Bronstein 2010.

60. For numerous other examples, see Project on Government Oversight 2018.

61. McCartney 2015: 41.

62. McCartney 2015: 41.

63. Miller, Capaccio, and Ivory 2013.

64. Berr 2005.

65. Quoted in McCartney 2015: 41.

Chapter 4: The Limits of Liberal Imperialism

1. Whitlock 2019. For a more detailed political economy discussion of the Afghanistan Papers, see Lambert, Coyne, and Goodman 2021.

2. Quoted in original source document: https://www.washingtonpost.com/graphics /2019/investigations/afghanistan-papers/documents-database/documents/johnson _thomas_ll_01072016.pdf?v=26.

3. Quoted in original source document: https://www.washingtonpost.com/graphics/2019/investigations/afghanistan-papers/documents-database/documents/background_ll_01_xx_carlisle_10292015.pdf?v=26.

4. Quoted in original source document: https://www.washingtonpost.com/graphics/2019/investigations/afghanistan-papers/documents-database/documents/marsden_david_ll_05_a2_12032015.pdf?v=26.

5. Quoted in original source document: https://www.washingtonpost.com/graphics/2019/investigations/afghanistan-papers/documents-database/documents/background_ll_01_xx_dc_08042015.pdf?v=26.

6. Quoted in original source document: https://www.washingtonpost.com/graphics/2019/investigations/afghanistan-papers/documents-database/documents/background_ll_01_xx_dc_11132014.pdf?v=26.

7. Quoted in original source document: https://www.washingtonpost.com/graphics/2019/investigations/afghanistan-papers/documents-database/documents/background_ll_03_xx_xx3_08242015.pdf?v=26.

8. Quoted in original source document: https://www.washingtonpost.com/graphics/2019/investigations/afghanistan-papers/documents-database/documents/copes_brian_ll_05_c15_02252016.pdf?v=26.

9. For a critical discussion of the invasion and occupation of Afghanistan, see Horton 2017.

10. Proponents of military occupation in the name of nation building often point to post-World War II Japan and West Germany as evidence of success. Coyne (2008a: 118-135) offers detailed discussion of the unique circumstances and events (especially those that were not planned or controlled by occupiers) that led to the positive outcomes in these cases.

11. The discussion of knowledge problems and political economy problems draws on Coyne and Wood 2020.

12. Quoted in Beschloss 2003: 137.

13. However, this same reasoning is not extended to non-ally governments who engage in similar foreign interventions. In stark contrast, foreign interventions by other, non-ally governments are met with condemnation. This was evident, for example, in the US government's response to the 2014 Russian invasion of Ukrainian territory. Then US Secretary of State John Kerry publicly condemned the invasion, calling it an "incredible act of aggression" while ignoring the extensive list of US government military interventions since its founding (see Torreon and Plagakis 2020). Seemingly oblivious to the more immediate US occupations of Afghanistan and Iraq, Kerry went on to note that "[y]ou just don't in the 21st century behave in 19th-century fashion by invading another country on completely trumped up pretext" (quoted in Dunham 2014). Interventionists view their own imperial actions and empire building as noble, righteous, and justified, while similar actions by others are viewed in harsh, negative terms.

14. See V. Ostrom 1991a: 242.

15. For a comprehensive critique of expert rule, see Koppl 2018.

16. Boulding 1978: 22.

17. Jervis 1976: 319.

18. I thank Ivan Eland for bringing to my attention this point about prior US interventions contributing to the emergence of al Qaeda and ISIS.

19. Hayek 1945: 521. See also Lavoie 1985b.

20. Coyne 2008a, 2013; Coyne and Mathers 2010; Coyne and Pellillo 2011; Duncan and Coyne 2015b; Coyne and Wood 2020; Lambert, Coyne, and Goodman 2021.

21. Coyne 2008a; Coyne and Pellillo 2011; Coyne and Duncan 2015b; Coyne and Wood 2020.

22. Shin 1994: 151.

23. See Boettke 2001: 248–265; Boettke, Coyne, and Leeson 2008; Coyne 2008a.

24. See Coyne 2008a.

25. Cook 2014: n.p.

26. Miesen 2013.

27. See Boettke, Coyne, and Leeson 2008; Coyne 2017.

28. Pritchett and Woolcock 2004: 197.

29. J. B. Murtazashvili 2016; I. Murtazashvili and J. B. Murtazashvili 2019; J. Murtazashvili and I. Murtazashvili 2020; J. B. Murtazashvili and I. Murtazashvili 2021.

30. Coyne 2013: 71–79.

31. Mises 1935, 1949; Hayek 1945; Lavoie 1985a, b, 1986.

32. Coyne 2013: 61–89.

33. See Easterly 2006, 2014.

34. Wood 2018.

35. ABC News 2004.

36. Cordesman, Loi, and Kocharlakota 2010.

37. Higginbotham 2010.

38. See Coyne 2008a: 66–70; Coyne and Boettke 2009; Flores and Nooruddin 2009; Coyne and Pellillo 2011.

39. Stewart 2010: n.p.

40. Higgs 1997b.

41. See Coyne and Boettke 2009; Coyne 2017.

42. Coyne and Pellillo 2011: 10–12.

43. Flores and Nooruddin 2009: 5.

44. US Department of the Army 2009: 1–29.

45. Montgomery 2004: 36.

46. Mises 1944; Tullock 1965; Niskanen 1971, 1975; Wilson 1989.

47. See Coyne 2008a, b, 2013; Coyne and Pellillo 2011: 13–15.

48. Diamond 2005: 28–29.

49. Phillips 2005: 7.

50. Mises 1944.

51. Tullock 1965; Coyne 2008b, 2013: 115–121.

52. USAID Office of the Inspector General 2008: 1, 6.

53. USAID Office of the Inspector General 2008: 8.

54. van Buren 2012: 3.

55. Gates 2014: n.p.

56. Coyne, Michaluk, and Reese 2016; Coyne and Duncan 2019.

57. See Coyne and Duncan 2019. For a general analysis of the fiscal commons, see Wagner 2012.

58. Coyne, Michaluk, and Reese 2016.

59. See Commission on Wartime Contracting in Iraq and Afghanistan 2011; Coyne 2008a, 2013.

60. See Posen 2014: 135–143; E. Cohen 2016: 173–194.

61. See Hobson 1902; Stromberg 2001; Maurer 2013.

62. Smith 1776 [2000] Book IV, Chapter VII: 663–693.

63. Röpke 1959: 87. Röpke was careful to point out that the operation of a market system does not require (or result in) military imperialism: "The idea that the economic system which rests upon the regulating function of the market and the separation of political sovereignty from economic activity is that which compulsorily drives nations into war, must be completely rejected" (1959: 88).

64. Hume 1963: 40, emphasis in original.

Chapter 5: Illustrating Public Bads: The War on Drugs in Afghanistan

1. Quoted in original source document: https://www.washingtonpost.com/graphics /2019/investigations/afghanistan-papers/documents-database/documents/flynn_michael _ll_11102015.pdf?v=26.

2. This chapter draws on Coyne, Hall, and Burns 2016.

3. See, for instance, Charles 2004: n.p.; Mili 2007; Karzai 2009: n.p.; Peters 2009.

4. United National Office on Drugs and Crime (UNODC) 2002: 4; UNODC 2003b: 15.

5. Special Inspector General for the Afghanistan Reconstruction 2018: vi.

6. Beith 2013.

7. It is important to note that this data is capturing an input into production (hectares of land) rather than an output. This is important because the connection between inputs and outputs will not necessarily be one-to-one, due to other factors such as rainfall, etc.

8. UNODC 2018: 5.

9. UNODC 2018: 5.

10. UNODC 2021.

11. Wellman 2020.

12. UNODC 2021: 10.

13. UNODC 2014: 21; Wellman 2020.

14. Dahl 2013.

15. Institute for Economics & Peace 2019: 2.

16. Institute for Economics & Peace 2019: 2.

17. Cooley 1999: 131.

18. Cooley 1999: 131. In the 1970s and early 1980s, the "Golden Triangle"—which includes Burma, Laos, and Thailand—produced an estimated 70 percent of the world's opium.

As of 2007, that area produced approximately 5 percent, with Afghanistan cultivating a majority of the world's supply (see Fuller 2007). There are a number of factors contributing to this change, including pressure from China and the international community on the governments of the countries in the Golden Triangle, state dysfunction and war in Afghanistan, and the efficiency of production in Afghanistan due to the climate and environment (see Fuller 2007).

19. Byrd and Ward 2004: 6.

20. Goodhand 2005: 199.

21. See Chouvy 2010: 151; Felbab-Brown 2011.

22. Komarow 2001.

23. UNODC 2002: 4.

24. Farrell and Thorne 2005: 81.

25. Farrell and Thorne 2005: 81. There had been previous deals between the international community and the Taliban to reduce opium cultivation, but the international community failed to follow through on its side of the deal (see Farrell and Thorne 2005). Farrell and Thorne (2005: 84–85) explain that the 2000 *fatwa* was effective because of incentive alignment. After its public announcement, the Taliban leadership had an incentive to carry through on the ban, since failure to do so would reflect negatively on their authority and leadership. This history highlights both the failure of the international community to deliver in the past, as well as the importance of incentive alignment when considering drug policy. Of course, we cannot know what the counterfactual would have been without the US intervention. It is possible that the Taliban's ban on opium may have been short lived for a variety of reasons, and that production may have again increased to pre-ban levels. And if the ban had continued, it is unclear how supply would have responded to the dramatic increase in price in the absence of foreign intervention.

26. For a comprehensive account of the US war in Afghanistan, see Horton 2017.

27. See B. Rubin 2004: n.p.

28. Berniker 2002.

29. Farrell and Thorne 2005.

30. United Nations Security Council 2001: n.p.

31. Goodhand 2005.

32. UNODC 2003a: 5.

33. UNODC 2004: 5. To at least some extent, this dramatic price increase is due to the Taliban's ban on opium in 2000. In addition, there may be external demand factors that contributed to the increase in price and output. For example, one factor may be the increase in opium-derived prescription drugs in the US (see Meier 2013 and Express Scripts Lab 2014). It is important to note that as the supply of opium increased in subsequent years, the farmgate price fell (see UNODC 2010: 149).

34. Blanchard 2009: 17.

35. See Byrd and Ward 2004.

36. See Integrated Regional Information Networks 2003.

37. Felbab-Brown 2009: 141.

38. Quoted in Risen 2007.

39. UNODC 2004: 1.

40. Tarnoff 2012.

41. Tarnoff 2012.

42. Risen 2007.

43. Tarnoff 2012: 20.

44. See Mercille 2013.

45. Beith 2013.

46. Risen 2007; Beith 2013.

47. Tarnoff 2012: 20.

48. UNODC 2006.

49. UNODC 2007: 20–21.

50. UNODC 2014: 21.

51. See UNODC 2005: 47; Kraeutler 2008.

52. Tarnoff 2012.

53. Quoted in Donadio 2009.

54. See US Department of State 2010.

55. Rubin and Rosenberg 2012.

56. Tarnoff 2012: 20.

57. See Embassy of the United States in Kabul 2014.

58. UNODC 2013: 5.

59. UNODC 2018: 5.

60. See Ingrahram 2014.

61. See Special Inspector for the Afghanistan Reconstruction 2014a: 2.

62. Special Inspector General for Afghanistan Reconstruction 2018: 55–57.

63. UNODC 2018: 8.

64. Special Inspector General for Afghanistan Reconstruction 2018: 57.

65. Sopko 2014: 2.

66. Special Inspector General for Afghanistan Reconstruction 2018: vii.

67. J. Clemens 2008. See also Kennedy, Reuter, and Riley 1993.

68. See J. Clemens 2013: 526.

69. Higgs 1997b.

70. Byrd and Ward 2004: 7.

71. B. Rubin 2004.

72. Stewart 2010: n.p.

73. See Felbab-Brown 2011.

74. See Becker, Murphy, and Grossman 2006 for a general discussion of this issue.

75. Moreau 2013: n.p.

76. Felbab-Brown 2009.

77. Moreau 2013.

78. Quoted in Paige 1991: n.p.

79. UNODC 2009: 2; Alcis, Mansfield, and Smith 2021: 34-5.

80. See Peters 2009: 23; Azami 2018; Sufizada 2020.

81. Special Inspector General for the Afghanistan Reconstruction 2014b; Standish 2014; Rowlatt 2019.

82. Felbab-Brown 2017: 98–103.

83. See Peters 2009; Chouvy 2010.

84. Peters 2009: 19.

85. Lobjakas 2007.

86. Although a rising GDP per capita (from $182 in 2002 to $614 in 2012, per World Bank estimates) in Afghanistan would suggest individuals are better off in terms of opportunities, such data is misleading. The reality is that the vast majority of the GDP increase is the result of external spending and foreign aid related to the US occupation and reconstruction (see International Monetary Fund 2012). As the Senate Foreign Relations Committee (2011: 2) noted, "According to the World Bank, an estimated 97 percent of Afghanistan's gross domestic product (GDP) is derived from spending related to the international military and donor community presence. Afghanistan could suffer a severe economic depression when foreign troops leave in 2014."

87. UNODC 2013: 23.

88. Quoted in National Public Radio 2013.

89. Quoted in National Public Radio 2013.

90. Quoted in Donadio 2009.

91. UNODC 2012: 5.

92. Quoted in Al Jazeera America and the Associated Press 2014.

93. Thornton 1991: 130.

94. See Becker and Murphy 2013.

95. Schweich 2006: n.p.

96. See Nordland 2013.

97. Nordland 2013.

98. See Risen 2008; Rubin and Rosenberg 2012.

99. Risen 2008.

100. Risen 2008.

101. Rubin and Rosenberg 2012.

102. Rubin and Rosenberg 2012.

103. See Coburn 2009; Rubin 2010.

104. See Leff 1964; Knack and Keefer 1995; Mauro 1995, 2004; Murphy, Shleifer, and Vishny 1993; Shleifer and Vishny 1993; Bardhan 1997; Zak and Knack 2001; Drury, Krieckhaus, and Lusztig 2006.

105. US Department of State 2008: n.p.

106. US Department of State 2008: n.p.

107. Piazza 2012: 213. Tests for causality suggest that the relationship runs from opium production to violence.

108. J. Clemens 2008, 2013.

109. Economist Melissa Dell (2015) studied the patterns of violence following increased antinarcotics efforts in Mexico, finding that initiatives to combat drug trafficking led to increased violence. This can be explained by outside traffickers attempting to secure territory

held by incumbent criminals, who are weakened by the government's interdiction efforts. Her findings provide evidence of the general relationship between interdiction efforts and increases in violence.

110. See Speri 2014.

Chapter 6: Illustrating Public Bads: Drones as Mechanized Terror

1. For a history of drone use in the United States, see Hall and Coyne 2014. For a discussion of the war on terror as an exercise in imperial policing, see Rovner 2017.

2. See Turse 2011; De Luce and McLeary 2016; Scahill 2016; Shaw 2016; Atherton 2020.

3. Quoted in Savage 2014: n.p.

4. See Singer 2009; Martin and Sasser 2010; Gregory 2011a, b; Benjamin 2013; Cronin 2013; Kaag and Kreps 2014; Calhoun 2015; Chamayou 2015; Cockburn 2015; Hall 2015; Plaw, Fricker, and Colon 2015; Woods 2015; Gusterson 2016; Kreps 2016; Scahill 2016; Atherton 2020.

5. The arguments in this chapter draw on Coyne and Hall 2018b as their foundation.

6. Boyle 2013: 21–22; Alkarama Foundation 2015. There are potentially other harms as well. For instance, Rigterink (2021) finds that terrorist groups increase the number of violent attacks after a successful drone strike on their leader.

7. Scahill 2016: 157.

8. See Hall 2015.

9. Obama 2013: n.p.

10. Brennan 2012: n.p.

11. Quoted in Shane 2011a: n.p.

12. Quoted in Economist 2015: n.p.

13. For a broader discussion of this point regarding the use of drones by governments around the world, see Lyall 2020.

14. Even the standard dichotomy of drone bombing versus conventional bombing is not as clear-cut as its proponents make it seem. According to one estimate, drone strikes conducted in Afghanistan from mid-2010 to mid-2011 were ten times more deadly for civilians, as compared to air strikes carried out by fighter jets (see Ackerman 2013; Zenko and Wolf 2016). Saif 2015 describes life in the Palestinian territories during the 2014 Israeli summer offensive. Among other things, he describes how the Palestinian population experienced different forms of bombing, saying that drones were no less terrifying than other forms of attack. This suggests that it is not the technology itself that is the determining factor of precision, but rather the manner and context in which technologies are employed.

15. Shane 2015.

16. Office of the Director of National Intelligence 2016.

17. See Zenko 2016.

18. See De Luce and McLeary 2016.

19. Singh 2013.

20. Scahill 2016: 157.

21. I am fully aware that the data collected on drone-related injuries and deaths—both targets and civilians—is highly imperfect. Some sources rely on news reports that may be incomplete or, in some instances, inaccurate. Others rely on interviews from locals or eyewitnesses who may lack context or have inaccurate information. Reporting and collecting information in a conflict zone is dangerous, making gathering accurate information difficult. In principle, this might lead to an under- or overestimation of injuries and deaths. For my purposes, the accuracy of the numbers presented are not as important as recognizing that there is reason to believe that innocent people are harmed by the use of drones, and that these costs must be taken into account when considering the use of drone technology.

22. Bureau of Investigative Journalism 2021.

23. Human Rights Watch 2013: 1.

24. Amnesty International 2013.

25. Amnesty International 2013: 56.

26. Human Rights Watch 2014: n.p.

27. Columbia Law School Human Rights Clinic and Sana'a Center for Strategic Studies 2017: 65

28. Amnesty International 2019: 6.

29. Amnesty International 2019: 6.

30. See Scahill 2016: 154–176.

31. Scahill 2016: 156.

32. Scahill 2016: 169.

33. For more on the human toll of US drone strikes, see Khan (2021a,b). It is important to note that innocent American citizens are not immune from death by their government's drone strikes (see Taylor 2015). In several instances, the US government has killed their own citizens in the name of protecting their citizens from foreign threats. An additional, often neglected, cost of drones is the perverse mental and health effects on drone operators (see Philipps 2022).

34. See Higgs 2006b; Coyne and Hall 2018a: 21–25.

35. The public's fear is often the result of threat inflation and government-produced propaganda (see Thrall and Cramer 2009; Coyne and Hall 2021).

36. Quoted in Scahill 2016: 169.

37. Rohde 2009: n.p.

38. See Rohde 2009, 2012.

39. Owen 2013: n.p.

40. Rohde 2012: n.p.

41. International Human Rights & Conflict Resolution Clinic and Global Justice Clinic 2012: 2.

42. International Human Rights & Conflict Resolution Clinic and Global Justice Clinic 2012: vii.

43. International Human Rights & Conflict Resolution Clinic and Global Justice Clinic 2012: 82.

44. International Human Rights & Conflict Resolution Clinic and Global Justice Clinic 2012: vii.

45. See Greenwald 2012a, b.

46. Quoted in McVeigh 2013: n.p.

47. Ackerman 2016: n.p.

48. Quoted in Madlena, Patchett, and Shamsan 2015: n.p.

49. Kilcullen and Exum 2009: n.p.

50. Human Rights Watch 2013: 26.

51. Kilcullen and Exum 2009: n.p.

52. Abbas 2013: n.p.

53. Rohde 2009: n.p.

54. It is important to note that there is a lack of consensus over the magnitude of the effect of drone strikes on terrorist recruitment and subsequent terrorist attacks. Among the issues are controlling for other relevant factors—grievances, weak governance, coercive recruitment—and issues of reverse causality. The key literature to date can be summarized as follows. Smith and Walsh 2013 find that US drone strikes in Pakistan have not reduced al-Qaeda's ability to disseminate propaganda, which is key to recruitment. Johnston and Sarbahi 2016 find that US drone strikes in Pakistan decrease the incidence and lethality of terrorist attacks. Jaeger and Siddique 2018 study the impact of US drone strikes in Pakistan and Afghanistan, finding that drone strikes in the former increase terrorist violence in the immediate term, while US drone strikes in Afghanistan have little effect on terrorist violence. Drawing on interviews and secondary sources, Shah 2018 finds no evidence that US drone strikes in Pakistan increase recruitment of militants. In contrast, Mahmood and Jetter 2019 find that US government drone strikes cause the Pakistani populace to sympathize with members of terrorist organizations.

55. Boyle 2013: 22–27.

56. See Coyne and Alshamy 2021 for a discussion of the negative, perverse consequences of the next iteration of drone technologies, Lethal Autonomous Weapons Systems (LAWS). LAWS refers to military systems that employ human-made algorithms to independently identify, search for, and engage targets.

57. This dangerous precedent has already been seized by former UK Prime Minister David Cameron, who used lethal drones to execute two British nationals located in Syria in August 2015. See Calhoun 2016. Also see Shane 2011b; Lyall 2020.

Chapter 7: Rethinking Empire

1. See Boettke 2001: 248–265; Coyne 2008a: 20–22.

2. On the pathologies of the state, see Coyne and Goodman 2021.

3. Higgs 2012: 16.

4. See Corwin 1947; Higgs 1987, 2004, 2007, 2012; Linfield 1990; B. Porter 1994; Rehnquist 1998; Stone 2003; Cole and Dempsey 2006; Cole 2008; Cole and Lobel 2009; Herman 2011; Walker 2012; Coyne and Hall 2018a.

5. Higgs 2012: 15.

6. See Astore 2018; Mueller 2021.

7. On the benefits of retrenchment, see Parent and MacDonald 2011; Glaser 2017; Mueller 2021. For an example of the benefits of retrenchment, see Blagden and Porter 2021, who argue that the United States should cease the goal of armed supremacy in the Middle East. Also see Astore 2018.

8. For a discussion of how markets serve as a social space which facilitates human relationships, reinforces ethical values, and allows for the development of trust, see McCloskey 2006; Storr 2008; Choi and Storr 2021.

9. See Blackwell and Harris 2016.

10. This is in line with Maull 1990: 101, who contends that "ours is no longer an international system of superpower hegemony, but one of cooperation and conflict among highly interdependent partners." Similarly, Milner 1991: 81–85 discusses the assumption of interdependence instead of anarchy in the international space. These analyses focus on interactions between nation-states. My contention is that we can extend this same logic to the individuals residing within nation-states, as well as the interactions between individuals residing in different nation-states.

11. See Kukathas 2003, 2021; McCloskey 2006; M. Clemens 2011; Caplan 2012; Coyne 2013; van der Vossen and Brennan 2018; Clausing 2019; Panagariya 2019; Storr and Choi 2019; McCloskey and Carden 2020; Nowrasteh and Powell 2021.

12. For a discussion of the importance of appeasement—or peaceful dealmaking—see Mueller 2021.

13. E. Boulding 2000: 1.

14. Tocqueville 1840.

15. See V. Ostrom 1991b.

16. See Buchanan 2005 for a discussion of the dire consequences of a citizenry "afraid to be free."

17. E. Boulding 2000: 1.

18. This and the following sections on polycentric defense draw on Coyne 2020; Coyne and Goodman 2020 as a foundation.

19. The concept of polycentricity was introduced by Michael Polanyi 1951, who argued that success in science required a certain organizational structure that allowed for the contestation of ideas through open inquiry and experimentation. For more details on the history of the concept of polycentricity, see Ostrom, Tiebout, and Warren 1961; V. Ostrom 1999, 2014; Aligica and Boettke 2009; Aligica and Tarko 2013; Tarko 2017; Wiśniewski 2018; Aligica, Boettke, and Tarko 2019. An open issue in the social sciences is the source of the overarching—or meta— rules governing human interaction. F. A. Hayek 1973 differentiated between two views of society—one based on designed order (what he termed "taxis"), and the other based on a self-governing spontaneous order (what he termed "cosmos"). From here, he differentiated between emergent law ("nomos") and designed legislation ("thesis"). For discussions of emergent law, see Ellickson 1994, Leeson 2014, Stringham 2015.

20. Musgrave 1939, 1941; Samuelson 1954, 1955. See also Hummel 1990; Hummel and Lavoie 1994; Coyne 2015 regarding the public good argument for the state provision of defense.

21. See Coyne and Lucas 2016.

22. See, for instance, Buchanan 1965; Ostrom and Ostrom 1977; Cowen 1985; E. Ostrom 2009; Rayamajhee and Paniagua 2021.

23. See Cowen 1985: 53; Hummel 1990; Hummel and Lavoie 1994.

24. See E. Ostrom 1990; V. Ostrom 1999 for examples of people overcoming the collective action problems associated with the tragedy of the commons, despite theoretical predications of the opposite.

25. On the importance of context-specific, tacit knowledge, see Hayek 1945.

26. Aligica and Tarko 2013; E. Ostrom 1996.

27. Goodman 2017.

28. Jacobs 1961.

29. See Scarry 2002.

30. On the role of public entrepreneurship and civil society, see E. Ostrom 2005; Aligica 2018.

31. See Tiebout 1956; Ostrom, Tiebout, and Warren 1961.

32. Cobb Jr. 2015; D. Beito and L. Beito 2017.

33. See Granick 2017; Coyne and Hall 2018a.

34. Sanger and Frenkel 2018.

35. Zetter 2014.

36. Coyne, Goodman, and Hall 2019.

37. See Aligica and Boettke 2009; Boettke 2018; Wiśniewski 2018; Aligica, Boettke, and Tarko 2019.

38. See Wiśniewski 2018: 43–62, who differentiates between different ranges of security goods. On the role of "selective" incentives in coordinating people in collective action situations, see Olson 1965; Tullock 1971; Lichbach 1994, 1998.

39. Ayres and Levitt 1998.

40. See Hill 2004; Umoja 2014; Cobb Jr. 2015.

41. Bennett, Holloway, and Farrington 2006: 439.

42. Bennett, Holloway, and Farrington 2006: 438. On the private provision of criminal justice, see Benson 1998.

43. According to one study, areas with community watch programs experienced a 16 percent reduction in crime versus control groups (Holloway, Bennett, and Farrington 2008: 24).

44. List of chapters and locations: http://guardianangels.org/safety-patrols.

45. See Coleman 2009.

46. This section draws on Ammons and Coyne 2018, 2020 as its foundation.

47. Sharp 1973, 1985, 1990, 2005; Schell 2003; Chenoweth and Stephan 2011. For a comprehensive review of the literature on nonviolent action, see Ammons and Coyne 2020.

48. Hume 1963: 29; de La Boétie 1975; Sharp 1973.

49. Sharp 1973: 11–12.

50. Sharp 1973: 19–23.

51. It is important to note that nonviolent action is distinct from, and does not require, a commitment to pacifism. Historically, many individuals engaged in nonviolent action were not committed to pacifism on religious or philosophical grounds. Pacifism is an ethical position, but nonviolent action is a tactic, a method of engaging in defense against a threat

(internal or external) without resorting to physical violence, or after physical violence has failed. It is a technique for providing security that, if practiced correctly, can be quite forceful and effective to control and combat powerful threats, even leading to the ouster of foreign invaders.

52. Sharp 1973: 657.

53. Sharp 1973: 69.

54. Sharp 1990: 9.

55. Gardner 2012: n.p.

56. Quoted in Roberts 2018.

57. Chenoweth and Stephan 2011: 7.

58. Kennan 1986.

59. See Higgs 1987; Hummel 2001; Buchanan 2005.

60. On the strategy of restraint, see Posen 2014.

61. On the nature and features of stable peace, see K. Boulding 1978.

62. K. Boulding 1978: 13.

63. E. Boulding 2000: 1.

64 K. Boulding 1978: 93.

65. E. Boulding 2000: 101. On the importance of bottom-up peace-building, see E. Boulding 1990; Autesserre 2021.

66. K. Boulding 1962: 336–337.

Epilogue: The Siren Song of Empire

1. Beckley and Brands 2021: n.p.

2. Kagan 2022: n.p.

3. Department of Defense 2018.

4. Colby 2021.

5. Colby 2021: 16–37.

6. Whitlock 2019.

7. Coyne 2015.

8. Colby 2021: 15.

9. Source: https://watson.brown.edu/costsofwar/figures/2021/BudgetaryCosts.

Selected Bibliography

Abbas, Hassan. 2013. "How Drones Create More Terrorists," *The Atlantic*, August 23. Available online: http://www.theatlantic.com/international/archive/2013/08 /how-drones-create-more-terrorists/278743/.

ABC News. 2004. "Soldiers Must Rely on 'Hillbilly Armor' for Protection," December 8. Available online: http://abcnews.go.com/WNT/story?id=312959&page=1.

Ackerman, Spencer. 2013. "US Drone Strikes More Deadly to Afghan Civilians than Manned Aircraft," *The Guardian*, July 2. Available online: https://www.theguardian .com/world/2013/jul/02/us-drone-strikes-afghan-civilians.

————. 2016. "After Drones: The Indelible Mark of America's Remote Control Warfare," *The Guardian*, April 21. Available online: https://www.theguardian.com /us-news/2016/apr/21/drone-war-obama-pakistan-cia.

Adams, Gordon. 1981. *The Politics of Defense Contracting: The Iron Triangle*. New York: Routledge.

Aikins, Matthieu. 2021. "Times Investigation: In U.S. Drone Strike, Evidence Suggests No ISIS Bomb," *New York Times*, September 10. Available online: https://www .nytimes.com/2021/09/10/world/asia/us-air-strike-drone-kabul-afghanistan-isis .html.

Al Jazeera America and the Associated Press. 2014. "U.S. General: Corruption, Not Taliban, the Worst Threat to Afghanistan," Al Jazeera America, April 30. Available online: http://america.aljazeera.com/articles/2014/4/30/afghanistan-corruptionrebuild .html.

Alcis, David Mansfield, and Graeme Smith. 2021. "War gains: how the economic benefits of the conflict are distributed in Afghanistan and the implications for peace. A case study on Nimroz province," ODI, London. Available online: https://l4p.odi .org/assets/images/L4P-Nimroz-study_main-report-13.08.21.pdf.

Aligica, Paul Dragos. 2018. *Public Entrepreneurship, Citizenship, and Self-Governance.* New York: Cambridge University Press.

Aligica, Paul Dragos, and Peter J. Boettke. 2009. *Challenging Institutional Analysis and Development: The Bloomington School.* New York: Routledge.

Aligica, Paul Dragos, Peter J. Boettke, and Vlad Tarko. 2019. *Public Governance and the Classical-Liberal Perspective: Political Economy Foundations.* New York: Oxford University Press.

Aligica, Paul Dragos, and Vlad Tarko. 2013. "Co-Production, Polycentricity, and Value Heterogeneity: The Ostroms' Public Choice Institutionalism Revisited," *American Political Science Review* 107(4): 726–741.

Alkarama Foundation. 2015. "Traumatising Skies: U.S. Drone Operations and Post-Traumatic Stress Disorder (PTSD) Among Civilians in Yemen." Available online: https://www.alkarama.org/sites/default/files/documents/Yemen_Drones_2015 _EN_WEB_FINAL.pdf.

Allen, John R., and Vanda Felbab-Brown. 2020. "The Fate of Women's Rights in Afghanistan," Brookings, September. Available online: https://www.brookings.edu /essay/the-fate-of-womens-rights-in-afghanistan/.

American Civil Liberties Union. 2018. "Stingray Tracking Devices: Who's Got Them?" Available online: https://www.aclu.org/map/stingray-tracking-devices-whos -got-them.

Ammons, Joshua, and Christopher J. Coyne. 2018. "Gene Sharp: The 'Clausewitz of Nonviolent Warfare,'" *Independent Review: A Journal of Political Economy* 23(1): 149–156.

———. 2020. "Nonviolent Action." In, Virgil Storr and Stefanie Haeffele (eds.), *Bottom-Up Responses to Crisis.* Cham, Switzerland: Palgrave Macmillan, pp. 29–56.

Amnesty International. 2013. "'Will I Be Next?' US Drone Strikes in Pakistan." Available online: http://www.amnestyusa.org/sites/default/files/asa330132013en.pdf.

———. 2019. "The Hidden US War in Somalia: Civilian Casualties from Air Strikes in Lower Shabelle." Available online: https://www.amnestyusa.org/wp-content /uploads/2019/03/The-Hidden-U.S.-War-in-Somalia.pdf?fbclid=IwARoeAXHk1e 64NAli7XVLoAY-LwKhAdk7vw6g-m7-3Of1obvzsDCmezNuE7w.

Anderson, Kevin M. 1995. "The Venezuelan Claims Controversy at the Hague, 1903," *Historian* 57(3): 525–536.

Astore, William. 2018. "Taking War Off its Pedestal," LobeLog, February 7. Available online: https://lobelog.com/taking-war-off-its-pedestal/.

Atherton, Kelsey D. 2020. "Trump Inherited the Drone War but Ditched Accountability," *Foreign Policy,* May 22. Available online: https://foreignpolicy.com/2020/05/22 /obama-drones-trump-killings-count/.

Atwood, Paul L. 2010. *War and Empire: An American Way of Life.* New York: Pluto Press.

Autesserre, Séverine. 2021. *The Frontlines of Peace: An Insider's Guide to Changing the World*. New York: Oxford University Press.

Ayres, Ian, and Steven Levitt. 1998. "Measuring Positive Externalities from Unobservable Victim Precautions: An Empirical Analysis of Lojack," *Quarterly Journal of Economics* 113(1): 43–77.

Azami, Dawood. 2018. "Afghanistan: How Does the Taliban Make Money?" *BBC*, December 28. Available online: https://www.bbc.com/news/world-46554097.

Bacevich, Andrew. 2002. *American Empire: The Realities and Consequences of U.S. Diplomacy*. Cambridge, MA: Harvard University Press.

———. 2005. *The New American Militarism*. New York: Oxford University Press.

———. 2009. *American Empire: The Realities and Consequences of U.S. Diplomacy*. Cambridge, MA: Harvard University Press.

Balko, Radley. 2013. *Rise of the Warrior Cop: The Militarization of America's Police Forces*. New York: PublicAffairs.

Baloyra-Herp, Enrique A. 1983. "Reactionary Despotism in Central America," *Journal of Latin American Studies* 15(2): 295–319.

Bamford, James. 1983. *The Puzzle Palace: A Report on America's Most Secret Agency*. New York: Penguin Books.

———. 2008. *The Shadow Factory: The Ultra-Secret NSA from 9/11 to the Eavesdropping on America*. New York: Anchor Books.

Bardhan, Pranab. 1997. "Corruption and Development: A Review of Issues," *Journal of Economic Literature* 35(3): 1320–1346.

Barfield, Thomas. 2010. *Afghanistan: A Cultural and Political History*. Princeton, NJ: Princeton University Press.

Baumol, William J. 1990. "Entrepreneurship: Productive, Unproductive, and Destructive," *Journal of Political Economy* 98(5): 893–921.

Bates, Adam. 2016. "Stingray: A New Frontier in Policy Analysis," Cato Institute Policy Analysis No. 809.

Beard, Charles A. 1936. "The Living Constitution," *Annals of the American Academy of Political and Social Science* 185(1): 29–34.

———. 1946. *American Foreign Policy in the Making, 1932-1940: A Study in Responsibilities*. New Haven, CT: Yale University Press.

———. 1949. *President Roosevelt and the Coming of the War, 1941: A Study in Appearances and Realities*. New Haven, CT: Yale University Press.

Becker, Gary S., and Kevin M. Murphy. 2013. "Have We Lost the War on Drugs?" *Wall Street Journal*, January 4. Available online: http://online.wsj.com/article/SB10001424127887324374004578217682305605070.html.

Becker, Gary S., Kevin M. Murphy, and Michael Grossman. 2006. "The Market for Illegal Goods: The Case of Drugs," *Journal of Political Economy* 114(11): 38–60.

Beckley, Michael and Hal Brands. 2022."The Return of Pax Americana?" *Foreign Affairs*. March 14. Available online: https://www.foreignaffairs.com/articles/russia-fsu/2022-03-14/return-pax-americana.

Beith, Malcolm. 2013. "A Single Act of Justice: How the Age of Terror Transformed the War on Drugs," *Foreign Affairs,* September 8. Available online: http://www.foreignaffairs.com/articles/139908/malcolm-beith/a-single-act-of-justice.

Beito, David T., and Linda Royster Beito. 2017. *T. R. M. Howard: Doctor, Entrepreneur, Civil Rights Pioneer.* Oakland, CA: The Independent Institute.

Bender, Bryan. 2010. "From the Pentagon to the Private Sector," *Boston Globe*, December 26. Available online: http://www.boston.com/news/nation/washington/articles/2010/12/26/defense_firms_lure_retired_generals/?page=full.

Benjamin, Medea. 2013. *Drone Warfare: Killing by Remote Control.* New York: Verso.

Bennett, Trevor, Katy Holloway, and David P. Farrington. 2006. "Does Neighborhood Watch Reduce Crime? A Systematic Review and Meta-Analysis," *Journal of Experimental Criminology* 2(4): 437–458.

Benson, Bruce L. 1998. *To Serve and Protect: Privatization and Community in Criminal Justice.* Oakland, CA: The Independent Institute.

Berger, Daniel, Alejandro Corvalan, William Easterly, and Shanker Satyanath. 2013. "Do Superpower Interventions Have Short and Long Term Consequences for Democracy?" *Journal of Comparative Economics* 41(1): 22–34.

Berniker, Mark. 2002. "Afghanistan: Back to Bad Opium Habits," *Asia Times,* December 25. Available online: https://web.archive.org/web/20160722071745/http://www.atimes.com/atimes/Central_Asia/DL25Ag01.html.

Berr, Jonathan. 2015. "Pentagon's 'Too Big to Fail' F-35 Gets Another $10.6 Billion," *Fiscal Times*, February 2. Available online: http://www.thefiscaltimes.com/2015/02/02/Pentagon-s-Too-Big-Fail-F-35-Gets-Another-106-Billion.

Beschloss, Michael. 2003. *Our Documents: 100 Milestone Documents from the National Archives.* New York: Oxford University Press.

Bessner, Daniel. 2019. "The Making of the Military-Intellectual Complex," *New Republic*, May 29. Available online: https://newrepublic.com/article/153997/making-military-intellectual-complex.

Bevins, Vincent. 2020. *The Jakarta Method: Washington's Anticommunist Crusade and the Mass Murder Program that Shaped Our World.* New York: PublicAffairs.

Blackwell, Robert D., and Jennifer M. Harris. 2016. *War by Other Means: Geoeconomics and Statecraft.* Washington, DC: The Council on Foreign Relations.

Blagden, David, and Patrick Porter. 2021. "Desert Shield of the Republic? A Realist Case for Abandoning the Middle East," *Security Studies* 30(1): 5–48.

Blanchard, Christopher. 2009. "Afghanistan: Narcotics and U.S. Policy," Congressional Research Service Report for Congress RL32686, August 12. Available online: http://www.fas.org/sgp/crs/row/RL32686.pdf.

Boettke, Peter J. 2001. *Calculation and Coordination: Essays on Socialism and Transitional Political Economy*. New York: Routledge.

————. 2018. "Economics and Public Administration," *Southern Economics Journal* 84(4): 938–959.

————. 2021. *The Struggle for a Better World*. Arlington, VA: Mercatus Center at George Mason University.

Boettke, Peter J., Christopher J. Coyne, and Peter T. Leeson. 2008. "Institutional Stickiness and the New Development Economics," *American Journal of Economics and Sociology* 67(2): 331–358.

Boettke, Peter J., Jayme S. Lemke, and Liya Palagashvili. 2016. "Re-evaluating Community Policing in a Polycentric System," *Journal of Institutional Economics* 12(2): 305–325.

Boot, Max. 2001. "The Case for American Empire: The Most Realistic Response to Terrorism Is for America to Embrace Its Imperial Role," *Weekly Standard* 7(5): 23.

————. 2002. *Savage Wars of Peace: Small Wars and the Rise of American Power*. New York: Basic Books.

————. 2003. "U.S. Imperialism: A Force for Good," *National Post,* May 13, p. 15.

Boulding, Elise. 1990. *Building a Global Civic Culture: Education for an Interdependent World*. Syracuse, NY: Syracuse University Press.

————. 2000. *Cultures of Peace: The Hidden Side of History*. Syracuse, NY: Syracuse University Press.

Boulding, Kenneth. 1962. *Conflict and Defense: A General Theory*. New York: Harper & Brothers.

————. 1978. *The Stable Peace*. Austin, TX: University of Texas Press.

Boyle, Michael J. 2013. "The Costs and Consequences of Drone Warfare," *International Affairs* 89(1): 1-29.

Brennan, Geoffrey, and James M. Buchanan. 1985 [2000]. *The Reason of Rules: Constitutional Political Economy*. In, *The Collected Works of James M. Buchanan*, volume 10. Indianapolis, IN: Liberty Fund.

Brennan, John. 2012. "The Efficacy and Ethics of U.S. Counterterrorism Strategy," Wilson Center, April 30. Available online: http:// www.wilsoncenter.org/event/the-efficacy-and-ethics-us-counterterrorism-strategy.

Brenner, Michael. 2014. "Ur Imperialism," *Huffington Post*, February 15. Available online: http://www.huffingtonpost.com/michael-brenner/ur-imperialism_b_4453714 .html.

Brooks, Risa, Jim Golby, and Heidi Urben. 2021. "Crisis of Command: America's Broken Civil Military Relationship Imperils National Security," *Foreign Affairs* 100(3): 64–75.

Buchanan, James M. 1965. "An Economic Theory of Clubs," *Economica* 32(125): 1–14.

―――. 1975. *The Limits of Liberty: Between Anarchy and Leviathan*. Chicago: The University of Chicago Press.

―――. 1980. "Rent Seeking and Profit Seeking." In, James M. Buchanan, Robert Tollison, and Gordon Tullock (eds.), *Toward a Theory of the Rent-Seeking Society*. College Park, TX: Texas A&M Press, pp. 3–15.

―――. 2005. "Afraid to Be Free: Dependency as Desideratum," *Public Choice* 124(1): 19–31.

Bueno de Mesquita, Bruce, and George W. Downs. 2004. "Why Gun-Barrel Democracy Doesn't Work," *Hoover Digest*, April 30. Available online: https://www.hoover.org /research/why-gun-barrel-democracy-doesnt-work.

―――. 2006. "Intervention and Democracy," *International Organization* 60(3): 627–649.

Bulmer-Thomas, Victor. 2018. *Empire in Retreat: The Past, Present, and Future of the United States*. New Haven, CT: Yale University Press.

Bureau of Investigative Journalism. 2021. "Drone Warfare." Available online: https:// www.thebureauinvestigates.com/projects/drone-war.

Burns, Sarah. 2019. *The Politics of War Power: The Theory and History of Presidential Unilateralism*. Lawrence, KS: University Press of Kansas.

Burton, James G. 1993. *The Pentagon Wars: Reformers Challenge the Old Guard*. Annapolis, MD: Naval Institute Press.

Bush, George W. 2001. "Address to a Joint Session of Congress and the American People," September 20. Available online: https://georgewbush-whitehouse.archives.gov/news /releases/2001/09/20010920-8.html.

―――. 2005. "President Bush's Second Inaugural Address," NPR.org, January 20. Available online: https://www.npr.org/templates/story/story.php?storyId=4460172.

Byrd, William, and Christopher Ward. 2004. "Drugs and Development in Afghanistan," Social Development Papers: Conflict Prevention and Reconstruction Paper No. 18. Available online: https://documents1.worldbank.org/curated /en/156391468740439773/pdf/30903.pdf.

Calder, Bruce J. 1984. *The Impact of Intervention: The Dominican Republic During the US Occupation of 1916–1924*. Austin, TX: University of Texas Press.

Calhoun, Laurie. 2015. *We Kill Because We Can: From Soldiering to Assassination in the Drone Age.* London: Zed Books.

———. 2016. *We Kill Because We Can: From Soldiering to Assassination in the Drone Age.* London: Zed Books.

Caplan, Bryan. 2012. "Why Should We Restrict Immigration?" *Cato Journal* 32(1): 5–24.

Carpenter, Ted Galen. 2019. *Gullible Superpower: U.S. Support for Bogus Foreign Democratic Movements.* Washington, DC: The Cato Institute.

Carpenter, Ted Galen, and Malou Innocent. 2015. *Perilous Partners: The Benefits and Pitfalls of America's Alliances with Authoritarian Regimes.* Washington, DC: The Cato Institute.

Castor, Suzy. 1974. "The American Occupation of Haiti (1915–34) and the Dominican Republic (1916–24)," *Massachusetts Review* 15(1–2): 253–275.

Chamayou, Gregoire. 2015. *A Theory of the Drone.* New York: The New Press.

Charles, Robert B. 2004. "Afghanistan: Are the British Counternarcotics Efforts Going Wobbly?" Testimony Before the House Committee on Government Reform Subcommittee on Criminal Justice, Drug Policy, and Human Resources, Remarks at Hearing. Washington, DC: US Department of State Archive.

Chenoweth, Erica, and Maria J. Stephan. 2011. *Why Civil Resistance Works: The Strategic Logic of Nonviolent Conflict.* New York: Columbia University Press.

Choi, Ginny Seung, and Virgil Henry Storr. 2019. "A Culture of Rent Seeking," *Public Choice* 181(1–2): 101–126.

———. 2021. "The Market as a Process for the Discovery of Whom Not to Trust," *Journal of Institutional Economics*, forthcoming.

Chouvy, Pierre-Arnaud. 2010. *Opium: Uncovering the Politics of Poppy.* Cambridge, MA: Harvard University Press.

Clausing, Kimberly. 2019. *Open: The Progressive Case for Free Trade, Immigration, and Global Capital.* Cambridge, MA: Harvard University Press.

Clemens, Jeffrey. 2008. "Opium in Afghanistan: Prospects for the Success of Source Country Drug Control Policies," *Journal of Law and Economics* 51(3): 407–432.

———. 2013. "An Analysis of Economic Warfare," *American Economic Review* 103(3): 523–527.

Clemens, Michael. 2011. "Economics and Emigration: Trillion Dollar Bills on the Sidewalk," *Journal of Economic Perspectives* 25(3): 83–106.

Cobb, Charles E., Jr. 2015. *This Nonviolent Stuff'll Get You Killed: How Guns Made the Civil Rights Movement Possible.* Durham, NC: Duke University Press.

Coburn, Noah. 2009. "Losing Legitimacy? Some Afghan Views, the Government, the International Community, and the 2009 Elections," Afghan Research and Evaluation Unit Post-Elections Brief 2. Available online: https://www.refworld.org /pdfid/4b162ee62.pdf.

Cockburn, Andrew. 2015. *Kill Chain: The Rise of the High-Tech Assassins*. New York: Henry Holt.

———. 2021. *The Spoils of War: Power, Profit and the American War Machine*. New York: Verso.

Cohen, Alexander. 2015. "Top Defense Contractors Spend Millions to Get Billions," The Center for Public Integrity, August 5. Available online: https://publicintegrity.org /national-security/top-defense-contractors-spend-millions-to-get-billions/.

Cohen, Eliot A. 2004. "History and the Hyperpower," *Foreign Affairs*, July/August. Available online: https://www.foreignaffairs.com/articles/united-states/2004-07-01 /history-and-hyperpower.

———. 2016. *The Big Stick: The Limits of Soft Power and the Necessity of Military Force*. New York: Basic Books.

Colby, Elbridge A. 2021. *The Strategy of Denial: American Defense in an Age of Great Power Conflict*. New Haven, CT: Yale University Press.

Cole, David. 2008. "No Reason to Believe: Radical Skepticism, Emergency Power, and Constitutional Constraint," *University of Chicago Law Review* 75(3): 1329–1364.

Cole, David, and James X. Dempsey. 2006. *Terrorism and the Constitution: Sacrificing Civil Liberties in the Name of National Security*. New York: The New Press.

Cole, David, and Jules Lobel. 2009. *Less Safe, Less Free: Why America Is Losing the War on Terror*. New York: The New Press.

Coleman, Gabriella. 2009. "Code Is Speech: Legal Tinkering, Expertise, and Protest Among Free and Open Source Software Developers," *Cultural Anthropology* 24(3): 420–454.

Columbia Law School Human Rights Clinic and Sana'a Center for Strategic Studies. 2017. "Out of the Shadows: Recommendations to Advance Transparency in the Use of Lethal Force." Available online: https://www.law.columbia.edu/sites/default/files /microsites/human-rights-institute/out_of_the_shadows.pdf?fbclid=IwAR1dTGM CE2BmkJETCJvj9wpBSe8KXM1gssyW--sfErRpPpTtvtt39rmCOCY.

Commission on Wartime Contracting in Iraq and Afghanistan. 2011. "Transforming Wartime Contracting: Controlling Costs, Reducing Risks." Available online: https://cybercemetery.unt.edu/archive/cwc/20110929213815/http://www.wartime contracting.gov/.

Congleton, Roger D. 2005. "The Political Economy of Crisis Management: Surprise, Urgency, and Mistakes in Political Decision Making," *Advances in Austrian Economics* 8: 183–204.

Connah, Leoni. 2020. "US Intervention in Afghanistan: Justifying the Unjustifiable?" *South Asia Research* 41(1): 70–86.

Cook, Steven A. 2014. "Washington Can't Solve the Identity Crisis in Middle East Nations," *Washington Post*, August 15. Available online: https://www.washingtonpost.com/opinions/washington-cant-solve-the-identity-crisis-in-middle-east-nations/2014/08/15/c72fc7e4-2254-11e4-8593-da634b334390_story.html.

Cooley, John. 1999. *Unholy Wars: Afghanistan, America and International Terrorism.* London: Pluto Press.

Cordesman, Anthony, H., Charles Loi, and Vivek Kocharlakota. 2010. "IED Metrics for Iraq: June 2003–September 2010," Center for Strategic and International Studies, November 11. Available online: https://csis-website-prod.s3.amazonaws.com/s3fs-public/legacy_files/files/publication/101110_ied_metrics_combined.pdf.

Corwin, Edward S. 1947. *Total War and the Constitution.* New York: Alfred Knopf.

Cowen, Tyler. 1985. "Public Good Definitions and Their Institutional Context: A Critique of Public Goods Theory," *Review of Social Economy* 43(1): 53–63.

———. 2011. *The Great Stagnation: How America Ate All the Low-Hanging Fruit of Modern History, Got Sick, and Will (Eventually) Feel Better.* New York: Dutton.

———. 2021. "Does Technology Drive of the Growth of Government?" In, Joshua Hall and Bryan Khoo (eds.), *Essays on Government Growth: Political Institutions, Evolving Markets, and Technology.* Cham, Switzerland: Springer, pp. 51–66.

Coyne, Christopher J. 2008a. *After War: The Political Economy of Exporting Democracy* Stanford, CA: Stanford University Press.

———. 2008b. "'The Politics of Bureaucracy' and the Failure of Post-War Reconstruction," *Public Choice* 135(1-2): 11–22.

———. 2011. "Constitutions and Crisis," *Journal of Economic Behavior and Organization* 80(2): 351–357.

———. 2013. *Doing Bad by Doing Good: Why Humanitarian Action Fails.* Stanford, CA: Stanford University Press.

———. 2015. "Lobotomizing the Defense Brain," *Review of Austrian Economics* 28(4): 371–396.

———. 2017. "The Law and Economics of Rule Reform." In, Todd J. Zywicki and Peter J. Boettke (eds.), *Research Handbook on Austrian Law and Economics.* Cheltenham, UK: Edward Elgar Publishing, pp. 92–108.

———. 2018. "The Protective State." In, Peter J. Boettke and Solomon Stein (eds.), *Buchanan's Tensions: Reexamining the Political Economy and Philosophy of James M. Buchanan.* Arlington, VA: Mercatus Center at George Mason University, pp. 149–169.

———. 2020. "Introduction: Symposium on Polycentric Systems in a Free Society," *Independent Review: A Journal of Political Economy* 25(2): 229–234.

Coyne, Christopher J., and Yahya Alshamy. 2021. "Perverse Consequences of Lethal Autonomous Weapons Systems," *Peace Review*, forthcoming.

Coyne, Christopher J., and Peter J. Boettke. 2009. "The Problem of Credible Commitment in Reconstruction," *Journal of Institutional Economics* 5(1): 1–23.

Coyne, Christopher J., and Rachel L. Coyne. 2013. "The Political Economy of Human Rights Scandals," *Homo Oeconomicus* 30(4): 101–126.

Coyne, Christopher J., and Steve Davies. 2007. "Empire: Public Goods and Bads," *Econ Journal Watch* 4(1): 3–45.

Coyne Christopher J., and Thomas K. Duncan. 2019. "The Unproductive Protective State: The U.S. Defense Sector as a Fiscal Commons." In, Richard E. Wagner (ed.), *James M. Buchanan: A Theorist of Political Economy and Social Philosophy.* New York: Palgrave Macmillan, pp. 235–261.

Coyne, Christopher J., and Nathan Goodman. 2020. "Polycentric Defense," *Independent Review: A Journal of Political Economy* 25(2): 279–292.

————. 2021. "Economic Pathologies of the State." In, Gary Chartier and Chad Van Schoelandt (eds.), *The Routledge Handbook of Anarchy and Anarchist Thought.* New York: Routledge, pp. 247–261.

Coyne, Christopher J., Nathan Goodman, and Abigail R. Hall. 2019. "Sounding the Alarm: The Political Economy of Whistleblowing in the US Security State," *Peace Economics, Peace Science and Public Policy* 25(1): 1–11.

Coyne, Christopher J., and Abigail R. Hall. 2014. "Perfecting Tyranny: Foreign Intervention as Experimentation in State Control," *Independent Review: A Journal of Political Economy* 19(2): 165–189.

————. 2016. "Empire State of Mind: The Illiberal Foundations of Liberal Hegemony," *Independent Review: A Journal of Political Economy* 21(2): 237–250.

————. 2018a. *Tyranny Comes Home: The Domestic Fate of U.S. Militarism.* Stanford, CA: Stanford University Press.

————. 2018b. "The Drone Paradox: Fighting Terrorism with Mechanized Terror," *Independent Review: A Journal of Political Economy* 23(1): 51–67.

————. 2019a. "State-Provided Defense as Non-Comprehensive Planning," *Journal of Private Enterprise* 34(1): 75–85.

————. 2019b. "Cronyism: Necessary for the Minimal, Protective State," *Independent Review: A Journal of Political Economy* 23(3): 399–410.

————. 2021. *Manufacturing Militarism: U.S. Government Propaganda in the War on Terror.* Stanford, CA: Stanford University Press.

Coyne, Christopher J., Abigail R. Hall, and Scott Burns. 2016. "The War on Drugs in Afghanistan: Another Failed Experiment with Interdiction," *Independent Review: A Journal of Political Economy* 21(1): 95–119.

Coyne, Christopher J., and Peter T. Leeson. 2004. "The Plight of Underdeveloped Countries," *Cato Journal* 24(3): 235–249.

Coyne, Christopher J., and Davis S. Lucas. 2016. "Economists Have No Defense: A Critical Review of National Defense in Economics Textbooks," *Journal of Private Enterprise* 31(4): 65–83.

Coyne, Christopher J., and Rachel L. Mathers. 2010. "The Fatal Conceit of Foreign Intervention," *Advances in Austrian Economics* 14: 227–252.

Coyne, Christopher J., Courtney Michaluk, and Rachel Reese. 2016. "Unproductive Entrepreneurship in U.S. Military Contracting," *Journal of Entrepreneurship and Public Policy* 5(2): 221–239.

Coyne, Christopher J., and Adam Pellillo. 2011. "Economic Reconstruction Amidst Conflict: Insights from Afghanistan and Iraq," *Defence and Peace Economics* 22(6): 627–643.

Coyne, Christopher J., and Garrett Wood. 2020. "The Political Economy of Foreign Intervention." In, Stefanie Haeffele and Virgil Storr (eds.), *Government Responses to Crisis*. Cham, Switzerland: Palgrave Macmillan, pp. 89–109.

Coyne, Christopher J., and Yuliya Yatsyshina. 2021. "Police State, U.S.A.," *Independent Review: A Journal of Political Economy* 26(2): 189-204.

Crawford, Neta C. 2021. "The U.S. Budgetary Costs of the Post-9/11 Wars," Costs of War Project, September 1. Available online: https://watson.brown.edu/costsofwar /files/cow/imce/papers/2021/Costs%20of%20War_U.S.%20Budgetary%20Costs%20 of%20Post-9%2011%20Wars_9.1.21.pdf.

Crawford, Neta C., and Catherine Lutz. 2021. "Human Cost of Post-9/11 Wars," Costs of War Project, September 1. Available online: https://watson.brown.edu /costsofwar/files/cow/imce/papers/2021/Costs%20of%20War_Direct%20War%20 Deaths_9.1.21.pdf.

Cronin, Audrey Kurth. 2013. "Why Drones Fail: When Tactics Drive Strategy," *Foreign Affairs* 92(4): 44–54.

Cummins, Lejeune. 1967. "The Formulation of the 'Platt' Amendment," *The Americas* 23(4): 370–389.

Dahl, Fredrik. 2013. "Afghanistan Risks Becoming 'Narco-State': U.N. Official," Reuters, October 9. Available online: https://www.reuters.com/article/us-afghanistan-drugs-un /afghanistan-risks-becoming-narco-state-u-n-official-idUSBRE9980OF20131009.

de La Boétie, Étienne. 1975. *The Politics of Obedience: The Discourse of Voluntary Servitude*. Montreal, Quebec, Canada: Black Rose Books.

Dell, Melissa. 2015. "Trafficking Networks and the Mexican Drug War," *American Economic Review* 105(6): 1738–1779.

De Luce, Dan, and Paul McLeary. 2016. "Obama's Most Dangerous Drone Tactic Is Here to Stay," *Foreign Policy*, April 5. Available online: http://foreignpolicy .com/2016/04/05/obamas-most-dangerous-drone-tactic-is-here-to-stay/.

Denison, Benjamin. 2020. "The More Things Change, the More They Stay the Same: The Failure of Regime-Change Operations," Cato Institute Policy Analysis No. 883.

Department of Defense. 2015. "Agency Strategic Plan: Fiscal Years 2015–2018, Version 1.0." Available online: https://cmo.defense.gov/Portals/47/Documents/Publications /ASP/FY2016_2018ASP.pdf.

————. 2018. "Summary of the 2018 National Defense Strategy of the United States of America. Available online: https://dod.defense.gov/Portals/1/Documents/pubs/2018 -National-Defense-Strategy-Summary.pdf

————. 2019. "Base Structure Report: Fiscal Year 2018 Baseline." Available online: https://www.acq.osd.mil/eie/Downloads/BSI/Base%20Structure%20Report%20 FY18.pdf.

Devins, Caryn, Roger Koppl, Stuart Kauffman, and Teppo Felin. 2015. "Against Design," *Arizona State Law Journal* 47(3): 609–681.

Diamond, Larry. 2005. *Squandered Victory: The American Occupation and the Bungled Effort to Bring Democracy to Iraq.* New York: Henry Holt.

Dobbins, James, John G. McGinn, Keith Crane, Seth G. Jones, Rollie Lal, Andrew Rathmell, Rachel M. Swanger, and Anga Timilsina. 2003. *America's Role in Nation-Building: From Germany to Iraq.* Santa Monica, CA: RAND Corporation.

Dobos, Ned. 2020. *Ethics, Security, and the War-Machine: The True Cost of the Military.* New York: Oxford University Press.

Donadio, Rachel. 2009. "New Course for Antidrug Efforts in Afghanistan," *New York Times,* June 27. Available online: http://www.nytimes.com/2009/06/28/world /asia/28holbrooke.html.

Donovan, James A. 1970. *Militarism, U.S.A.* New York: Charles Scribner's Sons.

Dorsen, Norman. 1989. "Foreign Affairs and Civil Liberties," *American Journal of International Law* 83(4): 840–850.

Douglas, William O. 1987. *The Douglas Letters: Selections from the Private Papers of Justice William O. Douglas,* Melvin I. Urofsky (ed.). Bethesda, MD: Adler & Adler.

Downes, Alexander B., and Jonathan Monten. 2013. "Forced to Be Free? Why Foreign-Imposed Regime Change Rarely Leads to Democratization," *International Security* 37(4): 90–131.

Drury, A. Cooper, Jonathan Krieckhaus, and Michael Lusztig. 2006. "Corruption, Democracy, and Economic Growth," *International Political Science Review* 27(2): 121–136.

Duncan, Thomas K., and Christopher J. Coyne. 2013a. "The Origins of the Permanent War Economy," *Independent Review: A Journal of Political Economy* 18(2): 219–240.

————. 2013b. "The Overlooked Costs of the Permanent War Economy," *Review of Austrian Economics* 26(4): 413–431.

————. 2015a. "The Revolving Door and the Entrenchment of the Permanent War Economy," *Peace Economics, Peace Science and Public Policy* 21(3): 391–413.

————. 2015b. "The Political Economy of Foreign Intervention." In, Peter J. Boettke and Christopher J. Coyne (eds.), *The Oxford Handbook of Austrian Economics*. New York: Oxford University Press, pp. 679–697.

Dunham, Will. 2014. "Kerry Condemns Russia's 'Incredible Act of Aggression' in Ukraine," Reuters, March 2. Available online: http://www.reuters.com/article /us-ukraine-crisis-usa-kerry-idUSBREA2I0DG20140302#9vhws43VahJWoFeA.97.

Dunne, J. Paul. 2013. "Military Keynesianism: An Assessment." In, Li Junsheng, Chen Bo, and Hou Na (eds.), *Cooperation for a Peaceful and Sustainable World* Part 2. Bingley, UK: Emerald Group Publishing, pp. 117–129.

Dye, Thomas R. 2001. *Top Down Policymaking*. New York: Chatham House.

————. 2014. *Who's Running America? The Obama Reign*. New York: Routledge.

Easterly, William. 2006. *The White Man's Burden: Why the West's Efforts to Aid the Rest Have Done So Much Ill and So Little Good*. New York: Penguin Press.

————. 2014. *The Tyranny of Experts: Economists, Dictators, and the Forgotten Rights of the Poor*. New York: Basic Books.

Economist. 2015. "Drone Strikes and International Law: Fallout Reaches the Ivory Tower," *Economist*, April 22. Available online: http://www.economist.com/blogs /democracyinamerica/2015/04/drone-strikes-and-international-law.

Edelson, Chris. 2016. *Power Without Constraint: The Post-9/11 Presidency and National Security*. Madison, WI: University of Wisconsin Press.

Ekirch, Arthur A., Jr. 2010. *The Civilian and the Military: A History of the American Antimilitarist Tradition*. Oakland, CA: The Independent Institute.

Eland, Ivan. 2019. *War and the Rogue Presidency: Restoring the Republic After Congressional Failure*. Oakland, CA: The Independent Institute.

Ellickson, Robert C. 1994. *Order Without Law: How Neighbors Settle Disputes*. Cambridge, MA: Harvard University Press.

Ellner, Steve. 1995. "Venezuelan Revisionist Political History, 1908–1958: New Motives and Criteria for Analyzing the Past," *Latin American Research Review* 30(2): 91–121.

Embassy of the United States in Kabul, Afghanistan. 2014. "U.S. Embassy Fact Sheet on the Good Performers Initiative." Available online: https://web.archive.org /web/20151010060212/http://kabul.usembassy.gov/pr-090114.html.

Enterline, Andrew J., and J. Michael Greig. 2005. "Beacons of Hope? The Impact of Imposed Democracy on Regional Peace, Democracy, and Prosperity," *Journal of Politics* 67(4): 1075–1098.

————. 2008. "Perfect Storms? Political Instability in Imposed Polities and the Futures of Iraq and Afghanistan," *Journal of Conflict Resolution* 52(6): 880–915.

Express Scripts Lab. 2014. "A Nation in Pain," An Express Scripts Report. Available online: https://corporate-site-labs-prod.s3.us-east-2.amazonaws.com/2019-08 /Opioid%20Report_0.pdf.

Farrell, Graham, and John Thorne. 2005. "Where Have All the Flowers Gone? Evaluation of the Taliban Crackdown Against Opium Poppy Cultivation in Afghanistan," *International Journal of Drug Policy* 16: 81–91.

Felbab-Brown, Vanda. 2009. *Shooting Up: Counterinsurgency and the War on Drugs.* Washington, DC: Brookings Institution Press.

_____. 2011. "War and Drugs in Afghanistan," *World Politics Review,* October 25. Available online: http://www.worldpoliticsreview.com/articles/10449 /war-and-drugs-in-afghanistan.

_____. 2017. "Organized Crime, Illicit Economies, Civil Violence and International Order: More Complex Than You Think," *Dædalus* 146(4): 98–111.

Feldstein, Martin. 2008. "Defense Spending Would Be Great Stimulus," *Wall Street Journal,* December 24. Available online: https://www.wsj.com/articles /SB123008280526532053.

Ferguson, Niall. 2003. *Empire: The Rise and Demise of British World Order and the Lessons for Global Power.* New York: Basic Books.

_____. 2004. *Colossus: The Rise and Fall of American Empire.* New York: Penguin Books.

Ferguson, Niall, and Moritz Schularick. 2006. "The Empire Effect: The Determinants of Country Risk in the First Age of Globalization, 1880–1913," *Journal of Economic History* 66(2): 283–312.

Fisher, Louis. 2013. *Presidential War Power.* Lawrence, KS: University Press of Kansas.

Fitzgerald, A. Ernest. 1972. *The High Priests of Waste.* New York: W. W. Norton.

_____. 1989. *The Pentagonists: An Insider's View of Waste, Management, and Fraud in Defense Spending.* New York: Harper & Row.

Flores, Thomas Edward, and Irfan Nooruddin. 2009. "Democracy Under the Gun: Understanding Post-Conflict Recovery," *Journal of Conflict Resolution* 53(1): 3–29.

Flynn, John T. 1944. *As We Go Marching.* New York: Doubleday.

Forbes, Ian L. D. 1978. "The German Participation in the Allied Coercion of Venezuela 1902–1903," *Australian Journal of Politics and History* 24(3): 317–331.

Fraenkel, Osmond K. 1946. "War, Civil Liberties, and the Supreme Court," *Yale Law Journal* 55(4): 715–734.

Fukuyama, Francis. 2005. *State-Building: Governance and World Order in the 21st Century.* London: Profile Books.

Fulbright, J. William. 1970. *The Pentagon Propaganda Machine.* New York: Vintage Books.

Fuller, Thomas. 2007. "Notorious Golden Triangle Loses Sway in the Opium Trade," *New York Times*, September 11. Available online: http://www.nytimes.com/2007/09/11 /world/asia/11iht-golden.1.7461246.html?pagewanted=all&_r=0.

Gans, John. 2019. *White House Warriors: How the National Security Council Transformed the American Way of War*. New York: W. W. Norton.

Gardner, David. 2012. "Do Not Despair Yet About Dictators," *Financial Times*, June 24. Available online: https://www.ft.com/content/737c74e4-bc53-11e1 -a836-00144feabdc0.

Gates, Robert M. 2014. "The Quiet Fury of Robert Gates," *Wall Street Journal*, January 7. Available online: https://www.wsj.com/articles/no-headline-available-1389128316.

———. 2020. "The Overmilitarization of American Foreign Policy," *Foreign Affairs* 99(4): 121–132.

Gilderhus, Mark T. 2006. "The Monroe Doctrine: Meanings and Implications," *Presidential Quarterly Studies* 36(1): 5–16.

Gilmartin, Mary. 2009. "Colonialism/Imperialism." In, Carolyn Gallaher, Carl T. Dahlman, Mary Gilmartin, Alison Mountz, and Peter Shirlow (eds.), *Key Concepts in Political Geography*. Los Angeles: SAGE Publications Ltd., pp. 115–123.

Gingeras, Ryan. 2010. "Last Rites for a 'Pure Bandit': Clandestine Service, Historiography and the Origins of the Turkish 'Deep State,'" *Past and Present* 206(1): 151–174.

Glaser, John. 2017. "Withdrawing from Oversees Bases: Why a Forward-Deployed Military Posture Is Unnecessary, Outdated, and Dangerous," Cato Institute Policy Analysis No. 816. Available online: https://www.cato.org/sites/cato.org/files/pubs /pdf/pa_816.pdf.

Glasgow, Roy Arthur. 1987. "The Birth of an American Empire," *Latin American Research Review* 22(1): 241–247.

Glennon, Michael J. 2015. *National Security and Double Government*. New York: Oxford University Press.

Goldberg, Jeffrey. 2016. "The Obama Doctrine," *The Atlantic,* April. Available online: https://www.theatlantic.com/magazine/archive/2016/04/the-obama-doctrine /471525/.

Goodhand, Jonathan. 2005. "Frontiers and Wars: The Opium Economy in Afghanistan," *Journal of Agrarian Change* 5(2): 191–216.

Goodman, Nathan. 2017. "The Coproduction of Justice." In, Chris W. Surprenant (ed.), *Rethinking Punishment in the Era of Mass Incarceration*. New York: Routledge, pp. 49–68.

Gopal, Anand. 2021. "The Other Afghan Women," *New Yorker*, September 6. Available online: https://www.newyorker.com/magazine/2021/09/13/the-other-afghan-women.

Gordon, Scott. 2002. *Controlling the State: Constitutionalism from Ancient Athens to Today*. Cambridge, MA: Harvard University Press.

Government Accountability Office. 2015. "High-Risk Series: An Update," Report to Congressional Committees, February. Available online: http://www.gao.gov /assets/670/668415.pdf.

Graham-Harrison, Emma. 2021. "How Mass Killings by US forces After 9/11 Boosted Support for the Taliban," *The Guardian*, September 10. Available online: https://www.theguardian.com/us-news/2021/sep/10/how-mass-killings -by-us-forces-after-911-boosted-support-for-the-taliban.

Granick, Jennifer Stisa. 2017. *American Spies: Modern Surveillance, Why You Should Care, and What To Do About It*. New York: Cambridge University Press.

Greenwald, Glenn. 2012a. "US Drone Strikes Target Rescuers in Pakistan—and the West Stays Silent," *The Guardian*, August 20. Available online: https://www.theguardian .com/commentisfree/2012/aug/20/us-drones-strikes-target-rescuers-pakistan.

———. 2012b. "New Stanford/NYU Study Documents the Civilian Terror from Obama's Drones," *The Guardian*, September 25. Available online: https://www .theguardian.com/commentisfree/2012/sep/25/study-obama-drone-deaths.

———. 2014. *No Place to Hide: Edward Snowden, the NSA, and the U.S. Surveillance State*. New York: Metropolitan Books.

Gregory, Derek. 2011a. "From a View to a Kill: Drones and Late Modern War," *Theory, Culture & Society* 28(7–8): 188–215.

———. 2011b. "The Everywhere War," *Geographical Journal* 177(3): 238–250.

Greve, Michael S. 2012. *The Upside-Down Constitution*. Cambridge, MA: Harvard University Press.

Grieb, Kenneth J. 1967. "The United States and the Central American Federation," *The Americas* 24(2): 107–121.

Griffin, Drew, and Scott Bronstein. 2010. "Defense Official Example of Revolving Door Between Governing, Lobbying," *CNN*, February 23. Available online: http://www .cnn.com/2010/POLITICS/02/23/broken.lobbyists/index.html.

Grossman, Richard. 2005. "The Blood of the People: The Guardia Nacional de Nicaragua's Fifty Year War Against the People of Nicaragua, 1927–1979." In, Cecilia Menjívar and Néstor Rodriguez (eds.), *When States Kill: Latin America, the U.S., and Technologies of Terror*. Austin, TX: University of Texas Press, pp. 59–84.

Gusterson, Hugh. 2016. *Drone: Remote Control Warfare*. Cambridge, MA: MIT Press.

Hall, Abigail R. 2015. "Drones: Public Interest, Public Choice, and the Expansion of Unmanned Aerial Vehicles," *Peace Economics, Peace Science and Public Policy* 21(2): 273–300.

Hall, Abigail R., and Christopher J. Coyne. 2013. "The Militarization of U.S. Domestic Policing," *Independent Review: A Journal of Political Economy* 7(4): 485–504.

———. 2014. "The Political Economy of Drones," *Defence and Peace Economics* 25(5): 445–460.

Hamilton, Lee H. 2009. "Relations Between the President and Congress in Wartime." In, James A. Thurber (ed.), *Rivals for Power: Presidential-Congressional Relations*. Lanham, MD: Rowman & Littlefield, pp. 285–308.

Hanson, Gail. 1994. "Ordered Liberty: Sumner Welles and the Crowder-Welles Connection in the Caribbean," *Diplomatic History* 18(3): 311–322.

Hanson, Victor Davis. 2002. "A Funny Sort of Empire: Are Americans Really So Imperial?" *National Review Online*, November 27. Available online: http://victorhanson .com/wordpress/a-funny-sort-of-empire/.

Harrison, Benjamin. 1995. "The United States and the 1909 Nicaragua Revolution," *Caribbean Quarterly* 41(3–4): 45–63.

Hartung, William D., and Mandy Smithberger. 2019. "America's Defense Budget Is Bigger Than You Think," *The Nation*, May 7. Available online: https://www.thenation .com/article/archive/tom-dispatch-america-defense-budget-bigger-than-you-think/.

Hayek, F. A. 1944. *The Road to Serfdom*. Chicago, IL: University of Chicago Press.

———. 1945. "The Use of Knowledge in Society," *American Economic Review* 35(4): 519–530.

———. 1973. *Law, Legislation and Liberty, Volume 1: Rules and Order*. Chicago, IL: University of Chicago Press.

Healy, David. 1991. "Rough Rider and Big Stick in the Caribbean," *Reviews in American History* 19(3): 402–407.

Hendrickson, David C. 2018. *Republic in Peril: American Empire and the Liberal Tradition*. New York: Oxford University Press.

Herman, Susan N. 2011. *Taking Liberties: The War on Terror and the Erosion of American Democracy*. New York: Oxford University Press.

Hexon, Daniel H., and Thomas Wright. 2007. "What's at Stake in the American Empire Debate," *American Political Science Review* 101(2): 253–271.

Higginbotham, Adam. 2010. "U.S. Military Learns to Fight Deadliest Weapons," *Wired*, July 28. Available online: https://web.archive.org/web/20191226120943/https:// www.wired.com/2010/07/ff_roadside_bombs/.

Higgs, Robert. 1987. *Crisis and Leviathan: Critical Episodes in the Growth of American Government*. New York: Oxford University Press.

———. 1997. "Regime Uncertainty: Why the Great Depression Lasted So Long and Why Prosperity Resumed After the War," *Independent Review: A Journal of Political Economy* 1(4): 561–590.

———. 2004. *Against Leviathan: Government Power and a Free Society*. Oakland, CA: The Independent Institute.

———. 2006a. *Depression, War, and Cold War: Studies in Political Economy*. New York: Oxford University Press.

———. 2006b. "Fear: The Foundation of Every Government's Power," *Independent Review: A Journal of Political Economy* 10(3): 447–466.

———. 2007. *Neither Liberty nor Safety: Fear, Ideology, and the Growth of Government*. Oakland, CA: The Independent Institute.

———. 2012. *Delusions of Power: New Explorations of State, War, and Economy*. Oakland, CA: The Independent Institute.

———. 2015. *Taking a Stand: Reflections on Life, Liberty, and the Economy*. Oakland, CA: The Independent Institute.

Hill, Lance. 2004. *The Deacons for Defense: Armed Resistance and the Civil Rights Movement*. Chapel Hill, NC: University of North Carolina Press.

Hitchman, James H. 1967. "The Platt Amendment Revisited: A Bibliographical Survey," *The Americas* 23(4): 343–369.

Hobbes, Thomas. 1904. *Leviathan, or The Matter, Forme & Power of a Commonwealth, Ecclesiasticall and Civil*. London: C.J. Clay and Sons.

Hobson, John A. 1902. *Imperialism: A Study*. New York: James Pott & Company.

Hogan, Michael J. 1998. *A Cross of Iron: Harry S. Truman and the National Security State 1945–1954*. New York: Cambridge University Press.

Holcombe, Randall G. 2013. "Crony Capitalism: By-Product of Big Government," *Independent Review: A Journal of Political Economy* 17(4): 541–559.

———. 2018. *Political Capitalism: How Economic and Political Power Is Made and Maintained*. New York: Cambridge University Press.

Holcombe, Randall G., and Andrea M. Castillo. 2013. *Liberalism and Cronyism: Two Rival Political and Economic Systems*. Arlington, VA: Mercatus Center at George Mason University.

Holloway, Katy, Trevor Bennett, and David P. Farrington. 2008. "Does Neighborhood Watch Reduce Crime?" Crime Prevention Research Review No. 3. Available online: https://journalistsresource.org/wp-content/uploads/2012/03/e040825133-res-review3.pdf.

Hopkins, A. G. 2007. "Capitalism, Nationalism, and the New American Empire," *Journal of Imperial and Commonwealth History* 35(1): 95–117.

———. 2018. *American Empire: A Global History*. Princeton, NJ: Princeton University Press.

Horton, Scott. 2017. *Fool's Errand: Time to End the War in Afghanistan*. Austin, TX: The Libertarian Institute.

Howe, Daniel Walker. 2007. *What Hath God Wrought: The Transformation of America, 1815–1848.* New York: Oxford University Press.

Howlett, Charles F. 1988. "Neighborly Concern: John Nevin Sayre and the Mission of Peace and Goodwill to Nicaragua, 1927–28," *The Americas* 45(1): 19–46.

Human Rights Watch. 2013. "'Between a Drone and Al-Qaeda': The Civilian Cost of US Targeted Killings in Yemen," HRW.org, October 22. Available online: https://www.hrw.org/report/2013/10/22/between-drone-and-al-qaeda/civilian -cost-us-targeted-killings-yemen.

———. 2014. "A Wedding That Became a Funeral: US Drone Attack on Marriage Procession in Yemen," HRW.org, February 19. Available online: https://www .hrw.org/report/2014/02/19/wedding-became-funeral/us-drone-attack-marriage -procession-yemen.

Hume, David. 1963. *Essays: Moral, Political, Literary.* New York: Oxford University Press.

Hummel, Jeffrey Rogers. 1990. "National Goods Versus Public Goods: Defense, Disarmament, and Free Riders," *Review of Austrian Economics* 4(1): 88–122.

———. 2001. "The Will to Be Free: The Role of Ideology in National Defense," *Independent Review* 5(5): 523–537.

Hummel, Jeffrey Rogers, and Don Lavoie. 1994. "National Defense and the Public-good Problem," *Journal des Economistes et des Etudes Humaines* 5(2-3): 353–377.

Ikenberry, G. John. 2012. *Liberal Leviathan: The Origins, Crisis, and Transformation of the American World Order.* Princeton, NJ: Princeton University Press.

Immerwahr, Daniel. 2019. *How to Hide an Empire: A History of the Greater United States.* New York: Picador.

Ingrahram, Christopher. 2014. "It's Official: The U.S. Drug War in Afghanistan is a $7.6 billion Failure," *Washington Post*, October 22. Available online: http:// www.washingtonpost.com/blogs/wonkblog/wp/2014/10/22/its-official-the-u -s-drug-war-in-afghanistan-is-a-7-6-billion-failure/.

Institute for Economics & Peace. 2019. "Global Terrorism Index 2019: Measuring the Impact of Terrorism." Available online: https://www.visionofhumanity.org/wp-content /uploads/2020/11/GTI-2019-web.pdf. Interview with Antonio Maria Costa, Head of the UN Office for Drug Control and Crime Prevention," The New Humanitarian, December 5. Available online: https://www.thenewhumanitarian.org/q-and/2003/12/05 /interview-antonio-maria-costa-head-un-office-drug-control-and-crime-prevention.

International Human Rights and Conflict Resolution Clinic (Stanford Law School), and Global Justice Clinic (NYU School of Law). 2012. "Living Under Drones: Death, Injury, and Trauma to Civilians From US Drone Practices in Pakistan." Available online: https://law.stanford.edu/wp-content/uploads/sites/default/files/publication /313671/doc/slspublic/Stanford_NYU_LIVING_UNDER_DRONES.pdf. "IMF

Data: Islamic Republic of Afghanistan Gross Domestic Product." Available online: http://www.imf.org/external/pubs/ft/weo/2012/01/weodata/weoapr2012all.xls.

International Security Advisory Board. 2015. "Report on Status of Forces Agreements." Available online: https://2009-2017.state.gov/documents/organization/236456.pdf.

Irons, Peter. 2005. *War Powers: How the Imperial Presidency Hijacked the Constitution.* New York: Metropolitan Books.

Jablonsky, David. 2002–03. "The State of the National Security State," *Parameters* 32(4): 4–20.

Jacobs, Jane. 1961. *The Death and Life of Great American Cities.* New York: Random House.

Jaeger, David A., and Zahra Siddique. 2018. "Are Drone Strikes Effective in Afghanistan and Pakistan? On the Dynamics of Violence between the United States and the Taliban," *CESifo Economic Studies* 64(4): 667–697.

Jefferson, Thomas. 1854. *The Writings of Thomas Jefferson,* volume VI. Washington, DC: Taylor and Maury.

Jervis, Robert. 1976. *Perception and Misperception in International Politics.* Princeton, NJ: Princeton University Press.

Johnson, Chalmers. 2004. *The Sorrows of Empire: Militarism, Secrecy, and the End of the Republic.* New York: Henry Holt.

Johnston, Patrick B., and Anoop K. Sarbahi. 2016. "The Impact of US Drone Strikes on Terrorism in Pakistan," *International Studies Quarterly* 60(2): 203–219.

Joint Economic Committee. 1969. "The Military Budget and National Economic Priorities," Hearings Before the Subcommittee on Economy in Government of the Joint Economic Committee Congress of the United States, First Session. Washington, DC: US Government Printing Office.

Jones, Garett, and Tim Kane. 2012. "U.S. Troops and Foreign Economic Growth," *Defence and Peace Economics* 23(3): 225–249.

Kaag, John, and Sarah Kreps. 2014. *Drone Warfare.* Malden, MA: Polity Press.

Kagan, Robert. 1998. "The Benevolent Empire," *Foreign Policy* 111 (Summer): 24–25.

———. 2012. *The World America Made.* New York: Vintage Books.

———. 2018. *The Jungle Grows Back: America and Our Imperiled World.* New York: Vintage Books.

———. 2021. "A Superpower, Like It or Not: Why Americans Must Accept Their Global Role," *Foreign Affairs,* March/April. Available online: https://www.foreignaffairs.com/articles/united-states/2021-02-16/superpower-it-or-not.

———. 2022. "The Price of Hegemony: Can America Learn to Use Its Power?" *Foreign Affairs.* May/June. Available online: https://www.foreignaffairs.com/articles/ukraine/2022-04-06/russia-ukraine-war-price-hegemony.

Kane, Tim. 2012. "Development and U.S. Troop Deployments," *Foreign Policy Analysis* 8(3): 255–273.

Karzai, Ahmed. 2009. "Inauguration Speech," Afghanistan-un.org, November 19. Available online: http://www.afghanistan-un.org/2009/11/president-karzai%E2%80%99s -inauguration-speech/.

Kelley, Robert. 1990. *The Transatlantic Persuasion: The Liberal-Democratic Mind in the Age of Gladstone.* New Brunswick, NJ: Transaction Books.

Kennan, George F. 1986. "A New Philosophy of Defense," *New York Review of Books,* February 13. Available online: https://www.nybooks.com/articles/1986/02/13 /a-new-philosophy-of-defense/.

Kennedy, Michael, Peter Reuter, and Kevin J. Riley. 1993. *A Simple Economic Model of Cocaine Production.* Santa Monica, CA: RAND Corporation.

Khan, Azmat. 2021a. "Hidden Pentagon Records Reveal Patters of Failure in Deadly Strikes," *New York Times,* December 18. Available online: https://www.nytimes .com/interactive/2021/12/18/us/airstrikes-pentagon-records-civilian-deaths.html.

———. 2021b. "The Human Toll of America's Air Wars," *New York Times,* December 19. Available online: https://www.nytimes.com/2021/12/19/magazine/victims -airstrikes-middle-east-civilians.html.

Kilcullen, David, and Andrew McDonald Exum. 2009. "Death from Above, Outrage Down Below," *New York Times,* May 16. Available online: http://www.nytimes .com/2009/05/17/opinion/17exum.html?pagewanted=all&_r=0.

Kindleberger, Charles P. 1981. "Dominance and Leadership in International Economy: Exploitation, Public Goods, and Free Rides," *International Studies Quarterly* 25(2): 242–254.

Kinzer, Stephen. 2007. *Overthrow: America's Century of Regime Change from Hawaii to Iraq.* New York: Times Books.

———. 2017. *The True Flag: Theodore Roosevelt, Mark Twain, and the Birth of American Empire.* New York: Henry Holt.

Kissinger, Henry A. 1969. *American Foreign Policy: Three Essays.* New York: W. W. Norton.

Knack, Stephen, and Philip Keefer. 1995. "Institutions and Economic Performance: Cross-Country Tests Using Alternative Institutional Measures," *Economics and Politics* 7(3): 207–227.

Knight, Frank. 1938. "Lippman's *The Good Society*," *Journal of Political Economy* 46(6): 864–872.

Komarow, Steven. 2001. "Afghan Drug Sellers Punished with Humiliation," *USA Today,* October 18. Available online: http://usatoday30.usatoday.com/news /sept11/2001/10/17/drug-dealer.htm.

Koppl, Roger. 2018. *Expert Failure*. New York: Cambridge University Press.

Kraeutler, Kirk. 2008. "U.N. Reports that Taliban Is Stockpiling Opium," *New York Times*, November 27. Available online: http://www.nytimes.com/2008/11/28/world /middleeast/28opium.html.

Kreps, Sarah. 2016. *Drones: What Everyone Needs to Know*. New York: Oxford University Press.

Kukathas, Chandran. 2003. *The Liberal Archipelago: A Theory of Diversity and Freedom*. New York: Oxford University Press.

———. 2021. *Immigration and Freedom*. Princeton, NJ: Princeton University Press.

LaFeber, Walter. 1984. *Inevitable Revolutions: The United States in Central America*. New York: W. W. Norton.

———. 1986. "The Evolution of the Monroe Doctrine from Monroe to Reagan." In, Lloyd C. Gardener (ed.), *Redefining the Past: Essays in Diplomatic History in Honor of William Appleman Williams*. Corvallis, OR: Oregon State University Press, pp. 121–141.

———. 1998. *The New Empire: An Interpretation of American Expansion 1860–1898*. Ithaca, NY: Cornell University Press.

Lal, Deepak. 2001. "Globalization, Imperialism, and Regulation," *Cambridge Review of International Affairs* 14(1): 107–121.

———. 2004. *In Praise of Empires*. New York: Palgrave Macmillan.

Lambert, Karras J., Christopher J. Coyne, and Nathan P. Goodman. 2021. "The Fatal Conceit of Foreign Intervention: Evidence from the Afghanistan Papers," *Peace Economics, Peace Science and Public Policy*, forthcoming.

Langley, Lester D. 1988. "Anti-Americanism in Central America," *Annals of the American Academy of Political and Social Science* 497: 77–88.

———. 2002. *The Banana Wars: United States Intervention in the Caribbean, 1898–1934*. Wilmington, DE: SR Books.

Langley, Lester D., and Thomas D. Schoonover. 1995. *The Banana Men: American Mercenaries and Entrepreneurs in Central America, 1880–1930*. Lexington, KY: University Press of Kentucky.

Lavoie, Don. 1985a. *Rivalry and Central Planning: The Socialist Calculation Debate Reconsidered*. New York: Cambridge University Press.

———. 1985b. *National Economic Planning: What Is Left?* Cambridge, MA: Ballinger.

———. 1986. "The Market as a Procedure for Discovery and Conveyance of Inarticulate Knowledge," *Comparative Economic Studies* 28 (Spring): 1–19.

Lawson, Marian L., and Emily M. Morgenstern. 2020. "Foreign Assistance: An Introduction to U.S. Programs and Policies," Congressional Research Service Report for Congress R40213, April 30. Available online: https://crsreports.congress.gov /product/pdf/R/R40213.

Leeson, Peter T. 2014. *Anarchy Unbound: Why Self-Governance Works Better Than You Think*. New York: Cambridge University Press.

Leff, Nathaniel H. 1964. "Economic Development Through Bureaucratic Corruption," *American Behavioral Scientist* 8(3): 8–14.

Lichbach, Mark I. 1994. "Rethinking Rationality and Rebellion: Theories of Collective Action and Problems of Collective Dissent," *Rationality and Society* 6(1): 8–39.

———. 1998. *The Rebel's Dilemma*. Ann Arbor, MI: University of Michigan Press.

Lieber, Robert J. 2005. *The American Era: Power and Strategy for the 21st Century*. New York: Cambridge University Press.

———. 2016. *Retreat and Its Consequences: American Foreign Policy and the Problem of World Order*. New York: Cambridge University Press.

Lindorff, Dave. 2018. "The Pentagon's Massive Accounting Fraud Exposed: How US Military Spending Keeps Rising Even as the Pentagon Flunks Its Audit," *The Nation*, November 27. Available online: https://www.thenation.com/article/archive/pentagon-audit-budget-fraud/.

Linfield, Michael. 1990. *Freedom Under Fire: U.S. Civil Liberties in Times of War*. Boston: South End Press.

Lobjakas, Ahto. 2007. "Afghanistan: NATO Downplays 'Conventional' Threat in South," *Radio Free Europe/Radio Liberty*, January 23. Available online: http://www.rferl.org/content/article/1074237.html.

Lofgren, Mike. 2016. *The Deep State: The Fall of the Constitution and the Rise of a Shadow Government*. New York: Penguin Books.

Lyall, Jason. 2020. "Drones are Destabilizing Global Politics: Simple Vehicles Make Conflict Tempting and Cheap," *Foreign Affairs*, December 16. Available online: https://www.foreignaffairs.com/articles/middle-east/2020-12-16/drones-are-destabilizing-global-politics.

Madison, James. 1865. "Political Observations, April 20, 1795." In, *Letters and Other Writings of James Madison*, volume 4. Philadelphia, PA: J. B. Lippincott & Co., pp. 485–505.

Madlena, Chavala, Hannah Patchett, and Adel Shamsan. 2015. "We Dream About Drones, said 13-year-old Yemeni Before His Death in a CIA Strike," *The Guardian*, February 10. Available online: https://www.theguardian.com/world/2015/feb/10/drones-dream-yemeni-teenager-mohammed-tuaiman-death-cia-strike.

Mahmood, Rafat, and Michael Jetter. 2019. "Military Intervention via Drone Strikes," IZA DP No. 12318. Available online: http://ftp.iza.org/dp12318.pdf.

Mahoney, James. 2001. "Radical, Reformist, and Aborted Liberalism: Origins of National Regimes in Central America," *Journal of Latin American Studies* 33(2): 221–256.

Maier, Charles. 2007. *Among Empires: American Ascendancy and Its Predecessors.* Cambridge, MA: Harvard University Press.

Martin, Matt J., and Charles W. Sasser. 2010. *Predator: The Remote-Control Air War over Iraq and Afghanistan: A Pilot's Story.* Minneapolis, MN: Zenith Press.

Mason, R. Chuck. 2012. "Status of Force Agreement (SOFA): What Is It, and How Has It Been Utilized?", Congressional Research Service Report for Congress RL34531, March 15. Available online: https://fas.org/sgp/crs/natsec/RL34531.pdf.

Matthews, Dylan. 2021. "20 Years, $6 Trillion, 900,000 Lives: The Enormous Costs and Elusive Benefits of the war on terror," *Vox*, September 11. Available online: https://www.vox.com/22654167/cost-deaths-war-on-terror-afghanistan-iraq-911.

Maull, Hanns W. 1990. "Germany and Japan: The New Civilian Powers," *Foreign Affairs* 69(5): 91–106.

Maurer, Noel. 2013. *The Empire Trap: The Rise and Fall of U.S. Intervention to Protect American Property Oversees, 1893–2013.* Princeton, NJ: Princeton University Press.

Mauro, Paolo. 1995. "Corruption and Growth," *Quarterly Journal of Economics* 110(3): 681–712.

_____. 2004. "The Persistence of Corruption and Slow Economic Growth," *IMF Staff Papers* 51(1): 1–18.

May, Ernest R. 1993. *American Cold War Strategy: Interpreting NSC 68.* Boston: St. Martin's Press.

McCartney, James. 1975. "11 Firms 'Primed' Pentagon," *Akron Beacon Journal*, October 25, p. 13.

_____. 2015. *America's War Machine: Vested Interests, Endless Conflicts.* New York: Thomas Dunne Books.

McChesney, Fred S. 1987. "Rent Extraction and Rent Creation in the Economic Theory of Regulation," *Journal of Legal Studies* 16(1): 101–118.

_____. 1997. *Money for Nothing: Politicians, Rent Extraction, and Political Extortion.* Cambridge, MA: Harvard University Press.

McCloskey, Deirdre Nansen. 2006. *The Bourgeois Virtues: Ethics for an Age of Commerce.* Chicago, IL: University of Chicago Press.

_____. 2019. *Why Liberalism Works: How True Liberal Values Produce a Freer, More Equal, Prosperous World for All.* New Haven, CT: Yale University Press.

McCloskey, Deirdre Nansen, and Art Carden. 2020. *Leave Me Alone and I'll Make You Rich: How the Bourgeois Deal Enriched the World.* Chicago, IL: University of Chicago Press.

McCoy, Alfred W. 2006. *A Question of Torture: CIA Interrogation, from the Cold War to the War on Terror.* New York: Metropolitan Books.

————. 2009. *Policing America's Empire: The United States, the Philippines, and the Rise of the Surveillance State*. Madison, WI: University of Wisconsin Press.

McVeigh, Karen. 2013. "Drone Strikes: Tears in Congress as Pakistani Family Tells of Mother's Death," *The Guardian*, October 29. Available online: https://www.theguardian .com/world/2013/oct/29/pakistan-family-drone-victim-testimony-congress.

Meier, Barry. 2013. *A World of Hurt: Fixing Pain Medicine's Biggest Mistake*. New York: New York Times Company.

Melman, Seymour. 1970. *Pentagon Capitalism: The Political Economy of War*. New York: McGraw-Hill.

————. 1985. *The Permanent War Economy: American Capitalism in Decline*. New York: Simon & Schuster.

Mercille, Julien. 2013. "Afghanistan, Garden of Empire: America's Multibillion Dollar Opium Harvest," Global Research, February 25. Available online: http://www.globalresearch .ca/afghanistan-garden-of-empire-americas-multibillion-dollar-opium-harvest /5324196.

Merton, Robert K. 1940. "Bureaucratic Structure and Personality," *Social Forces* 18(4): 560–568.

Miesen, Mike. 2013. "The Inadequacy of Donating Medical Devices to Africa," *The Atlantic*, September 20. Available online: http://www.theatlantic.com/international /print/2013/09/the-inadequacy-of-donatingmedical-devices-to-africa/279855/.

Mili, Hayder. 2007. "Afghanistan's Drug Trade and How It Funds Taliban Operations," The Jamestown Foundation, May 10. Available online: http://www .jamestown.org/programs/tm/single/?tx_ttnews%5Btt_news%5D=4145&tx _ttnews%5BbackPid%5D=182&no_cache=1#.VGJn7IvF9uA.

Miller, Kathleen, Tony Capaccio, and Danielle Ivory. 2013. "Flawed F-35 Too Big to Kill as Lockheed Hooks 45 States," *Bloomberg Business*, February 22. Available online: http://www.bloomberg.com/news/articles/2013-02-22/flawed-f-35-fighter -too-big-to-kill-as-lockheed-hooks-45-states.

Millett, Richard, and G. Dale Gaddy. 1976. "Administering the Protectorates: The US Occupation of Haiti and the Dominican Republic," *Revista Interamericana* 6(3): 383–402.

Mills, C. Wright. 1956. *The Power Elite*. New York: Oxford University Press.

Milner, Helen. 1991. "The Assumption of Anarchy in International Relations Theory: A Critique," *Review of International Studies* 17(1): 67–85.

Mises, Ludwig von. 1927 [1996]. *Liberalism: The Classical Tradition*. Irvington-on-Hudson, NY: The Foundation for Economic Education.

————. 1935. "Economic Calculation in the Socialist Commonwealth." In, F. A. Hayek (ed.), *Collectivist Economic Planning*. London: George Routledge & Sons, pp. 87–130.

———. 1944. *Bureaucracy*. New Haven, CT: Yale University Press.

———. 1949. *Human Action: A Treatise on Economics*. New Haven, CT: Yale University Press.

Mitchell, Nancy. 1996. "The Height of the German Challenge: The Venezuela Blockade, 1902–3," *Diplomatic History* 20(2): 185–209.

Mitchener, Kris James, and Marc Weidenmier. 2005. "Empire, Public Goods, and the Roosevelt Corollary," *Journal of Economic History* 65(3): 658–692.

Montgomery, John D. 2004. "Supporting Postwar Aspirations in Islamic Societies." In, John D. Montgomery and Dennis A. Rondinelli (eds.), *Beyond Reconstruction in Afghanistan: Lessons from Development Experience*. New York: Palgrave Macmillan, pp. 32–52.

Moreau, Ron. 2013. "The Taliban's New Role as Afghanistan's Drug Mafia," *Newsweek*, June 12. Available online: http://www.newsweek.com/2013/06/12/talibans-new -role-afghanistans-drug-mafia-237524.html.

Morris, Edmund. 2002. "'A Matter of Extreme Urgency': Theodore Roosevelt, Wilhelm II, and the Venezuela Crisis of 1902," *Naval War College Review* 55(2): 73–85.

Moya Pons, Frank. 1998. *The Dominican Republic: A National History*. Princeton, NJ: Markus Wiener Publishers.

Mueller, John. 2021. *The Stupidity of War: American Foreign Policy and the Case for Complacency*. New York: Cambridge University Press.

Mueller, John, and Mark G. Stewart. 2011. *Terror, Security, and Money: Balancing the Benefits, Risks, and Costs of Homeland Security*. New York: Oxford University Press.

———. 2012. "The Terrorism Delusion: America's Overwrought Response to September 11," *International Security* 37(1): 81–110.

———. 2016. *Chasing Ghosts: The Policing of Terrorism*. New York: Oxford University Press.

———. 2021. "Terrorism and Bathtubs: Comparing the Assessing the Risks," *Terrorism and Political Violence* 33(1): 138–161.

Munger, Michael. 2019. *Is Capitalism Sustainable?* Great Barrington, MA: American Institute for Economic Research.

Murphy, Frank. 1943. "Kiyoshi Hirabayashi v. United States, 320 U.S. 81, 113." Available online: http://caselaw.findlaw.com/us-supreme-court/320/81.html.

Murphy, Kevin, Andrei Shleifer, and Robert W. Vishny. 1993. "Why Is Rent-Seeking So Costly to Growth?", *American Economic Review Papers and Proceedings* 83(2): 409–414.

Murtazashvili, Ilia, and Jennifer Brick Murtazashvili. 2019. "The Political Economy of State Building," *Journal of Public Finance and Public Choice* 34(2): 189–207.

Murtazashvili, Jennifer Brick. 2016. *Informal Order and the State in Afghanistan*. New York: Cambridge University Press.

Murtazashvili, Jennifer, and Ilia Murtazashvili. 2020. "Wealth-Destroying States," *Public Choice* 182(3–4): 353–371.

Murtazashvili, Jennifer Brick, and Ilia Murtazashvili. 2021. *Land, the State, and War: Property Institutions and Political Order in Afghanistan.* New York: Cambridge University Press.

Musgrave, Richard A. 1939. "The Voluntary Exchange Theory of Public Economy," *Quarterly Journal of Economics* 53(2): 213–237.

———. 1941. "The Planning Approach in Public Economy: A Reply," *Quarterly Journal of Economics* 55(2): 319–324.

National Public Radio (NPR). 2013. "Afghan Farmers: Opium Is the Only Way to Make a Living," NPR.org, November 14. Available online: http://www.npr.org /blogs/parallels/2013/11/14/245040114/afghan-farmers-opium-is-the-only-way-to -make-a-living.

National Security Council. 1950. "NSC 68: United States Objectives and Programs for National Security," January 31. Available online: https://fas.org/irp/offdocs/nsc-hst /nsc-68-9.htm.

Niskanen, William A. 1971. *Bureaucracy and Representative Government.* Chicago, IL: Aldine-Atherton.

———. 1975. "Bureaucrats and Politicians," *Journal of Law and Economics* 18(3): 617–643.

Nock, Albert Jay. 1935. *Our Enemy, the State.* New York: William Morrow and Company.

Nordland, Rod. 2013. "Production of Opium by Afghans Is Up Again," New York Times, April 15. Available online: https://www.nytimes.com/2013/04/16/world/asia /afghanistan-opium-production-increases-for-3rd-year.html.

Nowrasteh, Alex, and Benjamin Powell. 2021. *Wretched Refuse? The Political Economy of Immigration and Institutions.* New York: Cambridge University Press.

Nugent, Walter. 2008. *Habits of Empire: A History of American Expansion.* New York: Knopf.

Obama, Barack. 2013. "Speech on U.S. Drone and Counterterror Policy," New York Times, May 24. Available online: https://www.nytimes.com/2013/05/24/us/politics /transcript-of-obamas-speech-on-drone-policy.html.

Office of the Director of National Intelligence. 2016. "Summary of Information Regarding U.S. Counterterrorism Strikes Outside Areas of Active Hostilities." Available online: https://www.dni.gov/files/documents/Newsroom/Press%20Releases/DNI +Release+on+CT+Strikes+Outside+Areas+of+Active+Hostilities.PDF.

Office of the Under Secretary of Defense (Comptroller). 2019. "National Defense Budget Estimates for FY 2020." Available online: https://comptroller.defense.gov/Portals/45 /Documents/defbudget/fy2020/FY20_Green_Book.pdf.

Olson, Mancur. 1965. *The Logic of Collective Action: Public Goods and the Theory of Groups.* Cambridge, MA: Harvard University Press.

Oppel, Richard A., Jr. 2010. "Tighter Rules Fail to Stem Deaths of Innocent Afghans at Checkpoints," *New York Times,* March 26. Available online: https://www.nytimes .com/2010/03/27/world/asia/27afghan.html.

Oppenheimer, Franz. 1922. *The State: Its History and Development Viewed Sociologically.* New York: B. W. Huebsch.

Organisation for Economic Co-operation and Development (OECD). n.d. "Statistics on Resource Flows to Developing Countries." Available online: https://www.oecd .org/dac/financing-sustainable-development/development-finance-data/statistic-sonresourceflowstodevelopingcountries.htm.

Ostrom, Elinor. 1990. *Governing the Commons: The Evolution of Institutions for Collective Action.* New York: Cambridge University Press.

———. 1996. "Crossing the Great Divide: Coproduction, Synergy, and Development," *World Development* 24(6): 1073–1087.

———. 2005. "Unlocking Public Entrepreneurship and Public Economies," Discussion Paper 2005/001. Helsinki: UNU-WIDER. Available online: https://www.wider .unu.edu/publication/unlocking-public-entrepreneurship-and-public-economies.

———. 2009. "A Polycentric Approach for Coping with Climate Change," Policy Research Working Paper. The World Bank. Available online: http://documents .worldbank.org/curated/en/480171468315567893/A-polycentric-approach-for -coping-with-climate-change.

Ostrom, Elinor, and Vincent Ostrom. 1977. "Public Goods and Public Choices." In, Emanuel S. Savas (ed.), *Alternatives for Delivering Public Services: Towards Improved Performance.* Boulder, CO: Westview Press, pp. 7–49.

Ostrom, Vincent. 1991a. *The Meaning of American Federalism: Constituting a Self-Governing Society.* San Francisco, CA: ICS Press.

———. 1991b. *The Meaning of Democracy and the Vulnerabilities of Democracies: A Response to Tocqueville's Challenge.* Ann Arbor, MI: University of Michigan Press.

———. 1999. "Polycentricity (Part 1)." In, Michael D. McGinnis (ed.), *Polycentricity and Local Public Economies.* Ann Arbor, MI: University of Michigan Press, pp. 52–74.

———. 2014. "Polycentricity: The Structural Basis of Self-Governing Systems." In, Filippo Sabetti and Paul Dragos Aligica (eds.), *Choice, Rules and Collective Action: The Ostroms on the Study of Institutions and Governance.* Colchester, UK: ECPR Press, pp. 45–60.

Ostrom, Vincent, Charles M. Tiebout, and Robert Warren. 1961. "The Organization of Government in Metropolitan Areas: A Theoretical Inquiry," *American Political Science Review* 55(4): 831–842.

Owen, Taylor. 2013. "Drones Just Don't Kill. Their Psychological Effects Are Creating Enemies," *Globe and Mail*, March 13. Available online: http://www.theglobeandmail .com/opinion/drones-dont-just-kill-their-psychological-effects-are-creating-enemies/ article9707992/.

Pagden, Anthony. 2005. "Imperialism, Liberalism & the Quest for Perpetual Peace," *Dædalus* 134(2): 46–57.

Paige, Randy. 1991. "Friedman & Szasz on Liberty and Drugs," Schaffer Library of Drug Policy. Available online: http://www.druglibrary.org/schaffer/misc/friedm1.htm.

Paltrow, Scot J. 2013. "Behind the Pentagon's Doctored Ledgers, a Running Tally of Epic Waste," Reuters, November 18. Available online: http://www.reuters.com /investigates/pentagon/#article/part2.

Panagariya, Arvind. 2019. *Free Trade and Prosperity: How Openness Helps the Developing Countries Grow Richer and Combat Poverty*. New York: Oxford University Press.

Parent, Joseph M., and Paul K. MacDonald. 2011. "The Wisdom of Retrenchment: America Must Cut Back to Move Forward," *Foreign Affairs* 90(6): 32–47.

Payne, James L. 2006. "Does Nation Building Work?" *Independent Review: A Journal of Political Economy* 10(4): 597–608.

Perez, Louis A. 1978. "The Platt Amendment and Dysfunctional Politics in Cuba: The Electoral Crises of 1916–1917," *West Georgia College Studies in the Social Sciences* 17: 49–60.

———. 1979. *Intervention, Revolution, and Politics in Cuba, 1913–1921*. Pittsburgh, PA: University of Pittsburgh Press.

———. 1984. "Dollar Diplomacy, Preventive Intervention and the Platt Amendment in Cuba, 1909–1912," *Inter-American Economic Affairs* 38(2): 22–44.

———. 1986a. "Aspects of Hegemony: Labor, State, and Capital in Plattist Cuba," *Cuban Studies* 16: 49–69.

———. 1986b. *Cuba Under the Platt Amendment, 1902–1934*. Pittsburgh, PA: University of Pittsburgh Press.

———. 1995. *Cuba: Between Reform and Revolution*. Oxford, UK: Oxford University Press.

Peters, Gretchen. 2009. *How Opium Profits the Taliban*. Washington, DC: United States Institute for Peace.

Philipps, Dave. 2022. "The Unseen Scars of Those Who Kill Via Remote Control," *New York Times*, April 15. Available online: https://www.nytimes.com/2022/04/15/us /drones-airstrikes-ptsd.html.

Phillips, David L. 2005. *Losing Iraq: Inside the Postwar Reconstruction Fiasco*. New York: Basic Books.

Physicians for Social Responsibility, Physicians for Global Survival, and International Physicians for the Prevention of Nuclear War. 2015. *Body Count: Casualty Figures after 10 Years of the War on Terror—Iraq, Afghanistan, Pakistan.* Washington, DC. Available online: http://www.psr.org/assets/pdfs/body-count.pdf.

Piazza, James A. 2012. "The Opium Trade and Patterns of Terrorism in Provinces of Afghanistan: An Empirical Analysis," *Terrorism and Political Violence* 24(2): 213–234.

Pickering, Jeffrey, and Mark Peceny. 2006. "Forging Democracy at Gunpoint," *International Studies Quarterly* 50(3): 539–560.

Plaw, Avery, Matthew S. Fricker, and Carlos R. Colon. 2015. *The Drone Debate: A Primer on The U.S. Use of Unmanned Aircraft Outside Conventional Battlefields.* Lanham, MD: Rowman & Littlefield.

Polanyi, Michael. 1951. *The Logic of Liberty.* Chicago, IL: University of Chicago Press.

Porter, Bruce D. 1994. *War and the Rise of the State: The Military Foundations of Modern Politics.* New York: The Free Press.

Porter, Patrick. 2018. "A World Imagined: Nostalgia and Liberal Order," Cato Institute Policy Analysis No. 843. Available online: https://www.cato.org/sites/cato.org/files /pubs/pdf/pa-843.pdf.

———. 2020. *The False Promise of Liberal Order: Nostalgia, Delusion and the Rise of Trump.* New York: Polity Press.

Posen, Barry R. 2014. *Restraint: A New Foundation for U.S. Grand Strategy.* Ithaca, NY: Cornell University Press.

Powell, Jim. 2006. *Bully Boy: The Truth About Theodore Roosevelt's Legacy.* New York: Crown Forum.

Priest, Dana, and William M. Arkin. 2011. *Top Secret America: The Rise of the New American Security State.* New York: Little, Brown and Company.

Pritchett, Lant, and Michael Woolcock. 2004. "Solutions When *the* Solution Is the Problem: Arraying the Disarray in Development," *World Development* 32(2): 191–212.

Project on Government Oversight. 2018. "Brass Parachutes: Defense Contractors' Capture of Pentagon Officials Through the Revolving Door." Washington, DC: Project on Government Oversight. Available online: https://s3.amazonaws.com /docs.pogo.org/report/2018/POGO_Brass_Parachutes_DoD_Revolving_Door _Report_2018-11-05.pdf.

Rayamajhee, Veeshan, and Pablo Paniagua. 2021. "The Ostroms and the Contestable Nature of Goods: Beyond Taxonomies and Toward Institutional Polycentricity," *Journal of Institutional Economics* 17(1): 71–89.

Rehnquist, William H. 1998. *All the Laws but One: Civil Liberties in Wartime.* New York: Vintage Books.

Reich, Robert. 2010. "America's Biggest Jobs Program: The US Military," *Christian Science Monitor*, August 13. Available online: https://www.csmonitor.com/Business /Robert-Reich/2010/0813/America-s-biggest-jobs-program-The-US-military.

Reich, Simon, and Richard Ned Lebow. 2014. *Good-bye Hegemony! Power and Influence in the Global System*. Princeton, NJ: Princeton University Press.

Ricard, Serge. 2006. "The Roosevelt Corollary," *Presidential Studies Quarterly* 36(1): 17–26.

Riddle, Donald H. 1964. *The Truman Committee: A Study in Congressional Responsibility*. New Brunswick, NJ: Rutgers University Press.

Rigterink, Anouk S. 2021. "The Wane of Command: Evidence on Drone Strikes and Control within Terrorist Organizations," *American Political Science Review* 115(1): 31–50.

Risen, James. 2007. "Poppy Fields Are Now a Front Line in Afghan War," *New York Times,* May 16. Available online: http://www.nytimes.com/2007/05/16/world /asia/16drugs.html?pagewanted=all.

———. 2008. "Reports Link Karzai's Brother to Afghanistan Heroin Trade," *New York Times,* October 4. Available online: http://www.nytimes.com/2008/10/05/world /asia/05afghan.html?pagewanted=2.

———. 2014. *Pay Any Price: Greed, Power, and Endless War*. New York: Houghton Mifflin Harcourt.

Roberts, Sam. 2018. "Gene Sharp, Global Guru of Nonviolent Resistance, Dies at 90," *New York Times*, February 2. Available online: https://www.nytimes.com /2018/02/02/obituaries/gene-sharp-global-guru-of-nonviolent-resistance-dies-at-90 .html.

Rohde, David. 2009. "A Drone Strike and Dwindling Hope," *New York Times*, October 20. Available online: http://www.nytimes.com/2009/10/21/world/asia/21hostage .html?pagewanted=all.

———. 2012. "The Drone Wars," Reuters, January 26. Available online: http://www .reuters.com/article/us-david-rohde-drone-wars-idUSTRE80P11I20120126.

Roosevelt, Theodore. 1910. *Presidential Address and State Papers*, volume III (Homeward Bound Edition). New York: Review of Reviews Company.

Röpke, Wilhelm. 1959. *International Order and Economic Integration*. Dordrecht, Holland: D. Reidel Publishing Company.

Rossiter, Clinton. 2009 [1948]. *Constitutional Dictatorship: Crisis Government in the Modern Democracies*. New Brunswick, NJ: Transaction Publishers.

Rovner, Joshua. 2017. "The War on Terrorism as Imperial Policing," War on the Rocks, November 2. Available online: https://warontherocks.com/2017/11 /the-war-on-terrorism-as-imperial-policing/.

Rowlatt, Justin. 2019. "How the US military's opium war in Afghanistan was lost," *BBC*, April 25. Available online: https://www.bbc.com/news/world-us-canada-47861444.

Rubin, Alissa J. 2010. "Afghans' Distrust Threatens U.S. War Strategy," *New York Times*, May 12. Available online: http://www.nytimes.com/2010/05/13/world/asia /13afghan.html?pagewanted=all&_r=0.

Rubin, Alissa J., and Matthew Rosenberg. 2012. "U.S. Efforts to Curtail Trade in Afghan Opium," *New York Times,* May 26. Available online: http://www.nytimes .com/2012/05/27/world/asia/drug-traffic-remains-as-us-nears-afghanistan-exit .html?pagewanted=all.

Rubin, Barnett R. 2004. "Drugs and Security: Afghanistan's Fatal Addiction," *New York Times*, October 28. Available online: http://www.nytimes.com/2004/10/28 /opinion/28iht-edrubin_ed3_.html?_r=0.

Ruiz, Bert. 2001. *The Colombian Civil War*. London: McFarland & Company, Inc., Publishers.

Saif, Atef Abu. 2015. *The Drone Eats with Me: A Gaza Diary*. Manchester, UK: Comma Press.

Salisbury, Richard V. 1997. "Great Britain, the United States, and the 1909–1910 Nicaraguan Crisis," *The Americas* 53(3): 379–394.

Samuelson, Paul A. 1954. "The Pure Theory of Public Expenditure," *Review of Economics and Statistics* 36(4): 387–389.

———. 1955. "Diagrammatic Exposition of a Theory of Public Expenditure," *Review of Economics and Statistics* 37(4): 350–356.

Sanger, David E., and Sheera Frenkel. 2018. "'Five Eyes' Nations Quietly Demand Government Access to Encrypted Data," *New York Times*, September 4. Available online: https://www.nytimes.com/2018/09/04/us/politics/government-access-encrypted -data.html.

Savage, Charlie. 2014. "U.S. Tells U.N. Panel of Steps to Revise Interrogation Policy," *New York Times*, November 12. Available online: http://www.nytimes.com/2014/11/13 /us/us-vows-to-stop-using-torture-against-terrorism-suspects.html?_r=0.

Scahill, Jeremy. 2016. *The Assassination Complex: Inside the Government's Secret Drone Warfare Program*. New York: Simon & Schuster.

Scarry, Elaine. 2002. "Citizenship in Emergency," *Boston Review*, October 1. Available online: http://bostonreview.net/forum/elaine-scarry-citizenship-emergency.

Schell, Jonathan. 2003. *The Unconquerable World: Power, Nonviolence, and the Will of the People*. New York: Henry Holt.

Schlesinger, Arthur M., Jr. 2004. *The Imperial Presidency*. New York: Mariner Books.

Schmitt, Eric. 2021. "A Botched Drone Strike in Kabul Started with the Wrong Car," *New York Times*, September 21. Available online: https://www.nytimes.com/2021/09/21 /us/politics/drone-strike-kabul.html.

Schrader, Stuart. 2019. *Badges Without Borders: How Global Counterinsurgency Transformed American Policing.* Berkeley, CA: University of California Press.

Schweich, Thomas. 2006. "Is Afghanistan a Narco-State?", *New York Times,* July 27. Available online: http://www.nytimes.com/2008/07/27/magazine/27AFGHAN-t .html?_r&_r=0.

Schweizer, Peter. 2013. *Extortion: How Politicians Extract Your Money, Buy Votes, and Line Their Own Pockets.* New York: Houghton Mifflin Harcourt.

Seligman, Lara. 2021. "'Tragic Mistake': U.S. Determines Kabul Drone Strike Killed Innocent Aid Worker, Nine Family Members," *Politico,* September 17. Available online: https://www.politico.com/news/2021/09/17/tragic-mistake-us-drone-strike-512586.

Senate Foreign Relations Committee. 2011. "Evaluating U.S. Foreign Assistance to Afghanistan," A Majority Staff Report, 112th Congress, First Session. Washington, DC: US Government Printing Office. Available online: http://www.foreign.senate .gov/imo/media/doc/SPRT%20112-21.pdf.

Senate Select Committee to Study Governmental Operations with Respect to Intelligence Activities. 1976. "Intelligence Activities and the Rights of Americans, Book II," Final Report, 94th Congress, Second Session. Washington, DC: US Government Printing Office. Available online: https://www.intelligence.senate.gov/sites/default /files/94755_II.pdf.

Sexton, Jay. 2011. *The Monroe Doctrine: Empire and Nation in Nineteenth-Century America.* New York: Hill and Wang.

Shah, Aqil. 2018. "Do U.S. Drone Strikes Cause Blowback? Evidence from Pakistan and Beyond," *International Security* 42(4): 47–84.

Shane, Scott. 2011a. "C.I.A. Is Disputed on Civilian Toll in Drone Strikes," *New York Times,* August 11. Available online: http://www.nytimes.com/2011/08/12/world /asia/12drones.html?_r=0.

———. 2011b. "Coming Soon: The Drone Arms Race," *New York Times,* October 8. Available online: https://www.nytimes.com/2011/10/09/sunday-review/coming -soon-the-drone-arms-race.html.

———. 2015. "Drone Strikes Reveal Uncomfortable Truth: U.S. Is Often Unsure About Who Will Die," *New York Times,* April 23. Available online: https://www.nytimes .com/2015/04/24/world/asia/drone-strikes-reveal-uncomfortable-truth-us-is-often -unsure-about-who-will-die.html.

Sharp, Gene. 1973. *The Politics of Nonviolent Action.* 3 parts. Boston: Porter Sargent.

———. 1985. *Making Europe Unconquerable: The Potential of Civilian-Based Deterrence and Defense.* Cambridge, MA: Ballinger.

———. 1990. *Civilian-Based Defense: A Post-Military Weapons System.* Princeton, NJ: Princeton University Press.

———. 2005. *Waging Nonviolent Struggle: 20th Century Practice and 21st Century Potential*. Boston: Porter Sargent.

Shaw, Ian G. R. 2016. *Predator Empire*. Minneapolis, MN: University of Minnesota Press.

Sherry, Michael S. 1995. *In the Shadow of War: The United States Since the 1930s*. New Haven, CT: Yale University Press.

Shin Doh Chull. 1994. "On the Third Wave of Democratization: A Synthesis and Evaluation of Recent Theory and Research," *World Politics* 47(1): 135–170.

Shleifer, Andrei, and Robert Vishny. 1993. "Corruption," *Quarterly Journal of Economics* 108(3): 599–617.

Shoup, David M. 1969. "The New American Militarism," *The Atlantic Monthly* 223(4): 51–56.

Singer, P. W. 2009. *Wired for War: The Robotics Revolution and Conflict in the 21st Century*. New York: Penguin Books.

Singh, Ritika. 2013. "Drone Strikes Kill Innocent People. Why Is It So Hard to Know How Many?" *New Republic*, October 25. Available online: https://newrepublic.com /article/115353/civilian-casualties-drone-strikes-why-we-know-so-little.

Slahi, Mohamedou Ould. 2015. *Guantanamo Diary*. New York: Little, Brown and Company.

Smith, Adam. 1776 [2000]. *An Inquiry into the Nature and Causes of the Wealth of Nations*. New York: The Modern Library.

Smith, Megan, and James Igoe Walsh. 2013. "Do Drone Strikes Degrade Al Qaeda? Evidence From Propaganda Output," *Terrorism and Political Violence* 25(2): 311–327.

Smith, R. Elberton. 1991 [1959]. *The Army and Economic Mobilization*. Washington, DC: Center of Military History, United States Army.

Sopko, John F. 2014. "Future U.S. Counternarcotics Efforts in Afghanistan," Testimony Before the Senate Caucus on International Narcotics Control. Available online: https://www.drugcaucus.senate.gov/sites/default/files/SIGAR%20John%20F%20 %20Sopko.pdf.

Sorensen, Christian. 2020. *Understanding the War Industry*. Atlanta, GA: Clarity Press.

Special Inspector General for the Afghanistan Reconstruction. 2014a. "Poppy Cultivation in Afghanistan: After a Decade of Reconstruction and Over $7 Billion in Counternarcotics Efforts, Poppy Cultivation Levels Are at an All-Time High," October. Available online: https://web.archive.org/web/20170519055649/https://www.sigar .mil/pdf/Special%20Projects/SIGAR-15-10-SP.pdf.

———. 2014b. "Quarterly Report to the United States Congress," October. Available online: https://www.sigar.mil/pdf/quarterlyreports/2014-10-30qr.pdf.

_____. 2018. "Counternarcotics: Lessons from the U.S. Experience in Afghanistan," June. Available online: https://www.sigar.mil/pdf/lessonslearned/SIGAR-18-52-LL .pdf.

Speri, Alice. 2014. "It's Spring in Afghanistan, Time for Taliban Fighting Season," *VICE News*, May 12. Available online: https://news.vice.com/article/its-spring -in-afghanistan-time-for-taliban-fighting-season.

Standish, Reid. 2014. "NATO Couldn't Crush Afghanistan's Opium Economy," *Foreign Policy*, November 13. Available online: http://foreignpolicy.com/2014/11/13 /nato-couldnt-crush-afghanistans-opium-economy/.

Staten, Clifford L. 2005. *The History of Cuba*. London: Palgrave Macmillan.

Stewart, Rory. 2010. "Afghanistan: What Could Work," *New York Review of Books*, January 14. Available online: http://www.nybooks.com/articles/archives/2010/jan/14 /afghanistan-what-could-work/.

Stockholm International Peace Research Institute. 2020. "USA and France Dramatically Increase Major Arms Exports; Saudi Arabia Is Largest Arms Importer," Sipri. org, March 9. Available online: https://www.sipri.org/media/press-release/2020 /usa-and-france-dramatically-increase-major-arms-exports-saudi-arabia-largest -arms-importer-says.

Stone, Geoffrey R. 2003. "Civil Liberties in Wartime," *Journal of Supreme Court History* 28(3): 215–251.

Stromberg, Joseph R. 2001. "The Role of State Monopoly Capitalism in the American Empire," *Journal of Libertarian Studies* 15(3): 57–93.

Storr, Virgil Henry. 2008. "The Market as a Social Space: On the Meaningful Extraeconomic Conversations That Can Occur in Markets," *Review of Austrian Economics* 21(2-3): 135–150.

Storr, Virgil Henry, and Ginny Seung Choi. 2019. *Do Markets Corrupt Our Morals?* New York: Palgrave Macmillan.

Stringham, Edward P. 2015. *Private Governance: Creating Order in Economic and Social Life*. New York: Oxford University Press.

Stuart, Douglas T. 2008. *Creating the National Security State: A History of the Law that Transformed America*. Princeton, NJ: Princeton University Press.

Sufizada, Hanif. 2020. "The Taliban Are Megarich—Here's Where They Get Their Money They Use to Wage War in Afghanistan," *Conversation*, December 8. Available online: https://theconversation.com/the-taliban-are-megarich-heres-where-they-get -the-money-they-use-to-wage-war-in-afghanistan-147411.

Tarko, Vlad. 2017. *Elinor Ostrom: An Intellectual Biography*. Lanham, MD: Rowman & Littlefield.

Tarnoff, Curt. 2012. "Afghanistan: U.S. Foreign Assistance," Congressional Research Service Report for Congress R40699, August 21. Available online: http://www.hsdl .org/?view&did=723512.

Taylor, Adam. 2015. "The U.S. Keeps Killing Americans in Drone Strikes, Mostly by Accident," *Washington Post*, April 23. Available online: https://www.washingtonpost .com/news/worldviews/wp/2015/04/23/the-u-s-keeps-killing-americans-in-drone -strikes-mostly-by-accident/.

Thornton, Mark. 1991. *The Economics of Prohibition*. Salt Lake City, UT: University of Utah Press.

Thorpe, Rebecca U. 2014. *The American Warfare State: The Domestic Politics of Military Spending*. Chicago, IL: University of Chicago Press.

Thrall, A. Trevor, and Jane K. Cramer (eds.). 2009. *American Foreign Policy and the Politics of Fear: Threat Inflation Since 9/11*. New York: Routledge.

Tian, Nan, Alexandra Kuimova, Diego Lopes da Silva, Pieter D. Wezeman, and Siemon T. Wezeman. 2020. "Trends in World Military Expenditure, 2019," Stockholm International Peace Research Institute. Available online: https://www.sipri.org/sites /default/files/2020-04/fs_2020_04_milex_0.pdf.

Tiebout, Charles M. 1956. "A Pure Theory of Local Expenditures," *Journal of Political Economy* 64(5): 416–424.

Tirman, John. 2011. *Death by Others: The Fate of Civilians in America's Wars*. New York: Oxford University Press.

————. 2015. "The Human Cost of War and How to Assess the Damage," *Foreign Affairs*, October 8. Available online: https://www.foreignaffairs.com/articles /middle-east/2015-10-08/human-cost-war.

Tocqueville, Alexis de. 1840. *Democracy in America. Part the Second: The Social Influence of Democracy*. Translated by Henry Reeve. New York: J. & H. G. Langley.

Tollison, Robert D. 1982. "Rent Seeking: A Survey," *Kyklos* 35(4): 575–602.

Tompkins, E. Berkeley. 1970. *Anti-Imperialism in the United States: The Great Debate, 1890–1920*. Philadelphia, PA: University of Pennsylvania Press.

Torreon, Barbara Salazar, and Sofia Plagakis. 2020. "Instances of Use of United States Armed Forces Abroad, 1798–2020," Congressional Research Service Report for Congress R42738, July 20. Available online: https://fas.org/sgp/crs/natsec/R42738.pdf.

Tullock, Gordon. 1965 [2005]. *The Politics of Bureaucracy*. In, Charles Rowley (ed.), *The Selected Works of Gordon Tullock*, volume 6: *Bureaucracy*. Indianapolis, IN: Liberty Fund, pp. 13–235.

————. 1967. "The Welfare Costs of Tariffs, Monopolies, and Theft," *Western Economic Journal* 5(3): 224–232.

————. 1971. "The Paradox of Revolution," *Public Choice* 11(1): 89–99.

Turse, Nick. 2011. "America's Secret Empire of Drone Bases," TomDispatch, October 16. Available online: https://www.tomdispatch.com/post/175454/tomgram%3A _nick_turse,_mapping_america%27s_shadowy_drone_wars.

————. 2021. "Will the Biden Administration Shine Light on Shadowy Special Ops Programs?", *The Intercept*, March 20. Available Online: https://theintercept .com/2021/03/20/joe-biden-special-operations-forces/.

Twight, Charlotte. 1975. *America's Emerging Fascist Economy*. New York: Arlington House Publishers.

Umoja, Akinyele Omowale. 2014. *We Will Shoot Back: Armed Resistance in the Mississippi Freedom Movement*. New York: New York University Press.

Unger, David C. 2012. *The Emergency State: America's Pursuit of Absolute Security at All Costs*. New York: Penguin Books.

United Nations Office on Drugs and Crime (UNODC). 2002. "Afghanistan Opium Survey 2002," Government of Afghanistan Counter Narcotics Directorate. Available online: https://web.archive.org/web/20210511143338/https://www.unodc.org/pdf /publications/afg_opium_survey_2002.pdf.

————. 2003a. "Afghanistan Opium Survey 2003," Government of Afghanistan Counter Narcotics Directorate. Available online: http://www.unodc.org/pdf/afg/afghanistan _opium_survey_2003.pdf.

————. 2003b. "Global Illicit Drug Trends," Office on Drugs and Crime, Vienna, Austria. Available online: http://www.unodc.org/pdf/trends2003_www_E.pdf.

————. 2004. "Afghanistan Opium Survey 2004," Government of Afghanistan Counter Narcotics Directorate. Available online: http://www.unodc.org/pdf/afg/afghanistan _opium_survey_2004.pdf.

————. 2005. "Afghanistan Opium Survey 2005," Islamic Republic of Afghanistan Ministry of Counter Narcotics. Available online: https://web.archive.org /web/20201213191939/https://www.unodc.org/documents/crop-monitoring /Afghanistan/afg_survey_2005.pdf.

————. 2006. "Afghanistan Opium Survey 2006," Islamic Republic of Afghanistan Ministry of Counter Narcotics. Available online: https://web.archive.org /web/20210201064850/https://www.unodc.org/pdf/execsummaryafg.pdf.

————. 2007. "Afghanistan Opium Survey 2007," Government of Afghanistan Ministry of Counter Narcotics. Available online: https://web.archive.org/web /20191113041015/https://www.unodc.org/documents/crop-monitoring/Afghanistan -Opium-Survey-2007.pdf.

————. 2009. "Addiction, Crime and Insurgency: The Transnational Threat of Afghan Opium." Available online: https://web.archive.org/web/20210201092528/https://

www.unodc.org/documents/data-and-analysis/Afghanistan/Afghan_Opium_
Trade_2009_web.pdf.

———. 2010. "World Drug Report 2010." Available online: https://www.unodc.org
/documents/wdr/WDR_2010/World_Drug_Report_2010_lo-res.pdf.

———. 2012. "Corruption in Afghanistan: Recent Patterns and Trends." Available online:
https://web.archive.org/web/20210817004225/https://www.unodc.org/documents
/frontpage/Corruption_in_Afghanistan_FINAL.pdf.

———. 2013. "Afghanistan Opium Survey 2013," Islamic Republic of Afghanistan
Ministry of Counter Narcotics. Available online: https://web.archive.org/web
/20201112003244/http://www.unodc.org/documents/crop-monitoring/Afghanistan
/Afghan_report_Summary_Findings_2013.pdf.

———. 2014. "World Drug Report 2014." Available online: http://www.unodc.org
/documents/wdr2014/World_Drug_Report_2014_web.pdf.

———. 2018. "Afghanistan Opium Survey 2018: Cultivation and Production," Islamic
Republic of Afghanistan Ministry of Counter Narcotics. Available online: https://
www.unodc.org/documents/crop-monitoring/Afghanistan/Afghanistan_opium
_survey_2018.pdf.

———. 2021. "Afghanistan Opium Survey 2019. Socio-economic Survey Report: Driv-
ers, Causes and Consequences of Opium Poppy Cultivation," Islamic Republic of
Afghanistan. Available online: https://www.unodc.org/documents/crop-monitoring
/Afghanistan/20210217_report_with_cover_for_web_small.pdf.

United Nations Security Council. 2001. "Agreement on Provisional Arrangements in
Afghanistan Pending the Re-Establishment of Permanent Government Institu-
tions." Available online: https://peacemaker.un.org/sites/peacemaker.un.org/files
/AF_011205_AgreementProvisionalArrangementsinAfghanistan%28en%29.pdf.

USAID Office of the Inspector General. 2008. "Audit of USAID/Iraq's Community
Stabilization Program," Audit Report No. E-267-08-001-P. Available online: https://
web.archive.org/web/20180905012929/https://oig.usaid.gov/sites/default/files/audit
-reports/e-267-08-001-p.pdf.

US Department of State. 2008. "Fighting the Opium Trade in Afghanistan: Myths,
Facts, and Sound Policy," Bureau of International Narcotics and Law Enforcement
Affairs. Available online: https://2001-2009.state.gov/p/inl/rls/other/102214.htm.

———. 2010. "U.S. Counternarcotics Strategy for Afghanistan March 2010." Available
online: https://2009-2017.state.gov/documents/organization/141756.pdf.

———. 2011. "Special Joint Press Briefing on U.S. Arms Sales to Saudi Arabia,"
Press Release, December 29. Available online: https://2009-2017.state.gov/r/pa/prs
/ps/2011/12/179777.htm.

————. 2020. "U.S. Arms Transfers Increased by 2.8 Percent in FY 2020 to $175.08 Billion," Bureau of Political-Military Affairs Fact Sheet, January 20. Available online: https://www.state.gov/u-s-arms-transfers-increased-by-2-8-percent-in-fy-2020-to-175-08-billion/.

US Department of the Army. 2009. *The U.S. Army Stability Operations Field Manual.* Ann Arbor, MI: University of Michigan Press.

Vagts, Alfred. 1937. *A History of Militarism: Romance and Realities of a Profession.* New York: W. W. Norton.

van Buren, Peter. 2012. *We Meant Well: How I Helped Lose the Battle for the Hearts and Minds of the Iraqi People.* New York: Metropolitan Books.

Vanden Brook, Tom, Ken Dilanian, and Ray Locker. 2009. "How Some Retired Military Officers Become Well-Paid Consultants," ABC News, November 18. Available online: http://abcnews.go.com/Politics/retired-military-officers-retire-paid-consultants/story?id=9115368.

van der Vossen, Bas, and Jason Brennan. 2018. *In Defense of Openness: Why Global Freedom Is the Humane Solution to Global Poverty.* New York: Oxford University Press.

Vine, David. 2015. *Base Nation: How U.S. Military Bases Abroad Harm America and the World.* New York: Metropolitan Books.

————. 2020. *The United States of War: A Global History of America's Endless Conflicts, from Columbus to the Islamic State.* Oakland, CA: University of California Press.

Vine, David, Cala Coffman, Katalina Khoury, Madison Lovasz, Helen Bush, Rachael Leduc, and Jennifer Walkup. 2021. "Creating Refugees: Displacement Caused by the United States' Post-9/11 Wars," Costs of War Project, August 19. Available online: https://watson.brown.edu/costsofwar/files/cow/imce/papers/2021/Costs%20of%20War_Vine%20et%20al_Displacement%20Update%20August%202021.pdf.

Waddell, Kaveh. 2015. "Who Is Spying on US Cellphones? Lawmakers Demand an Answer," *Defense One,* November 9. Available online: http://www.defenseone.com/technology/2015/11/who-spying-us-cellphones-lawmakers-demand-answer/123527/.

Wagner, Richard E. 2012. *Deficits, Debt, and Democracy: Wrestling with Tragedy on the Fiscal Commons.* Cheltenham, UK: Edward Elgar Publishing.

————. 2014. "American Federalism: How Well Does It Support Liberty?", Mercatus Center at George Mason University. Available online: http://mercatus.org/sites/default/files/Wagner_Federalism_v2.pdf.

Walker, Samuel. 2012. *Presidents and Civil Liberties from Wilson to Obama: A Study of Poor Custodians.* New York: Cambridge University Press.

Weingast, Barry. 1995. "The Economic Role of Political Institutions: Market-Preserving Federalism and Economic Development," *Journal of Law, Economics, & Organization* 11(1): 1–31.

Wellman, Philip Walter. 2020. "White House: Afghanistan Opium Yield Expected to Rise Even as Acreage Planted to Poppies Falls," *Stars and Stripes*, February 10. Available online: https://www.stripes.com/news/white-house-afghanistan-opium -yield-expected-to-rise-even-as-acreage-planted-to-poppies-falls-1.618240.

Wertheim, Stephen. 2021. *Tomorrow, the World: The Birth of U.S. Global Supremacy.* Cambridge, MA: Belknap Press of Harvard University Press.

Wessler, Nathan Fred. 2014. "Trickle Down Surveillance," Al Jazeera America, June 12. Available online: http://america.aljazeera.com/opinions/2014/7/surveillance -lawenforcementnsastringray3.html.

Whitlock, Craig. 2019. "At War with the Truth, The Afghanistan Papers: A Secret History of the War," *Washington Post*, December 9. Available online: https://www .washingtonpost.com/graphics/2019/investigations/afghanistan-papers/afghanistan -war-confidential-documents/.

Willers, Jack Conrad. 1977. "A Philosophic Perspective of Bureaucracy," *Peabody Journal of Education* 55(1): 45–50.

Williams, William Appleman. 1969. *The Roots of the Modern American Empire.* New York: Random House.

————. 1980. *Empire as a Way of Life.* New York: Oxford University Press.

Wilson, James Q. 1989. *Bureaucracy: What Government Agencies Do and Why They Do It.* New York: Basic Books.

Winn, Peter. 1999. *Americas: The Changing Face of Latin America and the Caribbean.* Berkeley, CA: University of California Press.

Wiśniewski, Jakub Bożydar. 2018. *The Economics of Law, Order, and Action: The Logic of Public Goods.* New York: Routledge.

Wood, Garrett. 2018. "The Enemy Votes: Bargaining Failure and Weapons Improvisation," *Economics of Peace and Security Journal* 13(1): 25–32.

Woods, Chris. 2015. *Sudden Justice: America's Secret Drone War.* New York: Oxford University Press.

Woodward, Ralph Lee. 1984. "The Rise and Decline of Liberalism in Central America: Historical Perspectives on the Contemporary Crisis," *Journal of Interamerican Studies and World Affairs* 26(3): 191–312.

Yarrington, Doug. 2003a. "Cattle, Corruption, and Venezuelan State Formation during the Regime of Juan Vicente Gómez, 1908–35," *Latin American Research Review* 38(2): 9–33.

————. 2003b. "The Vestey Cattle Enterprise and the Regime of Juan Vicente Gómez, 1908–1935," *Journal of Latin American Studies* 35(1): 89–115.

Young, Robert J. C. 2015. *Empire, Colony, Postcolony.* Chichester, West Sussex, UK: John Wiley & Sons.

Zak, Paul J., and Stephen Knack. 2001. "Trust and Growth," *Economic Journal* 111(470): 295–321.

Zenko, Micah. 2016. "Don't Believe the U.S. Government's Official Numbers on Drone Strikes and Civilian Casualties," *Foreign Policy*, July 5. Available online: http://foreignpolicy .com/2016/07/05/do-not-believe-the-u-s-governments-official-numbers-on-drone -strike-civilian-casualties/.

Zenko, Micah, and Amelia Mae Wolf. 2016. "Drones Kill More Civilians Than Pilots Do," *Foreign Policy*, April 25. Available online: http://foreignpolicy.com/2016/04/25 /drones-kill-more-civilians-than-pilots-do/.

Zetter, Kim. 2014. "New Movement Aims to 'Reset the Net' Against Mass Surveillance," *Wired*, May 6. Available online: https://www.wired.com/2014/05/reset-the-net/.

About the Author

CHRISTOPHER J. COYNE is Senior Fellow at the Independent Institute and Co-Editor of *The Independent Review*, Professor of Economics at George Mason University, Co-Editor of the *Review of Austrian Economics*, and Book Review Editor for *Public Choice*. He received his Ph.D. in economics from George Mason University. He has taught at West Virginia University and Hampden-Sydney College, and he has been the Hayek Visiting Fellow at the London School of Economics and Visiting Scholar at the Social Philosophy and Policy Center at Bowling Green State University.

His other authored books include *Manufacturing Militarism: U.S. Government Propaganda in the War on Terror* (with Abigail R. Hall); *The Economics of Conflict and Peace: History and Applications* (with Shikha Basnet Silwal, Charles H. Anderton, Jurgen Brauer, and J. Paul Dunne); *Defense, Peace, and War Economics*; *Tyranny Comes Home: The Domestic Fate of U.S. Militarism* (with Abigail R. Hall); *The Essential Austrian Economics* (with Peter J. Boettke); *Doing Bad by Doing Good: Why Humanitarian Action Fails*; *After War: The Political Economy of Exporting Democracy*; *Media, Development, and Institutional Change* (with Peter T. Leeson); and *Context Matters: Entrepreneurship and Institutions* (with Peter J. Boettke).

Professor Coyne is also a contributing author in over 30 volumes and over 150 articles and reviews in scholarly journals. And, his edited books include *In All Fairness: Equality, Liberty, and the Quest for Human Dignity* (with Robert M. Whaples and Michael C. Munger); *Interdisciplinary Studies of the Political Order: New Applications of Public Choice Theory* (with Donald Boudreaux and Bobbi Herzberg); *Exploring the Political Economy & Social Philosophy of*

James M. Buchanan (with Paul Dragos Aligica and Stefanie Haeffele); *Interdisciplinary Studies of the Market Order: New Applications of Market Process Theory* (with Peter J. Boettke and Virgil H. Storr); *Future: Economic Peril or Prosperity?* (with Robert M. Whaples and Michael C. Munger); *The Oxford Handbook on Austrian Economics* (with Peter J. Boettke); *Flaws and Ceilings: Price Controls and the Damage They Cause* (with Rachel Coyne); and *The Handbook on the Political Economy of War* (with Rachel L. Mathers).

His popular articles have appeared in such publications as *The Hill, Daily News, Boston Review, Fraser Forum, Detroit News, Cedar Rapids Gazette, Lafayette Journal & Courier, Herald Times Reporter, Des Moines Register, Green Bay Press Gazette, Shreveport Times,* and *Muscatine Journal.*

Index

Independent Institute Studies in Political Economy

Independent Institute Studies in Political Economy

INDEPENDENT
I N S T I T U T E

100 SWAN WAY, OAKLAND, CA 94621-1428

For further information:
510-632-1366 • orders@independent.org • http://www.independent.org/publications/books/